twochubbycubs
Saturated Fats

James and Paul Anderson

DEDICATION:
GRANDMA, WE LOVE YOU

This collection of nonsense, thoughts and laboured euphemisms about genitals is dedicated to the most wonderful of all people, my dear nana. She would have tutted and winced her way through all the bad language, acting aghast like she didn't know such words existed. Such a fibber – I heard her swearing like a trooper when she dropped her box of suet once.

She lived a long life full of tolerance, bone-dry pastry and badly-completed Take a Break puzzles. She shuffled off the mortal coil in her polyester slippers and the world lost a tiny bit of sparkle.

Always thinking of you, Dorothy B.

I SAID I'M ALWAYS THINKING OF YOU JEEZ NEVER MIND HAVE YOU EVEN GOT YOUR HEARING AID ON I CAN HEAR IT BLOODY WHISTLING

CONTENTS

twochubbycubs on: attending a wedding

A wedding. I dread them, but I had committed to it and we had elected to stay overnight to fully participate in all the glorious and luxurious details of the day? Well, being tight-arse Geordies, we were in the car with not a moment to spare to ensure that we could check in the very second it was available and get the full benefit of our rate. Our suits were hastily hung in the back of the car and with the DS3 out of action, it was into Paul's car for the hour long trip down to the wedding venue, a wonderful old hall in the middle of the countryside. All very elegant.

Of course, I spent the entire car journey clutching fitfully at my seatbelt and trying to a) persuade Paul that he really mustn't call anyone a knobhead as these were people I work for and b) we weren't taking part in the Gumball Rally and that we should really slow the fuck down. Both of these pleas fell on deaf, sweaty ears and he busied himself with the radio knob for pretty much the entire duration of the drive. It's a glorious road, the A68, and it should be of particular interest to anyone who enjoys looking at the back of nicotine-coloured caravans for long stretches at a time, whilst Ernie and Elsie Incontinent meander around each bend at a speed closer to an asthmatic turtle. It was lucky I wasn't driving as they would have been nothing more than matchsticks by the side of the road by the second turn. We arrived at the venue in excellent time and I really can't fault Paul's driving, save that he went too fast, went too slow, didn't change gears in time, failed to turn off his Tracy fucking Chapman for thirty minutes and the car air freshener was a mite too strong for my delicate nose. I don't have one of those clubber noses that have been sanded down and desensitised by years of ketamine and cocaine – I came from a poor family, remember. The closest we got to hard drug use was Calpol, and even that was the Netto own-brand stuff which I'm sure was just wallpaper paste with an Opal Fruit stirred in.

We did manage a little bit of excitement driving into the venue, with it's long, sweeping gravel drive which pulled across a field of sheep, one of whom started chasing the car. This was made surprisingly easy for the sheep as I was henpecking poor Paul again about not going too fast in case he chipped the paintwork. With an angry sheep building up quite the canter behind us, Paul knocked the car into fourth gear and revved away, peppering the poor little bugger with gravel and leaving a big old dust-cloud behind us in the middle of this beautiful nature scene. He pulled into the car park like the car was on fire and I was almost surprised he didn't fancy doing a few doughnuts in the car park to complete the look.

Naturally, with this wedding attracting lawyers and high-ups from all over the place, the car park was littered with the type of car that annoys me immensely

– white BMWs and Audis. I spend more time making wanker signs at them as they invariably demand to overtake than I do with my hand on the gearstick. Ah well. I have to admit, I felt incredibly out of place pulling up in our battered Micra with its go faster stripes and DON'T BLAME ME, I VOTED LABOUR bumper sticker. We both spend a lot of our time worrying that we're not 'up to scratch' but in situations like this, fuck it. Get drunk and have a nice day.

We were shown to a room in the stable block – very Mary and Joseph – and immediately set about picking up anything that wasn't nailed down and secreting it into our suitcases. Tissues, loo-roll, toiletries, even the little UHT milks (why? Seriously why? They always taste like pre-cum and end up sitting in our suitcase until the next holiday where we find them rolling around in a side-pocket, still as pristine and 'fresh' as the last time we saw them). Paul and I differ on the ethics of hotel room stealing – I always take a few things but try not to take the piss, whereas Paul would cheerfully ring Pickfords and have them load the settee and armoires into the back of a lorry before I'd even had a chance to flick the travel kettle on.

We christened the room the only way a young married couple can – a quick bout of sex and then a cup of free coffee, a cup of free tea, a cup of hot chocolate, a cup of green tea and eight packets of those tiny Walker's Shortbreads you always get. Paul had the immediate dilemma of needing to use the netty to 'drop the kids off' but not being able to because invariably other guests arriving would want to have a look at our room and I didn't want my co-workers to be met with the stench of death that normally follows Paul's visits to the bathroom. Instead we showered, shrieked a bit, use the tiny hairdryer to attempt to dry my back hair despite said hairdryer being so weak it barely shifted the top off my free cappuccino, and unpacked our suits.

Paul looked dapper. I however, did not. In all their infinite wisdom, the good numpties at Moss Bros had only gone and left the FUCKING SECURITY TAG hanging on the outside of my suit jacket. I hadn't spotted it because we'd been in such a flap the night before and anyway, surely that's a pretty fundamental part of selling a bloody suit? The air was blue, let me tell you. I rang up the shop and asked for advice only to be told there was no way of removing it without causing irreparable damage but that I could return it to the shop for my full money back. I pointed out that I had to wear the suit in twenty minutes only to be told there was nothing they could do without their manager. What the f**k would the manager do? Unless it was Uri Geller and he was going to use his mind to remove the stupid tag from afar, he'd be as useless as a trapeze artist with an itchy arse. I called him a word that my mother would still smack the back of my legs over and hung up. No jacket, then. I'd be the only one at the wedding not dressed to the nines.

To compound matters, I'd wildly misjudged my shirt and not realised quite how tight the collar was, meaning whenever I did the top button up a tiny life-belt of fat appeared over the top. So I couldn't wear a tie, either. At this point, all I could do was laugh, and Paul cheered me up by letting me have the last Options Hot Chocolate from the tray and ringing for further supplies. At least my shoes were polished and my hair was suitably mohawked. So, jacketless and tieless, I joined Paul and we headed into the hall. In retrospect, I should have just carried a tray of canapés around and pretended I was part of 'The Help'. Easy to be wise after the event.

I confess this now: I hate weddings. Don't get me wrong, I enjoyed seeing a co-worker look absolutely beautiful and beaming marry the love of her life, and the snacks, staging and entertainment were second to none, but it means making small talk with a lot of people I don't know and that means the potential for embarrassing myself is incredibly high. I've only ever been to four weddings – one was my own, one was a friend who then split up from her partner two months later and the other two weddings were family affairs where the bride wore a shellsuit. Both times, I kid you not. You've never heard Pachelbel's Canon until you've heard it accompanied by corned-beef thighs rubbing against polyester.

That said, it turned out to be a most pleasant day. Paul and I made effortless conversation with all those who deigned to talk to us, the wine flowed endlessly and I managed to eat my dinner without dropping an amuse-bouche down someone's cleavage or breaking wind during the speeches. I spotted that Paul had tears in his eyes and I thought he'd been touched by the heartfelt words of the speaker until I realised it was because they'd taken the tower of macaroons away from the table. The evening drew in and the drinks continued, with Paul and I deciding at 8pm to nip back to the room to "freshen up", which was actually just an excuse to go and get nasty, given we "were on holiday".

...

...

Well, that ended abruptly, didn't it?

Yep, so overflowing were we with bonhomie and expensive wine that we got back to the room, spilt a glass of wine on the carpet and fell asleep pretty much where we fell, which in Paul's case was actually bent over the bed with his arse hanging out welcoming the morning with regular, eye-wateringly pungent farts. I'd managed to fall asleep in a chair with a piece of Lego from the wedding favours stuck in my foot. Not very impressive. Everyone else had danced the night away in a celebration of love and we'd spent it – and the overnight stay in our £200 room – snoring and farting with the window open. Remember we were in a stable block too with other guests in adjoining rooms, it probably sounded like we were mixing cement all night. I was absolutely fucking mortified. We freshened up the best we could but still couldn't face everyone at breakfast, so we waited until our hangover had shifted a little and made a beeline for our car, raring down the gravel path like extras from Mad Max. We'd missed the hog-roast (though judging from my wincing when I sat down, I reckon we'd at least tried something similar ourselves), the first dance, the fireworks, the lot. Hell, we'd even missed the breakfast and that was the thing I had been really looking forward to.

We drove home in head-aching silence, fed the cats, and pretty much spent the rest of the day in bed feeling sorry for ourselves and writing passive-aggressive Twitter comments on Moss Bros' wall, until they blocked us.

Bastards.

See, I told you we're no good at weddings.

twochubbycubs on: colonic irrigation

WARNING: if you're a little squeamish, best skip a page. Seriously. Graphic and frank discussion about sex and poo lies ahead. Which you're going to read even if you're squeamish, but for goodness sake make sure you're not eating oxtail soup.

You may recall that back on my birthday Paul surprised me with a gift voucher for a colonic irrigation, which as birthday surprises go is like getting a card where someone has spat in it. Nothing says I love you, birthday boy like 'I think your bowels might need a good rinse'. I wouldn't care, I'm a gay man in a loving marriage and I've always prided myself on having a clean nipsy – there's nothing worse than go-faster-stripes on your willy after sex.

People think gay sex must be a messy affair but honestly, it isn't. As long as you're sensible and don't go for a quick morning putt after a night on the Guinness, you're generally alright. That said, we do have a friend who after pulling out of his one-night-stand had a sweetcorn kernel wedged in his japs eye. That'll teach him for going in without protection – you wouldn't go through a car wash with your windows down, after all. There is another who 'rinses himself out' – ah fuck it, let's not be delicate – he douches with a bottle of Evian, because clearly bog-standard tapwater won't do for his mudchute. I don't think anyone's ever got to the point of climax and said 'No no, I can't do this, I'm a Volvic man'. Horses for courses.

So yes, my bowels, and related to them, my colonic irrigation. I phoned up a week or so ago and booked myself in with an altogether too-cheery receptionist who took my details like I was enquiring about a secondhand sofa she was selling. I was to arrive at 11 for a quick chat with my 'therapist' who'd talk me through the procedure and then get to work. Those were her exact words – get to work – as if filling my bottom was akin a tough bit of plastering or knocking down a wall. Gracious. Paul hadn't even took the day off work to provide moral support, which was fair enough, but it meant I had to take my car to the clinic, and I spent most of the journey there wishing I'd had the wherewithal to bring a towel with me for the car-seat on the journey back. I can't imagine the good folks at the 'Best Handwash In Town' are that au-fait with dabbing bum-water out of a DS3's upholstery. Still, at least it distracted me.

They say to wear clothes that can easily be removed – I assumed they meant slacks and a t-shirt rather than a rip-off onesie that I could tear away like a magician's assistant. God knows why the top was so important but I spent a good ten minutes picking an outfit (something I genuinely never do, I normally just lean into my wardrobe and wear the first thing that falls on the floor). I didn't want to wear something too casual that would give the air of someone for whom having their bowel rinsed was nothing more than a mere afterthought at the end of a busy day, but nor did I want to go dressed like I was giving a sermon to poos past. I went with black jogging bottoms and a Disney t-shirt. Oh how we'd laugh together as the tube went up. Anyway.

Having found the place, I parked up, signed the forms and met my nurse, Jessica, which I thought was a terribly posh name for someone who spent most of their day peering at bumholes. She was pretty and pleasant and actually did manage to put me at ease somewhat, which was nice. Perhaps their choice of relaxing music was a bit off – it was eighties songs via the medium of panpipes, the sort of shite you'd find next to the till at a run-down garden centre. I'd forgotten to take my iPod out of the car so I was stuck with it.

She asked me to take off my trousers and get myself comfortable on the bed, on my side with my knees tucked up into my chest. This was the most excruciating bit – the moment her soft, blue eyes would come face to face with my rusty bullet hole. I thought I heard her sucking air in through her teeth like a builder but in retrospect it might have just been the foam mattress adjusting. I heard the familiar click of a lube bottle and pop, in went the speculum.

I resisted the urge to be mischievous and moan 'more, MORE' and push back. I kept still and listened to pan-pipe Bananarama. She talked me through the whole process of attaching the 'water in' tube and the 'poo out' tube though she did stop short of patting my flank with the back of her hand the way one might try and calm a worried horse. Then came the water.

And do you know, it was really quite pleasant. I'm not sure what I expected but it was just the gentlest of feelings. Don't get me wrong, I wasn't expecting her to come in with a fireman's hose and fill me with water 'til I rolled out like a mocha Violet Beauregarde, but I was still unsure of how much pressure she'd apply. What actually happens is that the water fills up your bowels gently until you've 'reached capacity', at which point the pressure is released your body gets rid of by essentially opening up the floodgate, sending all that water, poo and bits and bobs merrily down the tube.

It's odd – the water seems to vary in temperature, but that's not the water temperature changing but rather how my bowels were reacting to it, perhaps the same way I do when I get in an unreliable shower, shrieking and recoiling with every cold burst. Plus, because your body is trying to get rid of the water, your ringpiece starts clamping like an old camera shutter. Had I been more on the ball I could have cut the end off a celebratory cigar for Jessica and I to share afterwards.

Speaking of Jessica, she didn't stay with me throughout, the machine did most of the work, and I was thankful. Imagine making small talk with someone as the contents of your bowel shoot around the room in a clear tube. I had a vision of her standing holding the tube and announcing the contents as they whooshed past – 'POO, POO, WATER, POO, POO, LUDO PIECE, POO, WATER, THE Z TILE FROM POCKET SCRABBLE, POO, WATER, SIX OLD BUTTONS, CARRIAGE CLOCK, WATER, WATER, WE'RE DONE!' like she was on the smelliest version of The Generation Game. Thankfully, that didn't happen either. No, the whole procedure was over in around forty minutes, after I'd been inflated and rinsed out a good few times. Jessica pulled the speculum out gently, which I was thankful as I was dreading a loud 'POP' noise like someone bursting a balloon, and after I gingerly stood up, she advised me to get dressed and go sit on the toilet for a bit. I didn't know whether I should have slipped her a tip but my wallet was in the car so that answered that conundrum. I almost felt a little sad saying goodbye, like we'd been through an emotional journey together, but she was very brisk and professional and I was on my way. I spent ten minutes in the toilet making sure there were no trains outside the station and then I was on my way.

Was it fun? Hell no. Did I feel better for it? Actually, a little. I felt a bit unsteady on my feet (perhaps I'd lost my centre of balance, the 'out tube' did gurgle and strain for a good five minutes at one point) but I made it to the car and sat on an old Socialist Appeal which Paul had thoughtfully left. I now know how the cat felt when we took him to the vets when he couldn't poo and she squeezed him like an old tube of toothpaste until a tiny malteaser of turd came bursting out the other end. I know, it's a glamourous life. I spent the rest of the day watching Come Dine with Me with my stomach gurgling ominously until Paul came home to tend to me.

I say tend to me, he immediately wanted to try it out. All I can say is that I've never heard it 'squeak' before, like rubbing a cloth down a dry window. I'm surprised she didn't at least hang a 'New Car Smell' magic tree down there too. So there you go: that's a colonic. Done. I didn't want to say to Paul that it actually wasn't too bad because god knows what I'd end up getting for our anniversary – an acid peel, or a urethra swabbing? Bleurgh. That's an actual fetish, too.

Well done for those squeamish for getting through - have yourself a cup of badly mixed hot chocolate and think of me.

twochubbycubs on: countdown and coach trip

Can I explain one of my irrational dislikes? I'm a big quiz-show fan, so I'll often pull a 15-to-1 or Countdown out of the Sky planner to watch when I'm bored. I know I know, but we all have quirks. My annoyance stems from Countdown, and in particular, the precocious 'youngsters' they occasionally have on. I get that they are geniuses, but the sight of all their weird 'never-left-the-house' tics and pallid skin makes my skin crawl. They nearly always look like in ten years time they're going to be talked to by the police for masturbating into the coat of a lady in front of them on an escalator. Still, that's easy for me to say, I don't have the balls to go on, even though I'm pretty decent at anagrams. It's easier to sit at the computer and be a TOTLACNUT about people.

Actually, that's a fib. Paul and I did apply to go on Coach Trip and got put on the waiting list, but never got any further. Probably for the best, Paul has a potty mouth and I reckon the bus would barely have a chance to back out of the car-park before we'd be booted off and Channel 4 shut down. I find Brendan hysterical though – he's exactly what I imagine Paul will look like in twenty years, perhaps minus the tight shirts.

twochubbycubs on: lazy Saturday afternoons

Paul's actually off down in London at the 'Give Britain a Payrise' rally. I work in the private sector so my eyes tend to glaze over when he goes on about rallies and protests, but fair play to the bugger for campaigning. Last time I told him to try and keep a low profile, and he ended up headlining the 1pm news with a soundbite about pensions. Even worse, the last time his place of work went on strike, he threw himself in front of someone's car and called her a scab, without realising it was the Chief Executive inside. Oops. Anyway, he's coming back home now and the latest text I got was 'Missing you, dying for a shit', which I don't really know how to take but I'll assume it was meant as a compliment.

I spent all morning lying in bed and willing myself to get up, but I didn't quite manage it until 1pm. Which sounds lazy, but I've had a very long week and our bed is super comfortable. Actually, that's a bit of a fib as I got up once and managed to moon someone putting a leaflet through our front door at the same time. I should explain. I got up for a wee and noticed the postman had been. We sleep naked, but the curtains were drawn so I went to the front door and bent down, completely naked, at the same time someone pushed a takeaway leaflet through the letterbox. Luckily our front door has that weird frosted glass in it, but I'm still fairly sure he got a damn good view of my tea-towel holder winking at him as I scrabbled to pick up the post. Ah well. This afternoon I decided to take it upon myself to go to B&M to find an elusive curry mix that a lot of people rave about online. Now, I've never been in B&M before, and well, goodness me.

Let me caveat the following by saying that I'm no snob, I don't mind cheap shops and I don't care how much something costs. But honest to god, I've never seen so many people with missing teeth in one place. I felt like I was at a gingivitis support class. Plus, I don't think I've ever had so many polyester-mix fleeces rubbed against me as people rugby-charged past to get to the Playboy mirrors. I'm lucky I didn't come out of there sparking and jolting like Electro from Spiderman.

twochubbycubs on: an MRI scan

Today has been a testing day, I'm not going to lie. Normally I'd bury my face in a box of Milk Tray until every pore was filled with cheap, naff chocolate, but as I'm dieting I'm just going to vent a bit.

Firstly, some grotty little chav almost crashed his shitty little acne carriage into my new car this morning. Not quite sure why he thought that pulling out of a junction into my oncoming-at-60mph car would be the best move for him, but he did, then he had the temerity to beep his horn at me and give me the finger. Bah! Let's hope his next inevitable dose of roaccutane is a lethal one. Oh and for the record, you don't need a fucking spoiler on a ten-year-old Vauxhall Corsa. It isn't going to launch into the air straining to get to 70mph on the A1.

Then work happened.

After I was released from work, I had a pleasant day availing myself of the MRI scanner at North Tyneside Hospital. Nothing too dramatic, but I have to have a regular check on my heart as it's a bit dicky, and the last thing I want to do is collapse on the floor at work making Donald Duck noises like poor old Jim Robinson in Neighbours. I got there, and after finding the first available car parking space just outside of fucking Aberdeen and paying a kings ransom for the chance to park on a bit of windswept tarmac more pockmarked than the aforementioned chav's face, proceeded to mince to entirely the wrong department. How we chuckled and laughed as I launched myself red-faced to the correct reception desk with only a minute to spare, only to be told the machine had been malfunctioning (brilliant news! just what you want to hear) and they were running late. Forty minutes of browsing 'Your Kitchen' and not daring to turn on my phone in case it reacted with the MRI scanner next door and created a wormhole through space (though I'd probably get back to my car quicker that way) later, I was in.

Now, the staff were absolute loves. They really were. And going into an MRI scanner doesn't bother me, I find it quite soothing. But I can see why they're scary, considering it looks like you're being slid into a colossal metallic Samsung-branded anus. The day got better when they gave me a 'medium' gown to change into, meaning my hairy sarlacc pit was on show to all and sundry (as it happens, I managed to put it on the wrong way anyway, so had to change again so my moobs were showing). Then, two phrases I don't hear often enough in my life 'I hope you've got good veins, as we're going to need to put a canula in and inject you with a contrast' and 'trainee, I'm going to need you to shave him'.

Well for fucks sake. I've had a bit of a run with tests lately on my heart which have required me being shaved, and each one has resulted in a strip of my chest hair being removed. I'm very hairy, and seemingly my body hair is made out of steel wool, because the poor trainee hacked away at me with a disposable razor for a good few minutes without making much of a difference. You've never experienced awkward until someone is holding your left tit in one hand and scraping away at your chest with an NHS-Never-Shave with the other. Bless his heart, he did try making small-talk with me and kept up the eye-contact, but when he said 'I can't even grow a moustache, never mind a chest like yours' it quite killed the conversation dead.

So, there I was, lying on the metal tray, feet just poking into the machine and the last question I got asked was 'Would you like Michael Buble to listen to during the scan?'. I nearly fell off the tray in indignation. I wouldn't want to listen to Michael Buble if I was on fire and he was calling the fire brigade, let alone endure his dinner-party crooning for an hour complimented by the German-techno sounds of an MRI scan. I politely declined and they put The Eagles on instead.

The scan itself took an hour, and whilst yes it is a smidge claustrophobic, you're given what in all honesty looks like a douching bulb to squeeze at any time if you get frightened, at which point (I presume) the tray slides back out and you're given a hot cocoa and a reassuring cuddle. I'm a BIG guy, and I didn't feel trapped – your nose is about 10" from the top of the machine. I keep my eyes closed and imagine I'm lying on a beach somewhere. A beach that smells oddly of ozone and farts. You shouldn't really move, as the stiller you are the better the quality of the scans, but I can guarantee you'll need to pick your nose, your teeth or your arse just as soon as you like. There is a LOT of noise – lots of clanging and whirring and buzzing, but it isn't alarming and just a sign that the machine is doing its thing. The radiographers (not sure that's right) talk to you occasionally, in my case telling me to breathe in, breathe out, breathe in, breathe out, hold your breath (to see what my heart does under pressure) and breathe again. It's the same thing keeping that twat Joey Essex alive. Anyway, at one point the woman was clearly distracted and forgot to tell me to breathe again, meaning I went almost a minute without taking a breath. No wonder my heart is buggered!

After forty five minutes, the tray slides out, you're given a cup of water and a thunderous round of applause (only on BUPA) and sent on your way. I got halfway back to the carpark before realising I'd nicked off without them taking out my canula, meaning a trek back and a 'ooh what am I like' moment. The sight of my blood pumping out of my arm as I distracted the nurse with my witty chat about Renee Zellweger made my toes curl a bit. But that was that. I was unusual in that a cardiologist was there to have a quick neb at my results, but my doctor will get the full report in due course.

I stopped by the proctology department hospital shop

and chose a finger of fudge. I feigned a sugar crash with the old vinegar-tits on the till but she was having none of it, charging me 45p for a bloody Fudge bar. I mean I ask you. Yes I'm on a diet but I needed something sweet as they didn't give me a lollipop for being a brave boy. NHS cutbacks see.

So that was my day. Actually not that bad. I apologise that this isn't a post about Slimming World but this is a personal blog, after all, and if it gives a bit of insight to anyone going into an MRI scanner at some point that's no bad thing.

twochubbycubs on: the cat shed

Firstly, I want to get something off my chest. Those awful adverts for eyelids-in-crumbs dispensary Iceland where that creepy orange manchild Peter Andre dances around exclaiming about super-cheap nonsense food. Haway. Peter Andre would never, ever shop at Iceland. But, if there's one man who will be used to blowing his wad on a cheap prawn ring that can satisfy up to twenty punters at once, it's Jordan's ex, Peter Andre.

SO, enough of that. Today's post is introducing one of our secret weapons – the Shed!

When we moved into our current house, we were amazingly lucky – tonnes of space and storage. Well, actually, not that lucky, the old dear who lived here before us died mid-poo and bless her heart, hit her head off the loo on the way down – which was tragic, but also (whisper it) a smidge vexing as it caused a very slow leak and soaked the bathroom floor – what a way to go though, we call her Elvis. We live in a very 'keeping up with the Joneses' type of street, with pretentiously named houses such as 'Willow Cottage' and 'Tena Towers' (might be a fib, that one) lining the paths. So of course, we immediately endeared ourselves to them by changing the name of our house to something a little more graphic. Maha.

For the first year, we did nothing more than internal

redecoration and completely ignored the tip-top shed down the side of the house, which, when we ventured inside, was chock-o-block with old tins of paint, Presto carrier bags, British Telecom bills, boxes and boxes of old papers, white dog poo etc. Once we cleaned that out, however, we had ourselves an empty shed just ready to be filled with the inevitable accoutrements you'd expect from two manly, burly men living together – perhaps petrol lawnmowers, barbecues, chainsaws and other various penis-replacements. Nah. Not us.

No, we fitted a magnetic cat-flap, added a flower box, carpeted the inside, added water bowls and an automatic food-dispenser, spent £90 on a cat-tree and opened the 'Cat Shed' up to our cats, who were just at the stage of venturing out the house. We were worried that they'd get wet outside and mew sadly at our back doors. The stress was getting too much hence the Cat Shed. They loved it. Well, Bowser did, Sola is a snotty cow who still sleeps in the compost bin just so she can come in the house smelling of rotting grass and give us dirty looks.

Oh, actually, before I go, another Iceland advert with Peter Andre just came on the telly where he was travelling by bus. The permatanned human niknak would never travel by bus. But, if there's one man who will be used to riding a sweaty box capable of accommodating up to sixty men at once with an impressive top deck, it's Jordan's ex, Peter Andre.

twochubbycubs on: a lunch hour in Newcastle

Can I just say, I've never felt like more of a fat bastard than when I staggered out of Nandos last night with five full paper bags of food. Admittedly I was buying for eight co-workers but who isn't going to look and think 'REALLY, WITH THOSE TITS' at me. Bah.

Normally, on the extravagant sixty minutes that my chains are released and I am free to leave my desk during the working day, I will go to a quiet place, like my car or the park, to read, sleep, eat dinner or imagine various psychopathic fantasies upon the various degenerates of Newcastle. However, today, I made the fatal error of venturing into town in order to pick up a prescription. In half-term week. Ugh.

There's a shop in Newcastle called Fenwicks which you have to cut through the men's clothing department in order to get to the food hall. It's the worst possible experience for a fat bloke, let me tell you. It isn't the clothes that are the problem, though – I have long since accepted that my clothes come measured in metre increments rather than inches. No, it's the staff. The floor seems awash with those posing peacock men who strut around with their o-so-achingly styled facial hair and jeans so tight you can almost see their individual sperms wriggling around. Let me say something: men who have beards should be burly, rough men who thinking washing their arse is foreplay. They do not belong on 'men' whose idea of a bad day at work is someone raising an eyebrow and criticising the way they've stacked the XXS Fred Smith accent shirts. Perhaps I'm just jealous and/or paranoid, but it's like an explosive decompression on a plane with them sucking air through their teeth as I blunder across the floor and they catch sight of my two year old Florence and Fred shirt, let out trousers and wide shoes that look like I buy them from Build a Bear. Such attitude! Such pretentious, sneering attitude and it is completely unwarranted. I'm reminded of Edina from Absolutely Fabulous who said '...and you can drop the attitude love, you only work in a shop'. Spot on. I have no problem with people working in shops, I'm not a snob – but honest to God, you're selling the shirts, not designing them. You beanpole buggers. Lunch acquired, I went to get my MASSIVE DRUGS (betnovate actually, I have a tiny annoying bit of dry skin on my foot).

The pharmacy, of course, was full of the usual work shy reprobates who haunt town during the day like milky skinned vampires, shaking and clutching their methadone scripts like a winning Euromillions ticket. I fully admit that I judge people immediately on sight (and bugger off, because we all do), and when a woman easily in her forties, with that pinched arse mouth look that you can only get from ten billion Sterling Blue hurriedly choked down outside of a Mecca bingo hall, wants to push in the queue because she's in a rush...well she got short shrift from me. On top of that, I had to wait almost thirty minutes for them to spin the Medicine Wheel of Fortune and give me my bloody cream.

To top off that lovely hour, as I walked behind the building to climb the stairs into work, there was someone, not even a trampy looking fella, having a shit behind Sainsbury's.

Welcome to Newcastle folks, stay all week.

twochubbycubs on: my lovely nana

October 2014

I need to make an announcement that I'm really a terrible grandson. I had plans to visit my nana today (she only lives 30 miles away and it's a nice drive), but I didn't get round to it because I got caught up gardening and playing on the Xbox. It will probably do my diet the world of good anyway, as whenever Paul and I go and visit we get the same questions...'would you like a bit of quiche / eight kitkats / mince pie / mince and potato pie / sandwich / lovely bit of tongue (steady) / a Ferrari Racket chocolate from ALDI etc...' which, when met with polite refusal and cries of 'but no, we're on a diet' results in a look like you've taken a shit on the carpet and woes of 'It'll never get eaten, it's just me in this house' and 'a quarter inch thick layer of butter on your sandwich will do you no harm'. Honestly! And mind that's even if she hears your refusal, she's so tone deaf you could fell a tree in the living room behind her chair and she'd smile bemused at you and say EH.

My nana is amazing, mind, no doubt about that. She is totally accepting of the whole Paul and I being bummers situation, though she did once ask 'which one was the woman' which was slightly awkward, as I thought she meant which of us preferred an 'unexpected item in the bagging area' – but she was actually meaning who did the ironing/cooking etc (remember she's in her late eighties). Ha! So I'll go visit her on Tuesday with my usual refrain of 'I DIDN'T LIKE TO CHANCE LEAVING IT TOO LONG NANA, IN CASE I NEED TO GET MY FUNERAL SUIT DRY-CLEANED'. God, I love her to bits.

January 2015

What a lovely day! An hour spent bellowing at my nana – not out of malice you understand, but remember, she's tone deaf so you end up repeating things in incremental degrees of volume until you're screaming NO THANKS I DON'T NEED A METRIC TONNE OF MINT IMPERIALS I'M ON A DIET like you're trying a hail a taxi from the moon. Bless her, it would be quicker and easier for me to have my side of the conversation tattooed onto my body and relayed back to her via sign language than it is to have a two-way conversation punctuated only by the sound of her hearing aid whirring away like an old 56k modem. Bless her though, I'd not change a bit about her. Even the answers in her Puzzler are hilarious – when she doesn't know, she just adds random letters in like someone upending a Scrabble board.

February 2015

Well, that was an exciting afternoon. The parents have decided to spend a bit more of my inheritance and have buggered off to the Gambia for a week or two, leaving

Nana Dearest in the care of me and my sister. She's very independent but it's good to check in on her every day just to make sure she hasn't rolled a seven and shuffled off the mortal coil. So, fatty and I piled into the car today at half one and drove the thirty miles over to her house – in the ice and snow – to see that she was up and about and dutifully forgetting to take her tablets. Got there to find her curtains still shut in the bedroom and the door locked. At 2pm, and us without a key. The dog was scratching on the other side of the door. No amount of knocking and shouting got a reply. Naturally, we ~~raised the alarm~~ buggered off to do our weekly shop at Tesco with a view to coming back and trying again at half three. Still no reply. I had no key, remember. How do you attract the attentions of an eighty eight year old woman whose hearing aid would merely register a muffled bump if a plane crashed in her garden?

Well, here's how – you get a clothes prop from the garden. For those of you who aren't living in the 1940s, a clothes prop is a very long, very thin bit of wood that Geordies use to hoist their clothes line high up in the air so that villagers in another parish altogether can cast disdainful looks at the skidders on your knickers.

Of course, it would be altogether too easy for my gran's prop to be a strong, metal affair like the one pictures – no, hers was a manky old bit of wood that had been sitting in the snowy mud since the Battle of the Somme and was dangerously rotten. Nevertheless I pressed on and hoisting the bendy, rotten, 14ft prop into the air like a fucking pole vaulter and standing on the tops of my boots, I rapped it smartly against her window, tap tap tap, whilst Paul brayed on the front door, with each 'tap' of the stick leading another muddy print against her window. After ten bloody minutes, a wispy bit of white hair appears followed by a bemused face, then the window opens and she tells me off for leaving mud all over her window frame. Turns out she had gone to bed the night before and only just woken up at 4pm, which frankly sounds like my idea of heaven. Pills dispensed and a cup of tea later, she turns to me sagely and says 'You could have just rang the doorbell, you know'. I almost turned the one hobnob (well, Aldi equivalent of a hobnob – a notnob?) I'd allowed myself to dust in my balled up fists. She's a dear, an absolute dear, but unless I had rung the doorbell with the front of my fucking car she really, really wouldn't have heard.

Still, how Paul and I laughed as we made our way back home, our shopping defrosting merrily in the boot. I'd do it all again though.

February 2015

Can we get something right straight off the bat? Man-buns. There's a simple test – if you are male, and you've tied up your locks like some weird hairy sphincter on top of your head, you're a cock. And not a nice cock, mind – we're talking a fishy old schlong. In fact no – if you had a sphincter in the middle of your head, that would actually make you an arse. I can't bear it. It doesn't so much as make my skin crawl as force it inside-out through cringing. Back when I had long hair, the only 'style' I succumbed to was brushing it, and that was only when I felt there might be a boiled sweet in amongst the tangles. There's an advert on TV now for Trivago which ends with a supposedly-dreamy shot of a woman asleep in a man's arms as he carries her down a hotel corridor to bed. He wouldn't be bad looking, but because of the man bun, you know that night is going to end with her face-down on a pillow and him accidentally calling her Patrick at the height of climax. There's no masculinity, no ruggedness – a weak, effete affectation which should only end up one way – in an acid bath. Too far? I say not far enough!

Tonight's been a bit of a wash-out – I was originally supposed to be out for dinner with work colleagues to say goodbye, good luck and thanks for all the laughs to one of the partners I work for, but thanks to the incompetence of Northumberland Council and their inability to fit a bloody toilet correctly that didn't happen, as I was summoned to my gran's house. Water was leaking through the ceiling again where they incorrectly fitted the toilet. Well they didn't fit the toilet on the ceiling, obviously. Anyway, it turns out it had been leaking since Wednesday and she had been patiently waiting for the council to come out, completely unable to use her upstairs loo, and having to totter down the stairs and to the outside loo (it's a really old house, we're not that Northern) every time she needed a tinkle in the dead of night. I mean for fucks sake, she's a very slow mover – she can go upstairs with a fiver in her purse and by the time she's made it back downstairs it's only worth £4.50. So this was a crap situation, and after my sister and I spent a bit of time bellowing at the council, they remedied it. Bloody ridiculous. I had an image in my head of her sat on the outside toilet, Puzzler in hand, frozen in time like Jack Torrance at the end of The Shining. Thankfully that didn't happen, although...

Bless!

twochubbycubs on: exercising

My own story with exercising is somewhat predictable. I was a skinny little thing until my balls dropped, I grew a peach-skin 'tache and my voice dropped, upon which I grew a cracking set of tits and filled out my trousers. PE was a nightmare because I had an absolutely horrible PE teacher who took great delight in making all the fatties be on the 'skins' team, i.e jiggle and wobble our way around a basketball court without our shirts on. My prevailing memory of PE was me deciding I didn't want to do cross-country and shouting at him, across the changing room, that I had terrible diarrhoea and couldn't possibly join in. His reply, with his midget hand firmly on his bony old thigh, was to yell back 'WELL IT'LL MAKE YOU RUN FASTER'. I had to put the tears in my eyes down to the four hundred cubic metres of Lynx Africa that hung in the changing room.

Actually, in retrospect, I'll give him that one. He was still a prick, though. Plus he used to wear the same rancid running leggings day in day out – blue Foothold ones that were strained around the gusset. You shouldn't be able to tell if your PE teacher was Jewish or not just by accidentally glancing at his crotch. Tell you what, though – he was a cracking geography teacher. Odd that!

In high school, PE was no better, but by that point the teaching staff had essentially given up on the fat kids and we were allowed to sit on the mats and gossip. I mean honestly, the clues to my inevitable lifestyle choices were there. They did eventually tell us off when we brought scones, clotted cream and jam to our PE class – and that's not even a fib. So, unlike most of the other lads who were happy kicking a bit of leather around in the mud or running aimlessly towards Newcastle Airport and back under the guise of cross-country, an enjoyment of sport was never fostered in me.

<flashforward wishy-whoo noise>

Paul and I decided to join a gym back in January, and told ourselves that we would look around the various gyms the region had to offer. We looked at one, and signed up for a year on the basis that a) it had a pool and b) it had a scented steam room. Honestly. David Lloyd in Jesmond. We were very keen to begin with, but stopped going, predominately because the weights area was absolutely full of preening, roid-rage arseholes who spent more time grunting in the mirror than using the machines. It was intimidating and always smelled of onions. I remember quite clearly one man who screamed 'FUCK' every time he lifted a weight and then looked around each time to see who was looking at him. Arseache. He was also one of those men who strut around the changing room bollock-naked so you can see all of his muscles. And they weren't worth seeing. He had a cock like a mouse's ear for a start.

Also, for the money you pay, the machines are quite old – which is fine, but if I'm a gadget man and I like things to distract me from the crushing heart pains and the death-rattle breathing. I don't think it's particularly unrealistic to expect a top-end gym to have a bike machine whose foot-straps don't snap and break every time you use them. I mean, for crying out loud, I don't have hobbit feet. The pool was pleasant enough, even if we drew gasps and pained looks from the Henriettas and Lucilla lot as we hoisted ourselves out of the pool. We haven't been for a while.

The scented steam room was a joy though. I might have came out with a face like a baggy scrotum but I smelt like a Florida orangery – and that's what it's all about.

twochubbycubs on: lamenting for hairstyles past

You know what I miss most from the last two decades or so? My hair. I used to have amazing hair. My friends, family and everyone in existence would doubtless think otherwise, but I don't care. I grew my hair for a good three years or so, dyed it a myriad of different colours, and always had something fun to play with during those tricky times when having a wank just wasn't appropriate behaviour, such as sitting on a bus or the funeral of a loved one. It was thick, luxurious, well-maintained – I loved being able to lie in the bath and swish it around in the water, I loved being able to tie knots in it, hell, I even straightened it once with a pair of straighteners and it was like the second coming. I do want to say though – at no point did I ever have one of those awful fringes which covered the eyes and necessitated that awful neck-throwing action that seems to be everywhere. I was never an Emo McGee. Too fat for it, for one thing, and I didn't have the wherewithal to start cutting myself and putting shit poetry on Livejournal.

Of course, wistful recollection is a wonderful thing, but in reality, I probably looked like the abandoned child of Snape from Harry Potter and old 'why use one voice when nineteen layered over the top of each other will do' Enya. When I was thin, it fair suited me, but when I was a porky fella, I just looked like a hairy Christmas bauble. I remember going to France with a mate when I was eighteen, and during a daring bit of drunkenness, having all my hair removed – and we're talking hair down to the middle of my back shaved off and my head left as smooth as a bowling ball. My mum walked straight past me at the airport and then spent the next twenty minutes shrieking and telling me I looked normal again. Cheers mum. For the first time in years, I felt a draft around my ears that even now makes me wince and long for the comfort of my Fructis-scented wonderhair. Ah well. Those days are definitely behind me, given that I've got hair like Steve McDonald now, and it's easier just to cut it myself than see myself reflected in a barber's mirror, light bouncing off the smooth, hairless front where so many beautiful hairs once lay. Sigh. The reason for this hair chatter by the way was the simple, indubitable truth that if I was to grow my hair again, I'd look like the time Fat Heather from Eastenders dresed up as Meat Loaf.

Anyway, come on, enough about times past. I went to see Interstellar last night, hence no post – apologies. However, I've got a corking recipe below for meatloaf which is perfect homely food for these cold nights. Interstellar, by the way, is absolute bobbins. It starts off promising enough, but then descends into look-at-me schtick and aren't-I-clever writing. Plus, every time Anne Fucking Hathaway opened her mouth I started having internal flashbacks to her caterwauling through Les Misérables a couple of years ago and had to stop the shakes with my salted popcorn. I'm sorry, but I just don't like her – and I think my friend summed it up best when she said that 'the biggest black hole in the entire movie is when Anne opens her letterbox mouth'. Haha!

twochubbycubs on: fish and France

Tonight was supposed to be a lovely romantic night, filled with Amazing Race and cosiness on the settee. I was going to take the lock off the central heating and allow Paul to put the heating on – well, it was icy on my car this morning, I think I've been entirely Geordie enough about the temperature thing. We've got one of those god-awful 'why yes, I'm incontinent' gas fires that the previous old couple had installed and I hate it. It hisses and smells, rather like Paul – and has equally dangerous levels of combustible gas. Anyway. That idea was quite literally put to bed as, after I made him the delicious dinner you see below, he went to 'drop the kids off' and fell asleep on the toilet. So he's away for an early night (in bed, that is – he's not still on the netty) and I'm left to do the cleaning up, accompanied only by the sound of his snoring, gasping for air and death-rattle farting. He's lucky he's so deliciously squishy.

Actually, I say it's quiet, but I'm actually being tormented by Cat Number 2 (Sola), who is currently outside the house trying to get in. No problem, I'll open the door. Except when I do, she sits there meowing and runs off as soon as I go to pick her up. Now she isn't fucking Lassie, I know there's no-one trapped down a well (and plus she's an evil cat – she'd be at the top of the well having a shit over the rim rather than dashing for help), she's just doing it to torment me. I sit down at the computer chair, and I hear the scratching at the front door begin. Then, she sticks her paw in a loose bit of fixture on the door and pulls it back just enough to make a tapping sound. Again and again and again. I put up with it, I curse at her, then I eventually get up, open the door, and off she flees. My own cat is playing Knocky-fucking-Nine Doors with me! It's bad enough I wake up to the sight of her licking her pencil sharpener every single morning, now she's bullying me at night too! Bag. I might see if I can take her to the vet and get her un-spayed, just because she was so hilariously grumpy for the few days after her last op. That'll teach her.

I'm trying hard to get into fish for an evening meal, with the old adage of 'if it swims, it slims' ringing in my ears. But so far, only tuna has passed muster, with everything else being deemed too fishy by my sensitive tastebuds. People always do the same thing when I mention I don't like fish – have you tried swordfish, oysters, trout, blah blah – yes! I have! I'm not unadventurous when it comes to food – I'll try anything and never say I don't like something without trying it. So I'm working my way through more fish, but, you know if you were to put down a steak and a piece of fish, you'd be able to tell which was fish because of the taste? It's THAT taste I don't like. Not fishiness, just...non-meatiness!

Fish does remind me of a favourite memory, though. I used to go on holiday to Montreuil-sur-Mer with a very good mate, and despite us both being common as muck, we decided to see if we could get a table at the poshest restaurant in the area, the Château de Montreuil, a ridiculously uptight fine-dining affair, not quite our level. Well no, nowhere near our level. We managed to bluff our way through the million courses until we were served a tiny blini with what I imagine was very good caviar atop. At the precise moment my friend put it into his mouth, I made a snide comment about one of the waiters and, of course with me being so deliciously cutting, he promptly burst out laughing, with the barely digested blini and caviar arcing gracefully across the table and landing in my doubtless very-expensive glass of champagne. Well, that was it for me, I was beyond help, in veritable paroxysms of laughter, but he was momentarily ashen. What to do? All manner of French lemon-mouthed hoity-toitys had turned to look at us. So, cool as a chinese cucumber, he reaches across the table, lifts my glass and downs the lot – champagne, caviar and blini – in one full gulp and crashes the glass down on the table with a loud exclamation of 'DEE-LICIOUS'.

Good heavens.

It's no wonder other nations think we're such an uncultured bunch.

twochubbycubs on: radio

I'm at a difficult stage in my life. The hour long commute from my home to work has to be done in a car (well no, I could take the bus, but so do so many smelly people and I can't be done inhaling someone else's body odour for an hour whilst I try to prevent my cankles brushing theirs) and I'm having trouble selecting a radio station. See, I used to enjoy Radio 1, and I admit that I think Nick Grimshaw is fantastic in the morning, but oh god lord the music. Occasionally there will be a song I enjoy, but most of the time I'm wailing at the radio because of the standard of music. For example, they play Lorde all the god-damn time, and her heaby breathing and straining of every single syllable makes it sound like she's singing for gold in a COPD clinic talent show. So, I end up stabbing at the buttons and switching to Radio 2.

Radio 2 is alright. I used to chortle along with Moira but I find her braying fake laugh like nails on a blackboard now. The music is slightly better, though I've heard it classed as 90% period-pain music, 10% Take That, which I think sums it up nicely. I'm usually alright with this for most of the journey until they play HIM. Ed Fucking Sheeran. Good heavens no. His voice is alright, and his songs catchy, but there's something about him that really makes my skin crawl. Well, not so much crawl as sprint right off my flesh and through a shredder. For one, in nearly every single photo I ever see of him he's doing this incredibly vexing squint-smile combination, like he's trying to read a heartfelt message off the head of a pin. Plus, he looks the absolute spit of my ex, who spent more time in bed scratching his dry skin than anything else. And he was a good one! I dated a proper abusive dick for a good year called Neil, until his passive-aggressiveness and cheating ways ended up with me cutting his treasured pony tail off. Remember: what do you find when you lift up a pony's tail? An ARSE. He had a weird bone disease too which meant he had really long arms and legs – sex was like getting into a fight with a rotary drier. So yeah! Radio 2. Alright until that flame-haired moon-faced bumhole starts his warbling.

What's left? I'm not intellectual enough for Radio 4, I'm sick of hearing the same eight pieces of music on Classic FM and, as I'm not a taxi offender / habitual sex-offender, Smooth FM is out of the window. BBC Radio Newcastle consists of people ringing up talking about their ingrown toenails and Metro Radio, which used to be grand back in the day, is fronted by two thick people and a sound effects machine. Bah. I generally end up getting in a huff with myself and singing instead. I could put on a podcast or my own music but I'm too lazy to figure out how the bluetooth works on my car. Ah well.

twochubbycubs on: dads, eh

Before I start – Paul sat bolt upright in bed this morning (well as bolt upright as someone with a waterfall of fat on their front can do) and announced 'I just had a dream that I won the Eurovision Song Contest...representing Lebanon!' and went back to sleep. I couldn't sleep after that particularly gay announcement. Cheers Paul.

The title of this post comes from my father, who on entering any room, always say 'EH' like he's missed out on some juicy titbit of gossip. I endured this for eighteen years before I moved out (not because of the eh-ing I hasten to add) and he still does it even to this day. Brilliant.

I'm going to quickly post this and then head off to see The Unmentionables – well you have to, it's Father's Day. My dad is brilliant – he's like the antithesis of me in every single way. Where some people might call me quite fey, he's super-butch. I'm fat, he's thin. He has a Screwfix catalogue next to his bed, I had a copy of Salza: For Lover of Latino Inches hidden under my mattress. He can quite cheerfully throw up a set of shelves, remodel a kitchen and mend a broken car, whereas I can quite cheerfully call a handyman, joiner and mechanic in on my mobile.

He's always been one of those dads who knows how to

do everything – and although he always walks into my house and says it smells of something, which irks me no end – he can always be relied upon if I ever need anything done. He was great with me growing up, despite having to endure the veritable collection of freaks that I brought home…the ginger one, the scabby one, the one with the discus-shaped lip, the one with the question-mark spine, the one who looked like Richard Osman from Pointless, Silent Bob, the chap whose voice sounded like a bee caught behind a radiator…he made small talk and polite conversation with them all. I never once felt awkward, pressured or unsupported and that's testament to what a great father he is. I never tell him that, obviously. That would be far too awkward and non-manly. Feelings, right?

Paul has a similar relationship with his dad, although it's slightly more difficult for him as there's over 250 miles between them. However, we seem to have settled into a pattern of genial giving of gifts on special occasions – Paul's dad gets a cookbook or an atlas at Christmas, Paul gets money a week after his birthday. I've met him and can gladly say the old 'in-laws are horrible' stereotype doesn't apply, which is great. He's a thoroughly pleasant chap. Paul often tells me of how he came out to his parents – his mum reacted in a very 'mum' way, by making retching noises and almost-but-not-quite putting down her Puzzler in shock, whereas his dad said 'SO YOUR MUM TELLS ME YOU'RE GAY, SON' and went back to fussing around his Renault 19.

Parents are fun.

As for us, being fathers is the last thing we'd ever want to do. The mechanics of it are bad enough — we're not going to stand around popping our yop into a plastic cup and finding some suitable receptacle to carry our child, that's too stressful. But even if we got past that point, the idea of having a child to look after is my idea of genuine hell. I can barely remember to clip my own toenails and go to the toilet, having some screaming hellchild demanding regular food and access to my bank account fills me with dread. So: you'll never be reading the tearful account of us adopting and raising a child, though you can know that if we ever DID, it would have a proper bloody name. I've heard of a kid being called Lil'star and it makes my eyes shake with fury.

twochubbycubs on: interactive gay TV

Do you know, there's lots of things I enjoy about staying in an airport hotel – not just the excitement, cramping belly and visits to the can that flying the next day induces in me, oh no. I like having my soap in a handy dispenser in the shower, plus the added novelty (occasionally) of having a seat in the shower – the glamour of being able to soap myself down with absolute minimal effort.

But what we really love is Rabbit Gay TV. We don't get this channel at home because it's on Freeview and we suckle merrily on Sky's teat, so whenever we stay at a budget hotel we delight in the wares of the channels at the end of the Freeview EPG. Rabbit Gay TV is just the best. It's essentially a scrolling list of those adverts you get in lonely heart columns, only with pictures. And good heavens, the pictures.

Now, I've been through enough shenanigans to know not to judge anyone's sexual choices, but I've genuinely never seen so many lorry drivers, binmen and retired accountants dressed up as 1980s housewives in one place. They're always the same, bad nylon wig, dress from a charity shop, posing with their hands coquettishly over their mouth like some simpering never-been-kissed seamstress, though you rarely get a seamstress named Big Keith. The adverts are nearly always the same, lots of WLTM and TV and GSOH and VWE (because what else do you expect to see when you lift up a lace petticoat than a very well endowed cock winking at you) and the audio clips are ever weirder, with hushed proclamations of desire whispered out in the echoing sounds of their garage or Vauxhall Passat.

Paul and I once decided to text a reply to someone on there to see what would happen, and I'm not exaggerating when I say that within five text messages, he was asking whether we liked "playing with dogs". Which sorta summarises exactly the type of person on there. Mind you, Paul used to know a lad who was paid by an old geezer to come round to his flat, eat beans and fart in the man's face. Now as someone who enjoys money, likes beans and loves a good fart, that sounds like my ideal job, though perhaps not for the poor victim. One of my toxic bumtrumpets near his face would leave him looking like Harvey Dent from the Batman series when he had half of his face burnt off. In fact, it would look like the top of a well cooked frittata.

twochubbycubs on: eye-tests

I can't be the only one who finds eye tests incredibly stressful experiences, can I? I spend an hour or so beforehand obsessively chewing gum and using mouthwash because I know someone is going to be right up in the face and I don't want them laughing gaily in the Vision Express staffroom at my smelly breath and dry skin. I have a massive anxiety with people being too close to me so sitting there whilst someone leans over me tutting about my answers and adjusting my lenses is a major nono.

It all stems from my first eye test which I shamefully waited until I was 23 to have, after I spent the first two years of our relationship thinking Paul was actually Japanese. Well maybe it wasn't that bad but I really was blind. I had a very old, lovely but very fat optician who spent about thirty minutes actually pressed up against my chair peering into my eyes with that little light of hers. If I moved my head up, I'd have gotten stubble rash from her chin, and if I had turned my face in either direction I'd have nuzzled right into her boobs. I've never had someone be that close to me and not buy me a drink first. She also, bless her, had clearly been eating poo or something beforehand because her breath was bleaching my hair every time she exhaled. Since that arduous half hour, I've really worried about eye tests ever since. But I look so much better in glasses so it's a hard choice…

twochubbycubs on: volunteering

October 2014

We volunteered as dog-walkers today.

It was BRILLIANT. I love dogs (not as much as cats – it's my ambition in life (or rather death) that when I snuff it, I lie in a living room with eighty cats picking away at my carcass and eight pouches of Bite 'n' Chew in my birds nest hair) but we can't have one in our house. It wouldn't be fair, as we both work long hours and I'd spend all day worried that the dog was looking out the window with a doleful expression on its face, waiting for our DS3 to come bouncing over the speed-bump/her at Number 2 at the bottom of our street. So. How to get some body magic in and meet new dogs? Easy! We rang up a local cat and dog shelter (Brysons of Gateshead) (I'm not sure if that needs apostrophising and now I'm stressing, so if it does, I'm sorry) and asked if they needed people to walk their dogs – and they do, so we did!

After spending ten minutes doing my normal parking routine of driving into a parking space, leaving it, driving back in at one degree less than before, checking the lines, driving out, putting my wipers on instead of my indicators and then finally driving in another bay just up the road, we were there, and after handing over ID (lest we stole the dogs, I assume) we were given Max (a spaniel, I think) and Scout (a greyhound). Off we trotted, with the greyhound almost immediately pulling me over. I'm a big guy, but this bugger was strong! Paul had worn a shitty pair of old trainers so he was fine clarting around in the mud, but I'd inexplicably chose Chelsea boots to wear, and I pretty much skated my way through the mud along the Bowes Railway.

We spent ages trotting along with the dogs who were wonderfully behaved, giving them a good walk (and us some great body magic) and generally enjoying ourselves. The dogs seemed happy to be made of a fuss of and getting some fresh air, even if my dog (Max) spent a horrendous amount of time picking absolutely every bit of rubbish up off the ground and trying to eat it, followed by me trying to stop him – I don't think we'd be able to take dogs out again if I returned it with a Panda Pop bottle poking out of his bumhole.

Gorgeous little buggers. Great way to get more exercise and to help out a local charity. They also need cat cuddlers but I don't think my heart can take it.

February 2015

Honestly, today has been a great day. My work allow us to take two days off a year to spend at home masturbating and watching Jeremy Kyle, though not at the same time volunteering at local charities, so today I took them up on it and went along to the cat and dog shelter to volunteer. Dressed in my most fabulous tracksuit, I was given the job of walking Lulu, a tiny angry-looking staffie (and I normally say no thanks I prefer bigger to them, oh wait, a STAFFIE) which I set about with great gusto.

It was a great walk, but fuck me Britain, learn to take your litter home. Cans of Rockstar and spent johnnies I can sort of understand (because nothing says 'I right fancy a shag' like having to reposition yourself mid-thrust amongst the dogturds and needles) but some of the other litter was perplexing. Dumping an armchair down a back lane is one thing, but carrying it across a farmer's field and dumping it in the middle of a bridlepath? Bewildering. Even odder, there was around 20 'Happy birthday Brother-in-Law' cards blowing around in the hedges, all of different designs. Who not only buys these cards but then packs them into their bag and absent-mindedly loses them in the middle of absolute nowhere? They were all sealed too. Perhaps I could have sold them in my own little niche card shop – but then I'd need twenty people who wanted to wish their brother in law good wishes, but not enough of a good wish to give them a card that wasn't streaked with dog-piss and armchair tassles. Ah well. I walked far too far before reminding myself I needed to turn back, and even poor Lulu looked pissed off with me as we began the long, long, LONG, uphill walk back. Nevertheless, she was dropped off at the centre, puffing and panting.

The next job was washing out all the cat litter trays and cuddling the cats. This was fucking amazing. Well not the cat litter, that was literally shit, but cuddling the cats? Amazing. Each one was more grateful than the last – all purrs and clawing and rubbing. Their homes were warm, clean and full of toys, and that made me incredibly happy and rather grateful. I knew that had I gone there and the cats looked as though they were feral Fukushima cats, I'd have taken them all home. And well, I don't have good experience with cats in cars.

The first time we took Bowser to the vets he immediately retaliated by clawing his way out of his cat-carrier (it had a dodgy door) and set about hurtling around the inside of the car like a motorbike in a wall of death. Let me tell you, it's hard to drive along a motorway with a black and white angry blur running horizontally around the interior of the car, simultaneously hissing in your ear and trying to remove your eyelids with its claws. Anyway.

The next job was even better – I had to spend half an hour socialising with one of the kittens who had to live alone. Only temporarily – he was brought back because someone had adopted him and then returned him because he has stomach problems meaning he has diarrheah. Frustrating that someone returned a cat just because it has the skitters – they're testing him but apparently it'll fix itself. I wanted to take him home – we've got plenty of experience with cats going to the toilet in odd places too. For example, our old cat (Luma – who went to live with my neighbour) used to go to the toilet not because she needed to but because she spotted an opportunity to piss us off – she pissed on our sky box, she pissed on the top of our hob, she had a crap in the plughole in our bath which we only spotted when we turned the shower on and the water didn't drain away due to the little cat-poo floating around our feet. She remains the only cat I know who could turn Whiskas Bite and Chew into a weapon of mass destruction. Cow. Anyway, Starshine the Shitty Kitty (as I tactfully named him) spent half an hour climbing all over me, chewing my face, clawing my top, purring in my ear. He was amazing.

After helping tidy up a bit, I was asked to take another dog for a walk – this time it was Rascal, another staffie but this time she'd been treated for ringworm, meaning she came out of the kennel looking like a threadbare doormat. Naturally, despite having the freedom to shit away to her heart's content in his cage, she waited until I was five steps out of the door before curling one out that even made my eye's water. I didn't know whether to call back in and tell them she'd had a puppy. Anyway, I took this patchy little wonder for a walk down under the A1 and back (oh the glamour) before accidentally stumbling across the place where my ex and I had our first date. He wasn't out at the time (unsurprisingly, as when he did come out his parents held a screwdriver to his throat and told him they'd get the gay out of him, poor bugger) so we had to go for a walk in the country. Bless him. I thought he was shivering with cold, but he was just scratching away at the eczema on his elbows. I'm so grateful she was a staffie mind, because she quite literally pulled me back up the hill, me clutching at my chest and panting dramatically. See had it just been me and Paul, we would have stopped twice climbing up that steep hill to 'check the view' – actually a ruse to cover our panting and heart arrhythmias. I'm still out of breath now.

Upon returning poor Rascal, it was four o clock and time to go, but they had saved a special treat for me. They know I love cats and they let me into a back room where there was a mother nursing her four tiny, newborn kittens. Well, born a week ago. It was wonderful – they were tiny, whimpering and clicky-purring, suckling away on the mother cat who looked so content. She only moved to get a face-rub from me, and then she immediately lay back down on top of her cats. Wouldn't that just have been my luck to have four poor kitties killed on my watch? After ten minutes, I left them to it. Aw.

On a serious note – if you're looking for something to do, please volunteer at your local cat and dog shelter. The one I go to is amazingly well run but they're always looking for help, and the exercise can't help but improve my weight loss. Do some research and give it a go.

twochubbycubs on: our bed

We've bought a new bed on a whim! That's two incredibly impulsive things we've done in so many days – a big deal when you're like us and the idea of being cute and spontaneous is buying a different scented candle at the garden centre, and even then only if it's included in the BOGOF offer.

I woke up this morning full of piss and vinegar about the state of our pillows – I'd get more neck support if I rested my head on the jet of air from a hairdyer. I have a neck like a fucking Tetris piece and I'm forever clicking and cracking it, much to the chagrin of Paul. If I shake my head furiously I sound like one of those clacker toys. Plus our bed is awful. We bought it from ASDA or somewhere because we got a 'great deal' but a) it's too small (we had a Caesar bed previously, that's 8ft by 7ft) and b) the mattress is awful. It provides all the orthopaedic comfort of being mugged for your mobile in a backalley. We're fat lads and every time we turn over the springs pop and 'boing' with increasing malice – I know at some point I'm going to turn over to snooze the alarm clock and be impaled right up my hoop. Imagine that – cause of death: 'anal trauma caused by cheapskate John Lewis mattress'. I'd certainly be a wailing ghost.

Not only that, but because the bed is one of those awful ones with the drawers underneath, we spend the night being tormented by our cat constantly pulling at it, trying to get inside. That's vexing enough, hearing the drawer roll forward an inch and roll back over and over again, but when she does get inside, you're so highly-tuned to the slightest noise that you're treated to ten minutes of her tongue rasping over her mary for ten minutes before she goes to sleep. Bag.

So we did what any normal couple would do, and rang the Premier Inn to find out how to buy one of the beds they use in their hotel rooms. We ❤ Premier Inn and we just don't care. We sleep so well in a Premier Inn bed, and now we get to enjoy the experience at home without worrying about how many pockets of Gentleman's Hot Vanilla has soaked into the mattress. Our new bed arrives in four weeks and it's exactly the same beds they use in the hotel. Mind, I hope we don't wake up with Lenny Henry in the bed...though he is a fan of the larger form...so who know. I might book into one of their rooms and steal the purple Premier Inn comforter just to complete the look, together with a menu of fried breakfast items to sit on my bedside table.

We did have an amazing period last year where we had a bed which was comprised of two superking sized beds pushed together. It took up the entire bedroom and was necessary because I needed to sleep apart from Paul for a few weeks whilst I recovered from an operation. Of course, being lazy, we just kept it for almost a year and with two quilts, eight pillows and enough room to literally somersault* (which I'd do if I didn't think my neck would be turned to dust thanks to my corpulence), it was brilliant. It was a sad day indeed in The Sticky Patch (the name of our house) when we dismantled poor old Megabed and Paul dragged the mattress – which resembled a Jackson Pollock painting at this point – into the garage. Sniff.

twochubbycubs on: call centres

As jobs go, my current one suits me fine – it's busy, demanding at times and very occasionally, whisper it, fun. I know right? But how's this for temptation – I'm going to be sitting amongst £165 worth of pick and mix next week. I mean haway. I've also spent thirty minutes finding pictures of sprinkles, lambs and cold beer this evening, all for work, so not so bad. I've been thinking about my previous jobs recently, so with that in mind, let me take you back to the early 00's. Warning: this post contains the C-word, and it isn't chocolate.

My first job was working for a well-known british telecoms provider in the complaints department, which, as a fresh-faced young eighteen year old, was quite the eye-opener. I went in full of cheeriness and enthusiasm and left seven months later a broken husk of a man. There's only so many times you can be called a thieving cunt for charging 35p for Caller Display and still feel peppy about slipping on your work slacks of a morning. Actually, we did have a man who called up who was called Mr Kunt – and that's not me being crass, that was his 100% genuine surname, which we knew because we checked his record. Brilliant. Try fault-finding on someone's line when you're trying to squeeze his surname in at every opportunity. 'IS IT CRACKLING, MR KUNT?'. Haha.

I left on a hungover whim after a mutual agreement

with a friend that we'd see where we got to in the day after spending all night out and about – we got to 9.30am, and it was me who cracked first. I had some old spinster ring up, giving it the whole 'I'VE BEEN A CUSTOMER FOR FORTY YEARS' nonsense (she actually sounded old enough to sit on the party line with Alexander Graham Bell, but that's by the by). She was ringing up to complain because we'd changed the colour of the phone book spines from a mild purple to a deep purple, and that upset her because her phone book didn't match all the others. I shit you not, she not only collected phone books, she displayed them in her living room. There's no happy ending there – she'll be found face-down on a stack of newspapers with cats eating her feet. Anyway, she was so intently obnoxious and rude (as if I'd personally standing at the printer and changing the inks over myself, instead of sitting there looking up Mr Kunt and burping out little boozy burps) that I ended up telling her I'd immediately remedy the situation, then promptly ordered her a pallet of Aberdeen phonebooks, which I was sure she'd find incredibly useful in her hovel in Sussex. I bet her face was red. And fucking hell wouldn't THAT clash with her shelves of broken dreams.

There were also the usual games of trying to get Abba lyrics into customer phonecalls – surprisingly easy when they were complaining about the cost of phone-calls ('I can save you Money Money Money Sir...pardon?' or 'Saving YOU money is the name of the game,

Madam...eh?') but more challenging when they're ringing about interference on their microsockets ('So your broadband drops out when you're viewing German animal porn....er...Does Your Mother Know?') etc. Finally, good old squidfucker – how many times can you get the word squidfucker into a hastily read out script about direct debits? YOU-CAN-CANCEL-SQUIDFUCKER-THE-INSTRUCTION-AT-ANY-SQUIDFUCKER-TIME...

Ah, great times. I'd work for a call-centre again – I did like the camaraderie and sense of working as a team, but I don't miss having a set amount of time to go to the toilet and buy a Kitkat. Plus, the pay was shocking – was it any wonder that we used to put the phones on mute whenever Doctor Who was showing on a Saturday evening on the giant screen they used for showing stats? Top tip – when you're being transferred, don't mouth off about the adviser, they can still hear you and chances are you'll be rerouted to some automated menu somewhere. Oops. And if you mouth off about not wanting to speak to 'THOSE INDIANS', fully expect to be put through to the adviser best at doing Welsh accents...

twochubbycubs on: designer shops

I've had occasion to go into two places I'd never normally venture this week – a proper designer fashion shop and an expensive perfume place – normally places I avoid like the plague.

My first task was to buy some jewellery for my boss who was leaving – so in I minced to Vivienne Westwood, expecting to be immediately shooed back outside by some harridan with a broom with exclamations of 'WE DON'T WANT YOUR SORT IN HERE' like a stray cat in a butchers. I don't do high-end fashion. Hell, I don't do fashion at all – I buy most of my clothes from Tesco because I couldn't care less what I look like as long as I'm clean and warm. Now the interesting thing was that my preconceptions about the designer shop were entirely wrong – the assistant behind the counter could not have been more friendly, warm or welcoming, despite me standing there in my Florence and Fred shirt and elastic trousers. Actually, I did have expensive shoes on, if that helps. Us fat men can't spend money on normal clothes but by gaw can we put it away on bags and shoes if we need it. She asked me what tone my friend was, I had no idea, whether she liked silver or gold, I had no idea, whether she was classic or modern, I had no idea. She masked her exasperation impeccably. I did almost want to tip her over the edge by asking if they had shirts in my size – looking at the offerings on the rails the only way I could wear a Vivienne Westwood shirt is if I folded it in two and used it as a handkerchief. One jacket that I thought would have been suitable for my two year old nephew was hastily put back when I realised it was an Adult M. Nevertheless, after a fashion, we managed to pick out a tasteful piece of jewellery and whilst I cold-sweated my way through paying for it, I engaged in a polite chitchat with the assistant, until she told me that the rug I was standing on was worth £9,000 and all I could think is that I'd covered it in cat-hair from where I had set my rucksack down. The cats use my rucksack as a sleeping bag, see, and no, I don't have a fag-bag or a murse. So...

The next stop was a fancy-dan perfume shop for a different gift for a different friend. I hate these places at the best of times, because walking through a perfume department is like being pepper-sprayed by eighteen old ladies at once. I find most perfumes repellent and as a general rule, if you walk near me and it smells like you've had a bath in Charlie Red, things aren't going to end well. It didn't help that the lady behind the counter was clearly only flying with one engine because she kept repeating the last three words back to me like a parrot – I was asking for some advice on perfumes and it was like I was in an echoey tunnel. 'LIKE SOME PERFUME?' followed by 'DON'T KNOW MUCH' and then 'PAYING BY CARD' and 'FOR YOUR ASSISTANCE' got real vexing, real quickly. Plus, I know it's par for the course when you work on a make-up counter, but I swear she'd put her make-up on with an emulsion roller – it was on so heavy I felt like I was undergoing rorschach testing, I nearly shouted out throbbing cock when she bent down to check my card. You shouldn't be able to remove 90% of your face with a damp wet-wipe and to be honest, I'm yet to see someone who doesn't look 100% prettier when they don't have half of Superdrug on their face. Says he, the fucking oil painting. Ah but see, I MIGHT have a face like a bucket of burnt Lego, but I'm not bothered.

twochubbycubs on: what vexes us about each other

That title suggests that our marriage is heading for the rocks, with some almighty scrap on the front lawn or atop the bungalow like in Die Hard, but no. We'd both look dreadful in a vest, like cottage cheese being strained through a yard of muslin. We're an odd couple, we so very rarely argue, and when we do, it's always over in seconds because Paul pulls a stupid face at me until I stop moaning at him. We're both too laid back to argue – like everything else, if it gets us out of breath, it isn't worth doing. That said, we did have a disagreement yesterday over what flavour stock cube to use in a recipe (honestly, it's all go in this house) and it got me thinking of an idea of a blog article – those little tiny things that irk us about one another after being together eight years. So I asked Paul to compile his top five (and oh, because I'm the writer, I get a right to reply), and so...

Paul's five things that rile him about me:

I put things on top of the kitchen bin instead of putting them in

This one sounds reasonable to the reader until you realise my logic – I put big stuff on the top of the bin so I remember to take it to the outside recycling bin rather than clogging up the tiny kitchen bin with giant lemonade bottles.

I eat all of his 'lunch' ham -i.e. the expensive ham that he buys to put in his sandwiches for lunch instead of the wafer-thin shite we buy for the cats

Because it's tasty.

I don't put chicken on a plate when it defrosts

Because it's in a sealed, freezer-proof bag! Plus it means we have an extra plate to wash.

I play odd music whenever I'm typing the blog

This one is fair enough, but I do have a defence, I can't have the TV on because I get distracted, and I can't have music with lyrics playing because I start singing, so it has to be score music or soundtrack stuff. Admittedly, he might not enjoy the theme from Rollercoaster Tycoon playing whilst I type but it's infinitely better than hearing an almost-30-year-old-man caterwauling his way through the Cher back catalogue.

I always put my smelly feet on him whenever we sit and watch TV

I'm six foot one, they have to go somewhere, and the floor is cold, whereas Paul is like a little hot water tank pumping out heat – cheaper than slippers.

Things that annoy me about Paul:

He'll happily put the milk carton back in the fridge even if has the tiniest sliver of milk in it — not enough for anything practical but just enough to make sure I try and make a coffee and end up exasperated

He'll randomly and without warning decide he doesn't like a food that I've cooked plenty of times before, turning serving up a new recipe into a dangerous game of ingredient Russian roulette

He'll cheerfully announce to the room every time he's been to the toilet

He can't take a single comment on his driving
(although that's partly because I've made him so sensitive about it by hanging on like I'm Sandra Bullock in Gravity every time he goes round a corner at 35mph); and

He eats all the fucking cheese in the fucking fridge
For all that he bitches on about me eating ham every time I go to make an omelette or something I'll find the tiniest crumb of cheese left or even worse, a block with a great big crime-scene-esque tooth-print in it.

Well, if that's all we have to moan about, I say we're doing pretty well! At least we're not the Trevor and

Little Mo of the street, which is a shame because I do a brilliant Scottish accent. Weigh in tomorrow and I'm aiming just to maintain or put on a pound – my boss left us with a colossal box of Sports Mixture to work through, knowing my weakness is flavoured animal hoof. So we'll see.

I'm off to the cinema on Tuesday, though not to see 50 Shades of Grey. I can't genuinely think of a film I'd want to see less at the cinema, not least because I bet you can barely hear the audio over the sound of what sounds like 250 tiny pairs of bellows pumping away. Work that one out. I just don't get it, I really don't – the books were about as erotic as hearing an uncaring doctor telling a child that they're not going to make their teenage years. Sex as described by the perpetually celibate – I'd get more aroused ringing up the speaking clock for a phonewank.

twochubbycubs on: online arguments

Let me tell you what I'm not ready for though – idiots. I saw something today which almost made my heart explode, it was simultaneously so sad and so telling of the future to come that I could barely register it. On an online newspaper article, an argument broke out between someone with the inevitable - **MAMMYOVLILANGEL'** following her first name and some other painted idiot about spelling. Her reply? What broke my heart? '**WEL U DNT NEED GRAMAR THS ISN'T A BUK**'

I might have slightly paraphrased there, I was that aghast I couldn't let it sink in. Since when did it become socially acceptable to be thick and fucking proud of it? I'm not some snob who expects everyone to type like Mavis Beacon and never make an error, but it's just become 'alright' to be dense and not make any strides to fix the problem. I appreciate there are plenty of people out there who struggle, and that's fair enough, but everyone else, make an effort – don't revel in your stupidity like a dog rolling in fox shit. If I don't know something, I learn it. I don't have a go at the people who do know the answer. It's the equivalent of me going onto The Chase and if the Chaser got a question right and I didn't, launching myself up the table and calling poor Anne a **FAT SLAHG WIV A SHIT HAREKUT**. I find it repellent, and I make no apologies for it.

Pardon me a moment.

Ah that's better – our cat decided to be sick all over our living room carpet as a thank you for us letting her into the house and popping her bed near the fire to warm her up. Bitch. I wouldn't care but she could have gone outside to be sick but decided that right in the middle of the living room was truly the best place. It doesn't help that our living room carpet looks like a magic-eye drawing of a kaleidoscope pattern, so as soon as she was sick we immediately lost it amongst the pattern. It truly is a carpet that you'd expect an insane lorry driver to keep behind his cab to wrap his prostitute corpses in. Stare hard enough and you'll not only see patterns, you'll lose your fucking mind. We're too tight to have it replaced though because it's really quite decent carpet to walk on – easily the best shag this house ever had before us young bucks moved in, am I right?

twochubbycubs on: road rage

December 2014

Had a proper road rage moment driving home from some absolutely tiny man (seriously, I could just see the top of his male-pattern baldness peeking out over his steering wheel) in a BMW, who decided that because I was in front of him and doing the speed limit (actually, a shade over) that he had the right to get right up my arse and swear at me in the mirror. I have to admit, I love it, I can't fathom why people get so apocalyptically angry when driving, especially when he had nowhere to go but maybe 100 yards in front of me. I put it down to the fact he was driving a BMW and was sick of always being the last person to realise when it's raining. Actually, there seems to be a proper surfeit of arsehole drivers on the road at the moment — predominately those wankers who drive along on a clear night with their fog lights on and, in some cases, their side lights, full beam and the light off their phone lighting up the inside of the car. That's quite possibly my biggest bugbear. The fact that your 0.8l shitwagon is illuminated like a dressing room mirror doesn't add any points to your driving! I'm not irrational, but I can't help but feel it would be best to find them on fire in a ditch somewhere later down the road.

January 2015

I know I've twittered on about driving a lot lately but it does cause ever so much of the rage I have swirling around in me like violent, piss-coloured clouds. For example, every day I join the A1, and every single day I conscientiously allow someone in front of me at the congested slip-road at Seaton Burn, exactly like you're supposed to. Almost every bloody day the driver in front never acknowledges the fact I've slowed to let them in, and most of the time, you can see their oily face illuminated by their phone as they merge whilst checking Facebook. I wish they'd amend the Highway Code to make it legal to carry cement blocks in the passenger seat, and for me to launch said brick through their back window and stot it off the back of their heads. It really makes me fizz!

Mind, there's one thing worse than that and that's arseholes who don't indicate, which I know everyone moans about, but it makes me grind my teeth into an enamel mist. If I'm tootling along merrily overtaking people and some barely functioning addlepate – almost exclusively in a spotlessly clean white Range Rover, company-paid-for Vauxhall Insignia or a spunk coloured Seat Mii driven recklessly – pulls in front of me, I can actually feel my eyes push my glasses down my nose as they're bulging so much. Of course I immediately spend 10 minutes doing highly theatrical hand gestures like I'm guiding a plane to an airport gate in the pitch black, but it never soothes me. Someone actually shrugged their shoulders and did a 'BUT WHAT CAN I DO' expression with their hands. At a time like that, the only rational thing would be to accelerate my car through their back window, but sadly, the law is against me.

I feel better for typing that, actually – even though I had to restart halfway through as Sola climbed onto my keyboard to show me her teats and hit the backspace key, moving my page back. Bitch – I reckon it's another one of her classic passive-aggressive moves, like licking my face in the morning until I wake up and then immediately turning around and showing me her pencil-sharpener blinking in the dawn sunlight.

Anyway, enough talk about my cat's bumhole.

June 2015

We got into an argument today in the car-park of a fucking farm-shop. I mean seriously, a farm-shop, it doesn't get any more middle-class-on-a-Saturday than that. To complete the scene, we had only stopped to see if they sold duck eggs. Anyway, we had parked Paul's little Micra between the lines of the bay as any normal, educated people would do. Some Red-Leicester-coloured, wrinkly, pendulum-tittied tart got out her car to the left and crashed her door into the side of ours. 'Accidentally'. And didn't apologise.

I was foaming – not so much for any possible damage to the car (there was a bit of a scrape, but it's our 'scrappy' car so I don't mind, it only adds to the character) but more for her nonchalance.

When I pointed out that she'd hit our car, she told me (quote) "the fucking wind caught my door". Looking at her, her face had clearly caught a fucking sandstorm, but that's by the by. I asked her to be more careful only to be met with a volley of abuse as she stomped off into the shop. Seriously now what happened to manners? It wouldn't really look too good having two big bald men shouting at one woman so we couldn't continue, but it took all of my good breeding not to climb on top of her shitty Ford Ka (missing the letters AAAHNT) and take a dump on her windscreen.

I can't *bear* people like that. Accidents happen – she did – but fucking apologise, for crying out loud. Since when did it become OK to waltz through life without any personal responsibility? £10 says she's the type who thinks acting classy is hanging a Magic Tree from her inevitable clit-ring before she sets off for a prison visit. Gah.

twochubbycubs on: pub quizzes

I'm trying to be more social. Remember me saying how lazy I am a few posts back? That also applies to social events. I get asked to go to various things and usually decline because I'm a) shy and b) incredibly fond of lying on my sofa with a cat in my back hair and Paul squeezing my feet. It's what I live for. But see I could die tomorrow and I don't want people remembering me as the person who was always "washing his hair", despite having roughly the same amount of hair found on my head as you'd find in a Phil Mitchell tribute annual.

So in the spirit of socialising and trying not to die alone surrounded by cats and a stuffed Paul carcass grinning lopsidedly at me like a boss-eyed Humpty Dumpty, I went along to a pub quiz with a couple of friends from work and two other ladies, who turned out to be lovely. I'm glad I went, not least because it was hilarious.

For a start, it was awash with teams taking it far too seriously. I love this. It's a fucking pub quiz – you're answering questions about Miley Cyrus, if you get it wrong you're not going to be taken outside and shot by the Gestapo. The prize was £47! Even so, there was table after table of people in dire need of a wash and some love furrowing their brows and furiously debating which two countries has the most nuclear reactors. For the record, we got that answer correct – USA and France. I watch a lot of Discovery Channel.

That said, we didn't win. We came...second from last. We did however win an extra point for having the best team name: Bender and the Jets. I think you'll agree that is awesome, and I'm allowed to say bender, I've earned the right – I've quite literally taken one for the team on that front. Or back. It's certainly better name than We're The Winners or Quizmasters. Neither of those teams won anyway, so egg on their face. It'll go well with the cum stains on their trousers.

Oh, I also totally pulled. Now it goes without saying that I wouldn't anyway, but even if I'd been tempted by the suggestion, his face put me right off. Some drunken arse, easily into his sixties and with a face like a smashed crab, asked me if I wanted to know the answer to who sang 'The Joker' and then licked his lips lasciviously at me like he was the best offer I'd get all night. I'd get more aroused getting chatted up by the cigarette machine. Seriously, he looked like that guy from The Fully Monty who was in Corrie.

I wouldn't care, we got the answer wrong, so maybe I should have just succumbed to his greasy wiles. Boke.

Finally, our group got 'hushed' and then told to be 'bloody quiet' by some gangster granny with a nicotine fringe and a mean look about her because we had the temerity to talk DURING THE INTERLUDE. She was trying to play card bingo like the top prize was a couple of extra month's on a drip – I've never seen playing cards turned over with such ferociousness. She turned around again and said 'AH'M TRYING TO HEAR THE ANNOUNCER' (I could barely hear her through all the phlegm in her voice trying to scramble out) and we were kowtowed into silence. I wouldn't care, it's not as if we were tuning up a brass band or felling trees, we were just talking normally (perhaps with a slight bit of shrieking from me, I'd had liquor). Mardy cow. Oh! And she was cheating. She had her phone out during the countries round. The temptation for me to lean over and whisper 'Do you mind not cheating so loudly, I'm trying to hear the announcer' was almost too much.

Card bingo, by the way – you get given a few playing cards, the Quiz Man has a full deck (unlike some of the audience), he announces them randomly and when you've turned over your lot, you win. Well, you don't win. You lose. EVERYONE loses at bloody card bingo.

twochubbycubs on: being a male class attendee

Attending a slimming class as a man can be quite daunting, but go along with the mindset that you're another 'member' as opposed to anything different and you'll have a gas.

I attended my first class at the tender age of 16, despondent at the realisation that I had a more impressive rack than most of my female schoolfriends, and never looked back. My own idea of a class back then was that it would be full of people I couldn't relate to blaming their star weeks and crying into a rusk. Well, I've only been to one class where that's come up. Wakefield. I had a woman whose breath smelt like something had died in there three years previous tell me that *'appen ah've put on a pound but that's because ah'm on t'blob'*, before she dissolved into fits of nicotine-lacquered giggles, concreting my homosexuality an extra 2%. It's not always such a classy affair, mind.

I'm not going to lie, it is very female-focused, with the class being made-up predominately of women (at least in all the classes I've attended over the years) and most of the slimming class promotional literature consisting of carefully posed pastel photos of female models rollerblading and gaily laughing with one another like a tampon advert from the Eighties. But your gender is irrelevant – everyone is genuinely welcomed and taken into the group. There's no 'us and them' gender divide, with the men cowering on one side of the church hall looking at their cankles and the ladies sitting on the other side cackling and wiggling their little fingers up and down. Everyone is encouraged to chat for a bit whilst people get weighed, but then its fingers-on-lips and eyes forward as the consultant does their schtick, so if you're a little shy, don't worry. You can get away with looking at your phone or twiddling your thumbs or even hiding in the bogs for 10 minutes (just tell people you're losing a pound or two and watch them roll on the floor with unbridled laughter) if you're feeling particularly antisocial.

There is another hidden bonus to being male in a female-dominated slimming class – men seem to lose weight a little easier than ladies (thanks to those swinging lockers of gloopy testosterone), meaning you can adorn your slimming diary with 'Slimmer of the Week' stickers until the cows come home and you mince them into skinny burgers. Slimmer of the Week normally gets a basket made up of fruit that each member has hastily bought from the Londis next door before class, meaning a gorgeous gallimaufry of on-the-turn bananas, packets of Aldi rice and limp peaches could be yours every single week.

The in-class magazine is a bit of a bust, though, no pun intended. Catering strongly for their female readership, it's full of coy articles about menstruation, make-up and the menopause, with a token story about a man who has lost loads of weight posing in a pair of Topman cords and a lumberjack shirt filling in a couple of pages. They're always annoyingly twee too – losing weight because they don't want to gasp and wheeze pushing their kids on the swings, or wanting to fit onto a rollercoaster – how I'd love to read an article where a man said that he didn't want to have to be put on an oxygen feed after lovemaking, or he'd killed eight one-night-stands through accidental bingowing based suffocation. Joking aside, the magazine isn't compulsory and the internet is awash with the recipes you often find in there.

What it all boils down to is the simple fact that everyone is there for the same reason – to lose weight. You could be pernickety and argue that some people go to maintain their weight, but do shut up. I'm a naturally sarcastic writer and I may not have completely conveyed how welcoming the groups actually are, but take me at my word – you'll be made to feel like a friend in no time at all. Regardless of whether you're the only man in the room full of women, you'll find support, ideas, tips and motivation that really will help you along with your weight loss. If you still feel unsure, just go along to a class and have a go – worst that can happen is that you'll lose £10 and come away with some recipes and minor tinnitus.

Plus, normally, if you're the only man, you'll get a

proper fuss made out of you and you'll be a shoo-in for the 'Man of the Year' award in class. Which is nice.

twochubbycubs on: first aid

Here, what a day. It's been a dreadful day today for someone who dislikes a) people and b) being the centre of attention. See, I'm one of the first aiders at work, which generally means I get to have a big important first aid box full of plasters and the exciting knowledge of everyone's intimate maladies. It's a very responsible position indeed, with matters that are nothing less than life or death – do I issue a corn plaster or a waterproof plaster? Do I check NHS Direct via phone OR online? Do I hide in the toilets until another first aider is found? PRESSURE.

The downside of this responsibility is that I have to attend refresher courses on what to do in the case of an emergency – which to my mind is an easy enough question – flap, wave my arms around dramatically and call 999, although I'm told that's overkill if someone splashes a bit of hot water from the coffee machine across their hand. I can't bear these type of 'events', I really can't. I spend so long worrying about whether I'm going to get picked to 'demonstrate' that I only just take the information in. It's hard to concentrate when you've got forty factory-workers angrily staring at you and criticising your soft office shoes as an ex-ambulance driver tries to put your arm in a sling.

There's only one scenario where I'd enjoy being helped into a sling and I'd be disappointed if that occurred in a

20 minute refresher.

I've mentioned before about my personal space issues – if anyone comes within 3ft of me my shoulders go up and my head disappears into my shoulders like a tortoise with anxiety – so people tumbling me around the carpet and trying to get my body into a recovery position is my idea of a living hell. Plus, there's the added pressure of trying not to break wind as my right thigh is hoiked into the air with the gentle touch of an abattoir-worker and having to kneel down in front of everyone to practice CPR on a dummy that looks like a boiled ham with a crudely drawn crayoning of Sharon Osbourne's face plastered on it.

Of course, I immediately managed to embarrass myself by nipping to the gents for a couple of minutes before the class started, only to find on my return that everyone had left the lobby and decamped into one of the meeting rooms. I peered through the window and sensed some familiarity amongst the bald heads and let myself into the room, having to cross it to get to the only spare seat, whispering apologies and 'oh silly me' faces a-plenty. Ten minutes into the lecture on how to safely lift boxes in a packing facility I realised my mistake and had to walk back across the classroom with everyone's eyes burning into me. I'm surprised my hair didn't catch. I found a chair in the other class and glowed with embarrassment.

The three hours passed fairly quickly, although of course I was chosen almost immediately as an example of oxygen deprivation, giving the scenario of 'If I held a pillow over James' face, it would take four minutes for his brain to start dying'. Typical. Half an hour in and he's got me pegged as a pillow-biter.

Giving CPR presented a challenge, not least because I was picked to 'build' the dummy to practice on in front of the entire class. Social anxiety coupled with someone telling you to 'pick a face out of the box' and 'turn it inside out, clip his ears onto the dummy' makes for a very challenging ten minutes. I can't build tension, let alone a fucking latex approximation of some chisel-jawed corpse whilst twenty people stare down at me as I fumble around his plastic lips. It gets better – I then had to demonstrate how to pump the chest (30 presses, hand over hand, between the nips) which meant a good minute of me pistoning up and down, more than likely with the top of my arsecheeks peeping out over my belt in an accusatory manner. Didn't get any less awkward when someone else took over, because then I had someone's arse backing into my face as they tried to bring the dummy back to life.

I also made the mistake of asking the teacher some basic tips on how to deal with any possible emergency arising from having a pregnant lady in the office. Well look, I think it's better to be prepared, and it's not like I have an intimate understanding of how it all happens.

For all I know, it might ding like a microwave, the flaps swinging open like the prize-doors on Bullseye and a baby comes swooshing out like its on a log flume. Well, clearly taken with the fact that someone had actually asked a question, he addressed the whole process of giving birth in blistering detail. I was enthralled. I could tell everyone else was seething because they wanted to be away but I can honestly say I now feel confident delivering a baby. It sounds marvellous − sacks of fluid bursting, feet wriggling out, placentas sloshing out like the sponge in a car-wash − you just need Melanie and Martina and you'd have a brilliant Fun House round.

Ah well. At least I'm trained up if anyone faints, burns themselves, does a Jim Robinson or strokes out. That feels good. And, although I've been my usually sassy self about the whole thing, these First Aid courses are amazing. I learn a lot and the presenters are always fantastic. Considering my medical experience begins and ends at being scared of the 999 theme tune, the fact they manage to hold my interest for so long is testament to how good they are. Great work.

Eurgh. I put Paul in the shock position once. I used Durex Heat instead of Durex Tingle. Poor love had to pop a blue raspberry ice-pop in afterwards to fix his nipsy.

twochubbycubs on: egg curry

You can rather guess the effect it's had on the both of us, can't you? Yep. A colossal, vile, dramatic rise in the amount, pungency and volume of our *after-dinner hints*.

Every time I *field a benchwarmer*, I'm taking another layer of skin off my buttocks. I'm raw, I'm not kidding, and each time Paul *steams his knickers* I feel my face tighten. It's awful – quite genuinely the worst smell that's ever barrelled out of us. Now I'm no prude, I love a good *taint-stainer,* and other people's *seam-splitters* make me howl, but this is too much, even for me. We can barely type for gagging and even the cat has been licking his own *chutney-locker* for twenty minutes just to give his nose a break. I've never seen a cat cry until tonight.

Listen, I've talked about *puckered-chuckles* before and I'm not going to go into too much depth here, but everyone – I don't care how hoity-toity and prim you are – has been proud of one of their farts before. My favourite? I once broke wind on the London Eye, in the height of summer, in a full capsule. Imagine that, the heat blaring down, everyone panicking but being terribly polite about the whole affair. In my defence, I didn't think it would smell and I was more preoccupied with making sure it wasn't a full-on *cheek-rattler* that I didn't think about the consequences. I bet there's still fingernails scratched into the emergency exit of capsule

19.

Paul disagrees though, stating that my best pump was early on morning as I dozed in bed and he got ready for work. He asked me a question and in my slumber I let loose the loudest, squeakiest *arse-moo* he'd ever heard, to the point where I woke myself up thinking it was the bedside alarm. He had to get back into bed for laughing so hard and he still chuckles about it now. We're a classy pair.

Here, my favourite old fart joke. It probably only makes sense if you're of an era when Emmerdale used to be Emmerdale Farm and Jimmy Saville was just a cheeky tinker.

A bloke goes into a bar and asks for a pint of bitter with a head on it. He gets one from the barman, and then asks him to keep an eye on the pint whilst he nips to the bog. Barman agrees. Bloke comes back from the netty only to find the pint is still there but the head is missing.

"What happened to the head on my pint?!" he asks the barman, to which the barman replies, *"well, see that large athletic looking lady over there? While you were in the gents she came over and farted on your pint and blew the head off it"*.

"Right" says the angry customer, **"I'm going to have a word with her!"**.

He storms over to the lady and asks, "**Excuse me, fart in my Whitbread?**"
and she says...wait for it wait for it...
"No I'm Tessa Sanderson"

I'll get my coat.

twochubbycubs on: two chubby cubs

Right – a heads up, which may be a bad choice of words for the little bit of explaining that I'm going to be doing – this blog post might be a little saucy. Oh my! Skip the next lot of paragraphs if you'd rather just get to the good bit.

You have to be super careful typing our blog name into google. Why? Because it can bring up a lot of filthy results if it is incorrectly spelled, just like one slip of the keys can make a weekend in Scunthorpe altogether less palatable. Thanks to the traffic we receive to the blog, we're number one if you search for 'chubby cubs' but if you look down, there's a fair few blogs that aren't quite for vanilla eyes!

So let me explain the name of the blog – the two and the chubby bit is obvious, we're a couple of gentleman of generous scale. But the cubs bit might be less obvious. See, in the gay world, aside from all the rainbows, magic dust and blistering fisting sessions, there's a tendency to group male types by an animal name. Breaking them down, very very loosely, and tongue completely in (bum)cheek:

bear: a bear is a more masculine looking bloke – bearded, hairy, generally stocky or fat, normally has a wardrobe full of plaid shirts, fan of Kate Bush;

cub: a younger version of a bear, generally equally hairy, more stereotypically masculine in traits, might order a Guinness in a pub rather than a blue WKD and a fingering;

otter: more difficult — because not all bears are fat, stocky and of course you get people in all different shades, a thin hairy bear might be described as an otter. Presumably because he is generally 'otter than most people under all that hirsuteness;

chicken and twink: young, attractive, usually slender or physically fit slip of a man. Again, very generally speaking, perhaps camper than most, more effeminate.

Of course, all boundaries are meaningless and it's also a rather outdated way of looking at things — being able to grow a beard and light a cigar without coughing your lungs up doesn't make you more masculine, whereas knowing the lyrics to every Alcazar song in Swedish and English doesn't necessarily make you less of a man. Well...

Our problem is — we're almost at the tipping point where we'd probably be classed as 'bears' rather than 'cubs' because we're getting on, but frankly two chubby bears doesn't scan right. Two Busomesque Bears? Two Beefy Butterballs? Actually, I quite like that one, but fuck me our porn warnings would skyrocket.

Oh, as an aside, those girls who seem to only have gay men as friends? Like my ex-flatmate who exclaimed we could go shopping together and sort each other's hair out? She got short shrift. But they have many sarcastic terms too – fruit flies, fag hags, queer dears...

That's enough of that, anyway.

twochubbycubs on: school dinners

I haven't seen the word croquettes since I was at school and enjoying all the fruits and deliciousness of school dinners. Of course back then it wasn't fancy croquettes made with sweet potato and garlic breadcrumbs, they were made with ashen grey potato and rolled in radioactive-orange 'bread' crumbs. Wonderful!

I used to love school dinners and I hold no love for those who say they were awful. Perhaps they were, but at least you got your 100% of cigarette ash requirement with your turkey dinosaurs (I went to a posh school, they shaped their turkey arsehole-and-eyelids into stegosauruses instead of non-descript Twizzlers, see).

We did have the stereotypical mean old dinner lady, though – Connie (naturally we called her Ronnie to annoy her), and she ruled the hall with an iron fist. Actually, not quite true, she'd had polio as a youngster and didn't so much have an iron fist as a few ball-bearings. That's cruel but true. Perhaps that's why she was always so bloody mean to the kids, to stop them being mean to her...different perspective when you're an adult. We just used to push past her, risking serious moustache burns, and get in before all the smelly little kids claimed all the chocolate orange tart.

I do remember once going to get my wallet out of my blazer and a condom that I had gallantly/optimistically (sensibly given what I was up to with my 'close friend' at the time, well not literally at the time, I had my eyes on the battered sausage) went flying out of the back of my pocket and into the canteen of baked beans in front of me. I got a strong talking to for that, though again in retrospect they should have advised me against using flavoured condoms. It was grape flavour and lurid purple and my friend and I had to get them from the toilets at Newcastle Airport in case anyone saw us.

I feel I should point out that my school was next to the airport – we didn't have a day-trip out just to buy battercatchers.

It must have been a fairly posh school looking back, because I definitely remember after the pudding being allowed to go back to the canteen and getting cheese and coffee. Admittedly it was a lump of cheddar and a cup of Mellow Birds Brown Mountain Water but still, cheese and coffee at 13. In sixth form we naturally progressed to cigars, brandy and shooting metal pellets at poor folk. Pfft. I actually left sixth form because they tried to make us wear a suit to school . FIGHT THE POWER. Totally worth it.

twochubbycubs on: injuries

Previous readers may recall that a few months ago, I had to go for an MRI scan on my heart. Exciting. I described it at the time like being sucked into a Polo-coloured sphincter. Well, after weeks and weeks of fitfully looking at the letterbox waiting for news, I finally got a letter from my doctor yesterday which said everything was OK, heart was beating as it should be and I had nothing to worry about, bar being too handsome for most people to deal with. Typical NHS restraint. I've actually (touching wood) been remarkably lucky with my health so far – found a lump in my boob a year or so ago but it turned out to be nothing exciting (I'm surprised it wasn't an M&M, to be honest) and a couple of bouts of anxiety throughout the last few years. I don't want to dwell on anxiety, but it's a very funny thing – people who wouldn't take the piss out of you if you had a broken leg or lost the sight on one eye feel quite chipper making snide comments about anxiety behind your back. I don't see a mental illness as less important than a physical one, but the world has a long way to go before that status is reconciled.

Ah well.

The only injuries I've ever had of note both have typically me causes – I've got a scar on my forehead from ~~a killing curse launched at me by the greatest Dark Wizard who ever lived~~ cartwheeling into the side of a door. I remember going downstairs (the cartwheel having been done in my bedroom, which was surprising because it remains the only bedroom I've ever been in where I had to back out onto the landing to turn around) with a cartoon egg-shaped lump on my head only for my mum to hoy a big bag of peas on it and sat me down in front of Countdown until I stopped trying to make an 18 letter conundrum. The second time I tore my lip open and bent (but didn't break) (I don't think) my nose to the left by using my face as an impromptu braking device on my bike – forgot that my brakes didn't work as I thundered down a hill the only way a fat lad on an old bike can, hit the front brakes, bike stopped immediately and I sailed through the air like a clay pigeon. Only I landed on my face. This time, I think I was knocked out, as my only memory is my sister running home to get my mother who took me home, wrapped a tea-towel from the side in the kitchen around my face (I can still taste I Can't Believe It's Not Butter and strawberry jam if I lick the scar) and left it to sort itself out. I've got a big scar on my bottom lip which I can see if I push my lips flat against my teeth, but other than that I'm fine. Actually, reading all this back, it makes it sounds as though I grew up in Mr Bumble's workhouse, but that's far from the truth. My mum just didn't want the nurses to question all the other bruises and marks on my body.

And that's a joke too, before anyone tries to respectively put us on the register. I always received

medical aid where necessary and my parents were —
and are — very loving!

twochubbycubs on: having children

There was some discussion with colleagues today about babies and we often get asked the same thing – would we like to adopt? Well no, not there and then obviously, I don't have a car seat – but could we be one of those gay couples who have a child?

The answer is an emphatic no. Or an astounding nope. Or a camp NOOOOOO-WAY-HUNAAAAAAAY. I genuinely can't think of something I want less in my life than a baby. Paul is fine with them, cooing and marvelling over their ruddy cheeks, but I'm not – all I see is a red-faced, spewing, bawling bundle of energy that would leave me terrified and exhausted, the human equivalent of turning on the light in a gas-filled room. I seem to lack that warm, friendly gene that can look at a baby and think 'aw how sweet' – I just see about 1000 different ways that I'm going to accidentally damage the poor bugger – immediately drop it on the floor when I try to cuddle it, or rest my chin on their soft skull and make their skulls look like an ashtray, or suddenly develop a violent tremor and immediately end up in a Louise Woodward situation, or I'll sneeze and deafen the poor bugger. It's just awful, and to that end, I've spent my entire life avoiding babies – I'll go sit in the toilet at work if someone brings their child in because I'm terrified that my lack of emotion will shine through. People must think I have a hair-trigger bladder the way I dash to the gents as soon as I hear a Mama and Papas hatchback pushchair being wrestled with in the lobby. I think babies sense this unease because they just start crying as soon as they see my face, the same way doctors, close friends, family, beggars and other men do. My nephew, who admittedly is a gorgeous, funny little tyke, cried his eyes out at me for almost eighteen months, finally thawing at Christmas when I had shaved off my sex-offender beard and brought gifts.

Plus, we're entirely too selfish as a couple to even think about having a baby. We struggle to remember to wash and clean ourselves, let alone something pink and squashy and full of off-colour poo. At least the cats know enough to go outside for their craps and if they meow and rub along our feet often enough, the occasional pouch of Felix will be dropped in their bowls from on high. One of the many benefits of being gay, aside from all the cock and being able to wear each other's clothes, is the fact you don't have to spend money on anything but yourself. There's no school uniform to buy, there's no school trips to pay for – every penny can go on hobbies and fetishwear. It's just great, and I know I'd immediately resent something that I had to pay out for on a regular basis – I still shoot mean looks at my car for taking all our money. BAH. Finally, there's the biology of it all – the thought of having to yankee-doodle into a paper cup and mixing it with Paul's like some sort of bleach-smelling watercolour set puts me right off.

So no – no children. The Sticky Patch will remain forever more a two-man tent. And quite bloody right too.

twochubbycubs on: cleaners

We briefly flirted with having a cleaner last year. See, we are both generally out of the house from 7am to 7pm, and by the time we've got home, found a recipe, cooked it and done a blog post, we're knackered. The idea of pushing a hoover around (bad example, we've got a Roomba which makes sad little beep-boops every now and then – probably because it's clogged up with three cats worth of cat hair) or cleaning the bath fills us with dismay. So, we tried to get a cleaner. The first two turned up once and then never came back, which was mysterious – we actually live in a very clean house – it was just the 'bigger' tasks that needed doing. It's not a 'wipe your feet as you leave' sort of house – even the toilet is surprisingly free of skidders given two burly blokes live here. The third (and last) cleaner used to come, do a half-arsed job and go, but then charge us the full amount. We were too 'nice' to pull her up on it and she's been texting every now and then asking when to come back. Frankly, it was terrifying – all I could imagine her doing was rummaging through our drawers and criticising my choice of underwear / spices / sex toys. Because that's EXACTLY what I'd do.

I'm reminded of a friend who always liked to inspect the medicines cabinet of whoever she was visiting, until she managed to accidentally wrench the whole cabinet off the wall onto the floor after one particularly exciting snoop. How do you cover that up? Nonchalantly state you were looking for a tampon or diarrhoea relief? Or just admit to being nosy? You'd be disappointed if you looked in our bathroom cabinet, it's full of old shaving foam, heartburn tablets and smart-price netty paper. So yes – every time I knew she was in the house, I'd spend my time panicking I'd be tagged in some off-colour facebook post with her holding up a bottle of lube or our bank statements for all the world to see. We have managed to get rid of her with lots of 'Oh we can't afford you anymore' gubbins, but I bet she's had a neb at our bank statements so she probably knows that isn't true anyway. Not that we have a lot of money I hasten to add, we don't, but we're incredibly tight so she knows we don't spend a lot.

We also used to have an ironing lady, because neither of us can iron worth a damn and good lord, I'd sooner iron my own face than work our way through our ironing pile – we both work in an office, so there's ten formal shirts and six pairs of trousers just from work alone. Remember, we're somewhat elephantine, so it takes the two of us standing at opposite ends of the garden just to fold our underwear. Plus, we're both used to one another's gentle musk – the last thing we need is some hairy-chinned old dear passing out from the fumes released from our boxers as she tries to press in a crease.

One concession we do have is a gardener – when we were given the house, we were completely new to the concept of looking after a garden – and there's a massive lawn at the front and another big bugger at the back. Paul had a few valiant months of trying to mow the lawn before we accepted defeat and brought in a gardener. He's smashing, but not too good at following instructions. For example, there's a little flower bed in the middle of the lawn – tiny, but it holds a heather bush. That heather bush was planted by the mum of the guy who gave us the house (who himself lives up the street) and we always agreed we'd let it flower. Well, WE did. The gardener didn't – he ran the bloody lawnmower right over the top of it, scattering memories and heather all over the lawn. He claimed he didn't see it. We were too cowardly to 'tell him off' because he had a pair of shears in his hands when we noticed and he's built like a brick shithouse. So, it was a quick trip to the garden centre to replace the bush. I just hope her ashes weren't under there. If they are, they'd be in my green recycling bin. No wonder she haunts the house.

twochubbycubs on: the Geordie accent

Argh! My well-meaning neighbour has inadvertently pissed me off, at the end of a rubbish day. Our general waste bin was missed by the council so we put it outside today and arranged for them to come and empty it. Great! Got home today to find the bin neatly stood next to the back door and a note saying 'It's not bin day so I brought your bin in' – fuckity fuckfuck! I can't even be angry with him because he meant well but really, did he think I just wheeled my wheelie bin full of bloody manky old scraps of food, cat food wrappers and bloody Take a Break to the end of my drive as a bloody ornament? That I may stand by it and wave at people and say 'Oh won't you come and look at my rubbish?' Does he think I was trying to set off my iron railings with the glamour of a Northumberland County Council wheelie bin? Argh. Worst part is, you only get two "missed collections" every year before you have to start paying! If I didn't like him, I'd poo on his garden.

I was told today that I have a lovely telephone voice, which was pleasant – although I was always under the impression that as soon as I pick up a phone, my voice actually deepens and goes a bit more Geordie than I'd like. Paul tells me that I have no discernible accent – which is lucky, as a strong Geordie accent (to an outsider) sounds like Brian Blessed yelling nuclear launch codes into a Toblerone tube. All went well when

Paul first met my parents, aside from afterwards when he turned to me in the car, ashen-faced, and confessed that he'd spent the last two hours nodding politely at my dad and being completely unable to decipher the accent. My dad has a mild Geordie accent but the state of Paul's confused face would suggest he sounded like a water-damaged cassette recording of Auf Wiedersehen, Pet.

Actually, I've enjoyed good luck with my voice throughout my life. I certainly didn't go through the mandatory six months of sounding like failing car brakes when I was a teenager – I seemed to go to bed sounding like a Snowman-era Aled Jones and woke up again sounding like Madge out of Neighbours. In fact, puberty was great fun for me – whilst a lot of my peers were awash with spots and 'taches like they'd stuck a few errant pubes on their top lip, I could grow a pretty manly beard right from the get-go. Clearly such high levels of testosterone (and it helped that my levels were kept regularly topped up, EH, AM I RIGHT, NUDGE NUDGE WINK WINK) didn't lead to any especially manly pursuits, though I was fairly decent at rugby, presumably because I looked like someone had driven a minibus onto the pitch and stretched a Matalan jersey over the top of it. Ah well.

twochubbycubs on: smoking

I swear to God – our neighbour put my bin back for the second time today! Why did he think I'd put it again? Does he think I'm giving him a cardio workout or something? Ah he's so bloody nice it's impossible to be mad but I fear that the rough-hewn men at the council will be foaming – three times now they've had that bin lorry backed up our street and three times the bin hasn't been out. Oops. That'll be them putting Bowser into the rubbish compacter tomorrow.

So, today. I was unlucky enough to be caught behind a cluster of office workers waiting to cross the road today, all puffing away on their e-cigarettes. That said, it did afford me the opportunity to mince through the strawberry-scented fog like I was coming out of the doors on Stars In Their Eyes when the light changed. I'm not keen on those e-cigarette thingies – I'm of the belief that if you want to smoke, then man up and bloody smoke – it should be Capston Full Strength tabs or bust. Admittedly it's far nicer seeing someone misting away like a boiling kettle than it is seeing them bent double chucking their lungbutter all over the pavement but still. Plus the e-cigarettes always look so ungainly, like you're sucking nicotine from a nosehair trimmer, and it does attract a lot of quite smug people who say they are harmless – perhaps, but society thought thalidomide was 'armless once.

I gave up smoking two years ago using Allen Carr's Easy Way to Stop Smoking and it was a revelation. I was panicked thinking the cravings would be hell on Earth but I finished his book, put out my cigarette and hardly even thought about smoking again. He teaches you to examine what exactly you're doing when you smoke, and explains why you want to keep smoking, and then breaks down each reason/excuse that you use to rationalise your smoking. It's great – cost £6 and never looked back, and I was on a good 20 smokes a day.

Mind you, that's not to say I've become one of those fervent anti-smokers who cough that tinkly little cough if someone has the temerity to light up near them. That I absolutely can't stand, it's such an oddly British passive action to take – either ask them to put it out or fuck off – you wouldn't sit in a burning building sneezing at the fire, you'd take immediate action! Fair enough you might end up with a Richmond Blue smouldering in your eye-socket but you would have the comfort of not being a passive-aggressive tosser to soothe it.

twochubbycubs on: tramps

I got asked for five pounds by a tramp today.

Five pounds! Gone are the days when someone would come up to you and shakily ask for 25p because they were just shy on the metro fare home. When did it make the jump to a fiver? If it goes any higher it'll be cheaper for me to jump in the car and nip over to Gateshead to buy the smack myself. Oooh think of the weight loss. Actually, I'd be a shite smack addict, I start shaking like a shitting dog the day before I have bloods taken. I'm not averse to giving to the homeless and unfortunate, but his sheer cheek put me right off – I didn't even get to do my 'pretend to pat my pockets for non-existent change' dance, which never works anyway because I'm forever sticking all my change into one pocket so I'm jingling and jangling down the street like a friggin' pearly queen. Plus, to cap it all off, what I thought was a little lip piercing from a distance was a howking great pus-filled sore on his upper lip which made me gag. I can't BEAR anything like that, it really upsets me. I know that's an incredibly superficial and shallow attitude but I don't care who you are, everyone has a physical attribute that they can't stand in others – mine is pus spots. I hardly think that's irrational.

Newcastle has some great tramps as well as the usual chancers, mind. Paul and I actually managed to make an enemy out of one of Newcastle's less fortunate citizens when we lived down on the Quayside, who we christened Rory just because that's what he always did – roared. There was a little yellow bus which would take you into town from the Quayside and because he was mad, he used to spend all day travelling up and down along the route – it was only ten minutes long and never varied but nevertheless. He used to have eye-wateringly bad BO first thing in the morning and by the time he'd spent all day cooped up on a bus on a hot day, well, it was the only bus I knew where the driver lit a match when old Rory got off. Anyway, whenever Paul and I got on the bus, he'd roar (hence the name) TEAPOTS at us and stare at us with his googly-eyes and spittle-flecked beard. All the way into Newcastle. Occasionally blowing kisses. And we never, ever knew why – until we happened across him outside of the bus. He did his usual trick of shouting teapots, but this time bent over in his shit-crusted coat and made a spout motion with his arm and a handle motion with the other – then it clicked, he was taking the piss out of us for being gay and the teapot thing was his way of saying we were camp.

Well, we thought it was bloody hilarious. I mean honestly, I might be a friend of Dorothy but at least I can have a hot bath of the evening. Sadly, we moved away and we only see him now and again, although he still gives us the old swivel-eye if it clicks who we are.

twochubbycubs on: our anniversary and dogging

Good news, it's our anniversary today – four years of hard, solid marriage, and eight years of being together. The eight years is a bit of a fudge, we can't actually remember the date we got together, but eight years in gay years is almost a century, so we're doing well! We had such a romantic start, looking back. I was trapped in a Tyneside flat with a borderline psychotic flatmate who never cleaned up, paid her bills or washed – and worse (as we found out after she left), used to hide her used, bloody drip-trays behind the radiator rather than putting them in the bin. You can imagine how fragrant her room was when the heating came on. Meanwhile, Paul was a tenant in a mansion in Portsmouth, paying all of his meagre nursing wage to two old queens who had a sling set up in the same room as their chest-freezer, meaning there was every chance of seeing some turkey-necked, bollock-naked aged twiglet trying to get top value out of his black-market Viagra with some bought in piece of rent each time you went to get a box of fish fingers. Wow, there's a sentence I don't get to type often enough. We'd met previously through university friends, but after our first proper 'meeting', Paul got the Megabus back to Newcastle with me and never went home. In the spirit of Queer as Folk, he's quite literally the one night stand who never went away. And damn it, we work together very well. I don't say it often enough and I'm often a bit mean in my depiction of Paul but I'd really have him no other way.

118

Even if he is sulking a bit because I told him that hugging him when I'm sitting down and he's standing up feels like I'm trying to move a hot-water tank.

Our wedding was a very low-key affair, but deliberately so. We spent as little money as possible on our wedding and then thousands on our honeymoon and went to Florida for a month. Some might say that's selfish but actually, given we don't like any kind of fuss made over us, it suited us down to the ground. Now, because I like writing, I immediately typed all of that up in a book, and although it's four years old, if you're a fan of my writing (and who wouldn't be?) you can find it here on Amazon for a tiny £1.20. I'd die a happy man if people had a read and left a review. Other people immediately copied my idea but well there's only one me. So there!

Remember we were going out for a McRib yesterday? We went out at midnight and didn't get back until 2.30am, mainly because once we had enjoyed the McRib, we decided to go for a drive along the coast. I love driving at night, partly because I've got a bit of boyracer in me (Paul's anniversary present) and it's good to get it out of my system every now and then. So, naturally, we were enjoying the various ice covered car-parks in Whitley Bay. That said, we must be the first two chavvy types to be doing spins on ice in the car but with the 25th anniversary special recording of Grease coming out of the speakers. What a mix! Oh and we managed to drive into a clearly very popular dogging spot – St

Mary's Lighthouse car park, if you're curious. We parked up for a moment just to cause mischief – two bears in a DS3 screeching and cackling their way through Look At Me I'm Sandra Dee would stop anyone on the vinegar strokes. We left before things got nasty, although the sight of someone's cottage-cheese thighs wobbling away in the moonlight half-in and half-out of a Vauxhall Astra made me a bit bilious. Still, each to their own – no judgement here.

twochubbycubs on: the bathroom lights crisis

I was going to do a quick post about my deafness but a much graver situation has arisen – we're down to one light in our bathroom. Which sounds fine, but we should have six. We had our bathroom done out when we moved in, more out of necessity rather than choice since the previous occupant died in there, knocking her head on the shitter on the way down and causing a slow leak which ruined the walls (her last act of malice, bless her, she really didn't want the gays in). We had six of those flush spotlights built into the ceiling – I like a lot of light whilst I bathe so that I can gaze upon my beauty and really soak it in. The plumber was fantastic, catering to our every whim, though he did fail to install a gloryhole through to the built-in wardrobes in our bedroom so he gets a mark down for that.

Anyway, over the course of the year, the lights have steadily been going and now the lighting is critical – when the first went, that was no problem, five was more than enough to read Viz by and even when the second one went, as long as I had enough light to differentiate between my toothpaste and Paul's heavy-duty Preparation H cream I was fine. To be fair, Paul doesn't have piles, though given the pressure I put on him as soon as he has to go I'm rather surprised – I've been known to bust out the Countdown clock if we're watching something and he's taking an age. Yep. Then the third light went, and at this point we decided that we really must replace them, but once we realised that would mean finding the garage key and getting the tiny stepladders out, that got forgotten about. Four went a few weeks ago, but luckily, the light above the netty remains resolute, as did the one above the bath, meaning I could still crack on with my Bill Bryson books in relative comfort.

Until tonight – we're down to one light, and it's the one above the toilet, which means that every time we have to go and drop the kids off we're going to be sat in a dark room with a spotlight directly above us, illuminating us like a prize on a second-rate game-show. That won't do! But see this is where our inherent inability to do anything especially manly comes in, because we genuinely can't figure out how to change the bulbs. According to the Internet, we should just be able to unscrew the fitting and replace the bulb, but I've tried with all five, and none of them can be moved one jot. Part of me is anxious that we're going to have to go in the loft and replace them from up there – surely not though? Going into the loft causes incredible anxiety in this house, not least because of the way the ladder flexes and bends (I had never heard a ladder cry out in pain until we got on it) and the beams creak underneath us.

We're left with two options, both equally embarrassing. I can call my dad to come over and do it, but well, I feel like a tit being a 29 year old bloke and having to get his dad to effectively change a lightbulb for us. My dad would do it no problem and be entirely gracious about it, but I always feel just that little bit less masculine. The alternative is to pay someone to come and do it, but that is even worse – they'll invariably try and talk to me about tits or football or cars and I'll have to stand there with glazed eyes looking non-plussed. I once had a BT engineer comment on my then-flatmate's knickers which were drying (or rather, knowing her delight in shagging every other guest she checked in at the Travelodge, they were airing out) on our hallway radiator, until I cracked a joke that they were actually my evening knickers and he spent the rest of the visit ashen-faced and scrabbling away at the junction box. We do get a lot of 'OH SO YOU LIVE HERE WITH YOUR BROTHER DO YOU' and then thirty minutes of awkwardness and loaded mentions of their wives/girlfriends (just so we know, see, in case the sight of a pock-marked arse sticking out of a pair of paint-covered slacks framed by a copy of the Daily Sport is going to set our loins aflame).

So what do we do? Who knows. I'm just dreading the moment that I'm using the loo and the light above goes pop, meaning I'll be stuck in the dark until Paul comes home and hears my plaintive wailing from the bathroom, only to refuse to come in because it smells like something died. What fun!

twochubbycubs on: saying thank you

We're experiencing a very British problem – the endless thank you cycle. You may remember we've got three cars – one for me, one for fattychops and one gifted to us. Well, the third car doesn't get used and it was a shame to have it sitting in the garage with only our 'summer clothes' and the ghost of the lady who lived here before us to keep it company. Our lovely neighbours were going on about their grandson needing a car when suddenly a lightbulb went off above our heads and we said he could have our third car as a thank you for all the help our neighbours give us, especially when it comes to gardening and using up hours of our time on anecdotes. He's absolutely lovely (and his wife is terrific) but he talks like I write – why use two words when eighteen paragraphs and three side stories about being a butcher will do? Wouldn't swap them for the world though so it was really no bother at all.

So, car handed over with a big thank you from us for all of their help. But oh no! They wanted to say thank you to us, so we had a very awkward conversation full of 'it's no bother' and 'no really, you mustn't' but god bless them, they've bought us £100 in theatre vouchers (after a difficult chat about our interests, it didn't seem seemly to ask for leather chaps and a moustache trimmer). Worse, they've popped it through our door when we've been at work, meaning we'll have to do the very right thing and nip over to say thanks. BUT. This to me seems like too big of a present just to say thank you, so what do we do now? Get a card? Go over and do the 'OH YOU SHOULDN'T HAVE' dance? I'm terrified that if we buy a small bunch of flowers, we'll end up getting an even smaller thank you back – like a Lindt chocolate or a copy of Take a Break with the arrow-word completed. And then what happens? Do I go over with my last Rolo and a daisy? I can see this whole thing ending up with us grappling in the street, trying to outdo each other's politeness through our tears.

Ah what a thing it is to be British.

twochubbycubs on: smiling

I don't know if anyone watches The Middle but there's a character called Sue who is permanently happy – the very antithesis of me. She conducts an experiment where she smiled at people to see if a smile was as contagious as a yawn. It WASN'T. But, you know, we don't smile enough, so I thought I'd do the same thing – smile at random people as I trundled around M&S before work this morning. Well, fuck me, that whole stereotype of Geordies being a friendly bunch couldn't be further off the mark – at least first thing on a rainy Tuesday morning. At best, most people reacted like they'd seen their own bumhole and didn't care for the colour, at worst I felt like I was at considerable risk of being stabbed in the beck. It doesn't help that I don't have a natural smile, one of those egregious, winning grins that can melt the stoniest of hearts and set gussets aflutter – it's more a lopsided leer that looks like I'm simultaneously dropping off my yoghurt and trying not to fart. No wonder no-one smiled back save for one lady, and she had a better beard than I did.

But isn't that a shame? I love it when people smile heartily at me or engage me in idle chit-chat. Put me in a room where I'm supposed to socialise and I'll stand there like the world's gayest hat-stand, all mute and agog. Stick me next to an old biddy in a bus-stop and I'll be waxing lyrical in no time, revelling in her bawdy tales of bus delays and the minutiae of her family tree. I can chat away to the checkout assistant in a supermarket until the cows come home, are milked, that milk sold for negative value and put back in my trolley for me to go 'OOOH the price of milk' at the cashier. Interestingly, I've had it pointed out that my accent changes depending on who I talk to – I got out of a taxi the other day and it took me about five minutes to stop talking like Jimmy Nail shouting a warning across a quarry. I find that if I'm in a situation where I'm not sure how someone is going to take my sexuality (up the arse, generally), I'll 'man up' the voice a bit – not that I sound like some lisping Monroe-esque harlequin you understand, but because I don't want to be found with my face caved in on an abandoned industrial park. You never know.

The problem with doing this is that it then invites some pretty bleak persiflage between me as a passenger and them as a driver. The last taxi driver I encountered asked me what car I drove – when I answered with 'White, DS3' he immediately dismissed it as a pussy car and told me to get a decent motor to 'attract the lasses'. Because, you know, his Skoda Octavia in syphilis yellow was clearly a clit-magnet. Nothing says sex machine like a beaded seat cover, poorly-masked body odour and Smooth FM playing over the speakers. Moron. Not the worst taxi driver I ever had mind – I once got the offer to 'pay my fare' an alternative way with the altogether more direct result of the taxi driver pulling over two hundred yards from my front door and getting his knob out – I wouldn't have been as offended if there had been miles on the clock but he'd only driven me around the town moor – two miles at best. I'm surprised he'd had time to turn his indicators off. I politely declined – well, as politely as you can when someone offers to effectively pay you £4.40 for oral sex – and threw a fistful of coins at him. Plus, on a purely shallow note, it looked like he had half a smoked cigarette sticking out of his zip. I mean make it worth my while, honestly. It looked like the whistle on an aeroplane lifejacket.

twochubbycubs on: having a bad day

I woke up in a proper huff today. No particular reason, just I wanted everyone I saw outside of my immediate circle of friends to be immediately blinked out of all existence. Humanity seemed to be doing its bit to bring me to my knees – if I'd had a shotgun and could carry off a leather knee-length coat with any sort of panache then there could have been genuine trouble. Things got off to a sour note as soon as I checked my facebook over my morning banana – which isn't as filthy as it sounds – and saw...

...people queueing up outside of Iceland to get a ready meal. I mean for heaven's sake. You need to understand that I wouldn't queue up outside of a shop if they were giving away free blowjobs and pug-faced kittens, but I can just about see the point of it if you're desperate for a bargain. But for a fucking ready meal? I've seen trolleys awash with them like each one contains a mini Margaret who will come and jiggle your fat-shelf up and done to tone it whilst you watch Eastenders. I apologise profusely if there are any readers out there who queued and enjoyed themselves but I find it despairing – like Black Friday but sweatier. Plus the sausages look like an old poo in a condom, though admittedly I'm basing that on a photo that Ray Charles himself seemingly took using a potato. Nevertheless, each to their own and all that. So...

Every song on the radio into work was the wrong one. My iPod wouldn't bluetooth up to the car music system meaning I couldn't have my music on. Every person in every single other car on the road was driving like an arsehole – either too slow, reading their phones, or swerving all over the road trying to get their iPod to bluetooth up to their car music system. Well, honestly. I nearly ran someone over who thought stepping out in front of the bus was the best way to continue their life and then I got stuck behind a bin-lorry who had parked up in a single-lane street so the driver could have a cigarette. And you can't remonstrate with a binman, everyone knows that. That was just the journey in.

Work was work.

Lunchtime came and by this point, all I wanted to do was eat my lunch and doze for half an hour in peace so I picked up my Thermos of bloody awful watery vegetable soup (I had nowt in last night to make something fancy) (Paul calls it care home broth) and made my way over my car in the multi-storey in Newcastle's Chinatown. No sooner had I poured my soup when some piss-eyed old bugger tapped on my window and told me to move my car as they were doing electric works on the lamppost behind. I duly obliged, working my way through my entire bank of swearwords as I moved around to find a space whilst all the while holding a cup of soup in one hand. Having done so, I finished my 'delicious' dinner and was about to nod off for twenty minutes when what sounded like the entire country of China paraded through the street below, banging drums and making noise. They were practising the Chinese New Year march and it was like being under attack. I would have had a more restful half hour if I'd managed to set my face on fire with the car lighter. Dejected and tired, with a fetching orange stain on my shirt from where I'd jumped the first time around, I headed back in.

But no! The joy didn't end there. Work continued being work. Over the rest of the day I managed to drop my pass into the toilet when I went for a piss and then drop it again down the stairs on the way out of the building. I also managed to leave my car parking ticket on my desk at work, meaning I had to go back for it, and then, the final insult, I got stuck behind the only AUDI driver in existence who DOESN'T think they need to go 150mph in their shite company car who was tootling merrily along the 60mph road at 30mph where the bends and hills precluded any overtaking. I like to think she at least heard the sound '**UUUUUUUUUUUUUNNNNNNNNNT**' as I finally overtook.

Anyway, I'm home now. Deep breath. I appreciate that this entry is one long moan but I needed it, and now I feel better. We're cooking doner kebabs tonight. Normally I'd shy away from a doner kebab, believing it's only really suitable for soaking up bile and half-digested carrot before promptly being upchucked in a technicolour yawn by some drunken trollop in the Bigg Market before she settle downs in an alleyway for a foamy piss and regretful sex.

twochubbycubs on: growing up

I heard Boy George on the radio driving back and it nudged a memory out of me – I once threw my sister's Culture Club CD down a well (apparently I lived in Amish country)– frankly the best place for it, but I got a proper telling off for it. But see now she used to do the same thing that Paul does now – hears a song, likes it, plays it over and over and over and over again. Not too bad when it's a decent ditty but Karma fucking Chameleon? Even now the opening chords of that song transport me right back to my teenage years in a bedroom that smelled slightly of bleach and Boy bloody George caterwauling through the floorboards.

I grew up in a tiny village in the middle of nowhere, Northumberland – the type of village where a minority of the locals still pointed at planes in the sky, mouthing the word dragons with spittle on their lips. It didn't have a corner shop (and still doesn't) but it did have two pubs and a kitchen and bathroom centre. You couldn't buy a pint of milk but you could buy a fabulous bespoke oak cabinet to store it in. It was a pleasant enough place to live but definitely somewhere you'd go to die rather than thrive.

My sister and I, and the other children of the village (or corn), spent most of our time building dens and treehouses. Well, I'd watch them build treehouses, I was always too fat to climb a tree and the one time I did

I got stuck up there for several hours before promptly falling out, like a sleepy owl dressed in a knock-off Diadora tracksuit. Looking back, our dens were amazingly creative – a stack of pallets hidden up a tree, a stack of pallets hidden in the woods, a stack of pallets hidden amongst the pallets on the building site when they built the new houses. We lit a fire once inside one of these enclosed dens which has to be the height of stupidity, but filled with the childlike sense of invincibility we carried on, and mind it gets worse – we used a tyre as a make-shift fire-pit. How the hell we survived that I have no clue – nothing says good country living like breathing in smoke and the fumes from a singeing tyre. Perhaps we'll be able to launch a criminal case against Dunlop in years to come for all of our defects but frankly, I don't have Julia Robert's three-cock-gob so I'd make a shite Erin Brockovitch.

twochubbycubs on: saving money

I'm alone in the house tonight as Paul's down South. I'm not too good at being in the house by myself, and it doesn't help that I've got the score from Scream 2 playing as I type. If my ex and Paul's mother burst through the door waving a knife at me then at least I can say I died doing what I love, typing with one hand and scratching my balls with the other. Though I do hate the thought of being discovered in my 'lay around the house' boxer shorts with the hole burnt in the behind – from an errant cigarette back when I used to smoke, not from any particularly violent flatus.

No recipe tonight, but instead, a response to the many posts I've seen dotted around saying how expensive SW is, especially for new joiners. So, I thought I'd rattle off a few ways around saving money on slimming world – our shopping bill normally comes in at around £50 a week, and we generally shop at a combination of Waitrose, Tesco and Morrisons. I'm just going to scattershot type the article mind, so don't expect structure and hilarity – I'm sitting here freezing my bollocks off but if I don't type it before my bath I'll never bother! I also plan to turn this into a pinned page at the top and keep adding to it. Oooh I'm the gift that keeps on giving!

Bulk buy the staples

Long time readers may remember The Cat Hotel – we

cleared out our shed, fitted shelving and use it to store bulk purchases of anything that is either on a considerable discount or cheaper to buy in bulk. So to this end we always have masses and masses of Slimming World staples – chopped tomatoes, beans, pasta, spaghetti, chickpeas, tinned veg, stock cubes, salt, vinegar, sauces, rice. We generally buy these in bulk from Costco – to give you an example of savings here, you can pick up 24 tins of excellent quality chopped tomatoes for around £7, or 28p a tin. Yes, you can buy them cheaper in Tesco if you go down to the 'Aren't I a cheapskate' range, but you're getting red piss in a tin with a tomato crust. There would be more tomato flavour if you sucked the tomato on the tin wrapper. Bulk buying nearly always pays for itself in the end plus you've always got something in – many a time Paul and I will just have a tin of beans for dinner because we're too busy illegally downloading TV shows and living the life of Riley. By the way, our cats don't bother with it, and why would they? Yes it's warm, safe and dry, but they'd much rather crap in my flowerbeds and track their muddy paws across our white tiles.

Cook twice, freeze once!

Most of our recipes can easily be doubled or halved – but if I say it serves four, then cook for four and freeze two portions – or serve three portions and take one for lunch the next day as we normally do. You're cooking the meal anyway so it's no hardship at all to freeze a bit up.

ALDI/LIDL

You can save money in these shops, but I don't like them. I have tried, I swear I have. We went to an Aldi once and it was just too stressful – I don't like a shop that puts garden shears next to petit pois tins and tumble drier balls next to the Daily Malk chocolate. I find it too confusing, with all the off-brand rip-offs and impossible layout – it's like an Escher puzzle of abject poverty. Plus when you go to pay for your items the cashier throws them through the checkout like she's going for gold for Great Britain's curling team. I like small talk and chit-chat, not fucking carpet burns from a pack of floor wipes swishing past my hand at the speed of light. If you can deal with the above, all the very best to you, you'll definitely save – but if not...

Don't be afraid to scrabble in the bargain bin

Listen, I used to avoid the bargain bin like the best of them, but since I discovered that my local Tesco actually do decent meat reductions, I'll happily get in there and elbow an old biddy in the face for £2 off a pork shoulder. You've got to be savvy though – get what you need, rather than what you think is a decent deal. If you weren't going to buy that six pack of yoghurt reduced to 8p because the fork-lift ran over it and a fox shagged the strawberry crunch, it's not a bargain. But the flipside of this is – don't be one of those fucking awful people who grab items as soon as the poor supermarket worker has stuck the reduced sticker on it. Have a touch of class. Yes, you might have a trolley so full of reduced bread that you could use it to stop a raging river, but what price dignity? I've mentioned before that I've seen people actually fighting and nothing is worth that.

twochubbycubs on: walking

Paul's back tomorrow. It's been odd without him in the house – the air smells fresher, certainly, and the toilet is remarkably un-pebbledashed, but it's been quiet and my feet have been getting cold during the night. We very rarely spend the night apart – I can genuinely only think of 6 nights, in over eight years, where we haven't been burbling sleepy nonsense in each other's ears and dutch-ovening our way through the night. I'll be glad to have him back, I'm about three days away from dressing in rags and wailing around the street in the rain like Eponine from Les Mis. In the meantime, a little bit about walking – I've walked for years.

I don't know how well any of you know Newcastle, but there's a town moor just outside the main city – a lovely, open field with a well-lit path cutting right across it. Well, to help improve my fitness, I've taken to walking across there into work and back in the evenings a couple of times a week – four miles in total. I'm not doing this to boost my weight-loss but rather to get back to a decent level of fitness. You don't need to exercise for SW to work, but well, it can't do any harm.

Of course, the town moor, by the very nature of its name, is also used by lots of other people, and has four unique problems – cyclists, walkers, dog-walkers and cows. Let's take cyclists first.

A few years ago, you'd be lucky if a cyclist had anything more than two wheels and a handlebar as they went past you. Times have changed, not least because you can now sense their self-satisfied attitudes before you see them, drifting ahead of their bike like a breath on your neck. I'm not a fervent anti-cyclist – admittedly, I don't see the point, but the 'Professional' cyclist does wind me up.

Now its not the helmet-cam that gets me cross, although it's just so needlessly passive-aggressive – the Halfords equivalent of wearing a sign saying Telltale Tit on it. It's not even the lycra, which clings to every wrinkle and takes away the mystery of whether a man has a matt or gloss finish. No…it's the lights that wind me up – I used to cycle merrily in the dark along country roads with only the little reflector that came free with my box of Frosties lighting the way, with my long black coat and my shit goth black hair billowing behind me like the gayest Scottish Widow you've ever seen. Now you see cyclists coming towards you looking like a tiny mobile oil-rig, all shiny helmets (admittedly not the first time I've had one of them come at me of a morning) and blinking lights morse-coding 'YES, I AM A TWAT' on the front. It's lucky I'm not epileptic, I'd be twitching halfway to Sunderland by the time I finished my walk.

Then see there's other walkers – I'm an incredibly competitive person but also someone who is fundamentally lazy, a dangerous combination. I don't like to be 'outwalked' by anyone, but I'm too fat and slovenly to move beyond a speed that could be best described as 'god bless him, he's trying'. If I see someone coming up behind me (admittedly not the first time I've had that happen of a morning, either) I'll immediately try and quicken my pace, but I'll sharp need to slow down as my trousers start smoking and the smell of bacon wafts around me. I'll lump joggers and runners in with this lot – fair play to anyone who wants to improve their fitness, it's all good fun, but why do so many need to run towards you with that weird cum-face thing going on?

Dog-walkers are even worse, though. I don't mind dogs, but only if they're decent, dog-sized dogs – not cats that bark. As a rule, if you can lift up a dog with one hand, it's too small for me. I like walking a dog to be a battle of wills, see. But by the by, it's those people who let the dog run up to you and jump up on my work trousers – I don't particularly like dogs I don't know at the best of times, but I could really do without a muddy pawprint over my crotch. Oh how the owners laugh gaily as I shoo their little shitmachine away from me, all 'OH HE'S REALLY NO BOTHER' and 'OH HOW HE LIKES YOU'. I'd love to reply 'DO YOU THINK I COULD DROP-KICK HIM OVER ST JAMES PARK FROM HERE?' but of course I'm too British so I just laugh nervously and call them rude words as soon as they turn their back. Keep your dog on a leash if you're incapable of calling them back, it's really that simple.

The final problem is cows. For eight months of the year, there are about two hundred cows milling around on the moor. No-one else seems fazed by them but they make incredibly nervous. I grew up in the country and was never fazed, but one day I was walking across the town moor with my headphones on, in a world of my own, when a cow 'crept' (I say crept, a cow weighs around 100 stone or so, so she did well) up behind me and nudged my side with her nose. I got such a fright that I actually screamed out loud like a jessie and well, now I'm terrified of them! There's only one place in Newcastle for 100-stone beasts with insanely long eyelashes and pendulous titties and that's the Bigg Market. I console myself by eating their brethren with a smug smile.

twochubbycubs on: religion

For some reason, Jehovah's Witnesses have taken to standing around outside of Eldon Square of a lunchtime, thrusting copies of The Watchtower at me as I shuffle past with my headphones in and trying desperately not to catch their eye. I feel like I can't be mean to religious people in the same way I often am with chuggers – I usually just point at my ears and pretend I'm deaf, and I once told someone collecting for Alzheimer's Research that she'd spoken to me just a few minutes before, didn't she remember...she called me a very unsavoury name, and perhaps rightly so. But the JWs are a bit creepy – too earnest with the smiles, too keen to stop people and try and engage them, too comfortable with being told to fuck off. Perhaps tomorrow I'll rock up to them and ask what they can do for me, as a blood-giving (sssh), civil-partnered sodomite who believes in abortion and hard living.

I've never been a religious person – the only time I went to church growing up was at Easter to get a free Easter egg (although it was always a Spar special egg, dead cheap with white bloom on the chocolate) or Christmas for the same reason, substituting egg for a chocolate jesus. It didn't help that the guy delivering the sermons had an almighty lisp, which as a child was immensely hilarious. I know, cruel, but there you go. Actually, unusual disability seems to have followed me around through religion – our RE teacher in middle school was

143

amazing (used to let us watch South Park rather than read the bible) but he had a tremor in his left hand, which combined with his hand all clawed up through arthritis, looked like he was wanking all the time. Awful I know, but that also used to cause much hilarity during lessons – teacher twittering on about God whilst calling him a wanker with his left hand.

I haven't had much experience with other religions either, sadly. As part of a cultural exchange, our class had to go and visit Newcastle Hindu Temple – the idea being our minds would be broadened by their lavish food, colourful buildings and pleasant atmosphere, whereas young Hindu children would get to come and sit on the rock hard pews and listen to a man in a frock lisp his way through All Thingth Bright and Beautiful. Well see it was all going swimmingly until we had to sit cross-legged on the floor and listen to the brahmin explain Hinduism – champion. Except I, coming from an environment where the only spice I consumed belonged to Ginger, Baby, Scary, Sporty and Posh, was having a bad reaction to the pakora we had been given at the start and, genuinely accidentally, let out a fart that, pushed between my flabby schoolboy bumcheeks and the hard, polished floorboards, was ridiculously loud. And long. Once it was coming, there was no stopping it – at least ten seconds easily of earth-shattering, hair-burning fart. It sounded like the police helicopter was hovering overheard, it truly did. No-one believed me that it was a genuine accident and I got made to stand outside, although to be fair that was probably to give my nipsy a chance to cool off in the autumn air. I got detention and summarily bollocked for that little incident. It's no wonder there's so much tension these days — if only there'd been a bit more tension in my sphincter, eh.

twochubbycubs on: birds

For most blokes, the idea of having a soaking wet bird angrily thrashing around on their face first thing in the morning would be an entirely wonderful way to wake up. Well, admittedly, we're not "most blokes" but let me tell you, it's not all that. Nevertheless, that's how we started the day, with my cat bringing a bird in through our bedroom window and throwing it against my face. Normally we're woken very gently by our fancy alarm clock that fades unnatural light into the room like a sunrise but clearly Bowser thought that was far too decadent and we needed a new alternative.

There was a LOT of screaming. I screamed, Paul screamed, the bird was screaming and the cat got such a fright at our apparently ungratefulness that he puffed up into Giant Cat Form, picked up his prey and took off with the bird in his teeth into the living room, leaving a lovely smear of blood across the floor from where it's wing was hanging off. We spent the next ten minutes trying to remove Bowser from the room and rescue the bird and, after much flapping around (by all of us) and some judicious use of a tea-towel, I slingshotted the poor bugger out of the living room window. He survived for all of about ten seconds before Sola, our other cat, jumped from the roof (we live in a bungalow remember, she's not THAT good) and tore his head off. In all, we'd gone from sleeping peacefully in our beds to watching a violent murder on our front lawn, with all the screaming and dramatics that entails, within fifteen minutes.

My heart was still racing as I backed the DS3 off the drive.

Of course, the fun didn't stop there, as when Paul posted a dramatic recollection of the encounter on Facebook, he was immediately set about by someone telling him off for not taking the bird to an animal hospital. Paul was being terribly polite and British about the whole thing but I immediately weighed in on the argument to point out that *'the Sparrow Ambulance was tied up attending to a coal tit with hurt feelings'* and that I lamented the fact I hadn't had the foresight to fashion the poor bugger *'a tiny sling from a spent match and a doll's shoelace'*.

I think we can agree that I won the argument.

twochubbycubs on: DIY

Look, here's the deal. Come hell or high water, by the end of today we are going to have new curtains installed in our bedroom. It needs to happen. See a while ago I took our blinds apart so that I could paint the little bit of wall behind them, then promptly lost the chain that holds them together so that now, every tiny gust of wind and they splay around in all directions, rattling and bumping into each other. That wouldn't be so bad, except we have to leave our windows open in our bedroom at night – how else could the cats deliberately go outside, get wet and then get under our duvet at 3am and press their tiny wet noses against our bumcheeks? We can't build a cat-flap into our doors as they're the wrong type. So given how windy and cold it is, our bedroom at night is always a) freezing and b) like sleeping through a particularly budget production of Stomp. It's lucky that we're both the type of person who likes to be entangled up in each other when we're asleep – I reckon one morning we'll just wake up as one person, melded together like the wax in a lava lamp. Fuck me, that would make typing this blog difficult.

Plus, god knows what our neighbours must think – our windows being open all night and us being in a bungalow means every fart, mumble, snore and sleep-cough echoes around the street. No kidding, I once finished an overtime shift at work and upon getting out the car at 3am I couldn't understand what the strange rattling noise coming from the engine was until I realised it was Paul's snoring from over 100 yards away. Worse still is that I'm forever talking and laughing in my sleep – Paul's recorded me merrily singing Cerys Matthew's bits from The Ballad of Tom Jones whilst deep in slumber. Plus, we're always talking incoherently to each other, normally burbling away merrily about being too hot, too cold or 'don't fart, the cat's in the bed and you'll gas the fucker'.

So, whilst the neighbours would still be treated to the cacophony of noise from our bedroom, we can solve the blinds rattling – and that's today's project. You may recall that we're both equally shit at DIY (remember our current bathroom situation?) so I can only assume this will end up with one of us in A&E and our home left a burnt out shell. We have to be the only couple out there who has a £200 drill and exactly 0 clues about how to use it.

Ah well, wish us luck.

twochubbycubs on: drinking

Now see here, I'm not a big drinker – I tend to be an all or nothing sort of guy, so if I start drinking, I'm on it until I'm bundled into a taxi / arrested for lewd behaviour / do a Winehouse and choke on my vomit. It was supposed to be a civilised night, actually, and it certainly started off that way, with champagne in Hotel Indigo. That civilised chatter lasted about fifteen minutes before talk about bumhole waxing, black fluff and 'dripping' got underway and then the night never really got the glamour back. Brilliant night though, even if my mate did end up telling some poor, haggard looking woman with eighties hair and a very cats-arse-mouth (she was tutting at our conversation and rolling her eyes) that she looked like Enya. Taxi!

I like to think I'm a pleasant enough drunk – I'm certainly not an angry drunk or – worse – the moaning, miserable sort – if anything I just become way too affectionate towards Paul.

God he puts up with a lot, doesn't he? I was texting him at all hours of the night and I was clearly hammered pretty quickly looking back at the text messages. In my defence, if there is one, my phone has a smashed glass screen so it's hard to type properly. Yeah, that'll be it. I can't remember anything from after Paul bundled me into the Micra, though he tells me:

- I kept falling asleep / passing out on the twenty minute drive home, intermittently burping and slouching over onto his shoulder, meaning he had to keep jerking the car to the left at high speed to tilt me the other way;

- I spent a lot of time telling no-one in particular to fuck off; and

- when I got home, he opened the car door and I went tearing out like my arse was on fire because I was about to have a technicolour yawn, went headfirst straight into the side of the shed – and then was sick all over our front lawn.

twochubbycubs on: junk food kids

Please tell me someone else caught Junk Food Kids: Who's To Blame on Channel 4 last week (and still on their catch-up service, now)? It takes a lot to get me screaming at the TV – normally it's thick people on gameshows, or if Jeremy Kyle's incredibly botoxed and exceptionally punchable face looms into the foreground like a possessed fleshy iron. But this documentary really took the biscuit, and gave it to a fat kid.

It was ostensibly a programme designed to look carefully at all sides of the argument over why Britain's kids are getting fat, with several different streams running throughout focusing on different children, but what got my blood pressure rocketing even more than my swollen ankles usually manage was poor Tallulah (which I'll spell correctly, even if your mother couldn't quite manage all the requisite L's needed to inscribe her own daughter's name correctly in copperplate on her neck) and her oil-slick of a mother, Natalie. The kid was fat – not podgy or puppy-fat – but fat. She was in constant pain because her teeth had rotted down through so much sugar at the age of four, which ultimately resulted in her having to go under the knife and have 6 of her baby teeth removed.

It didn't take long for the same old excuses to be trotted out, either – the poor lassie was fat because of her 'fi-royd'. Fuck off, unless the thyroid was being deep-fried and served with a side of chips, we could probably rule that out. She gives her daughter Ribena at night instead of water because the alternative is 'she'd (the mother) be up all night'. Boo hoo! It's called parenting – you can't expect Professor Weetos and Dr Pepper to look after your kid. She then missed an appointment at the dental hospital for her daughter because she couldn't be bothered to roll out of bed of a morning. I despair.

It makes me enormously nettled when no-one dare say the truth to these parents – it's YOUR fault. You're feeding them crap and then wondering why their teeth are black and rotten. You choose to let them brush their teeth only when they want to and give them full sugar Ribena instead of cuddles and attention. You're trying to be a friend instead of a parent and as a result, your child is fat and in pain. But instead of remedying this, you blame everyone else but yourself. I can't fathom it – I love my cat, and if I thought he was in pain, I'd do anything I could to fix it – and I didn't push him out of my vagina after nine months of nurturing. I don't even HAVE a vagina. I know Natalie loved her kid – but you're supposed to, loving your kid doesn't make you an amazing parent – nurturing and making sure they are healthy and happy does that.

There were others too, including a truculent little madam who sat through her dietitian appointment with her mobile in her hand, barely acknowledging or respecting the learned doctor, instead playing on Facebook whilst her mother looked on with a 'well what can I do' face on. Here's what you do – you take the mobile out of your daughter's hand, you drive 7 miles away and put it by the the side of the road. If it goes missing, tough titty, daughter learns a lesson. If it doesn't, that's a fourteen mile walk for your daughter and think of the weight-loss. If I'd disrespected someone like that when I was a kid – and I'm not some gosh-darn-it eighty-year-old, I'm only in my late twenties – my arse would have looked like a bag of raw mince from the back of my parent's hands. But instead the mother kowtowed to her daughter's moods and inclinations like some shaking shrew and then wondered why the daughter didn't respect, acknowledge or follow her.

Of course, like most of Channel 4's documentaries, it was pretty sneaky filming – they played the usual trick of letting the subject say something like 'AH'VE NO IDEA HOW LITTLE BELLABRUSCO GOT CHUBBY' and then panning the camera across a sea of off-brand crisps (Sprinters) and Aldi chocolate bars (N&Ns). I know it was designed to make the viewer annoyed and I know that I played along by getting irate and shaking my head in disbelief – I had to take a Stugeron afterwards because I felt seasick.

twochubbycubs on: why Paul is fat

Paul is writing today's entry.

I'm usually the 'behind the scenes', younger, more handsome (*James edit: he's not*) half of Two Chubby Cubs – I tend to cook the meals whilst James works his magic on them fancy words in the posts. I don't mind, I quite enjoy cooking (though I'm still very much an amateur) and I can never be arsed after a day typing at work to then do the same at home. And, it lets me catch up on my boring programmes that James whinges about (look, Korean war bunkers ARE interesting. I don't care what everyone says) (*James edit: they're not*).

I've had a bit of a backward route into cookery, it has to be said. At school I can remember making shortbread and rolls, and the rest of the time was spent gossiping and trying to stealthily hit the 'Emergency Stop' button for the electric ovens so we didn't have to do anything (90%+ success rate, btw) and could go back to yakking. It's only really been in the last few years that I've had a stab at anything other than the plastic film on a ready meal and bunging into the microwave.

I suppose I can blame my mother for that, mealtimes at home at their most exotic never ventured past a jar of Uncle Ben's Sweet and Sour Sauce poured over a pack of slightly-frosty Kwik-Save Chicken Wings in a Pyrex dish. She did dally with switching to BBQ Sauce somewhere in the mid-90's but realised the error of her ways and went back to the lesser of the two evils. The chicken was never pre-cooked and whilst I'm not sure if that mattered it always had a slight pink hue and a chewy texture that made you feel like you had a corner of a baby wipe in your mouth. To this day I still can't eat chicken that has any bones. For the only time in my life I'm solely a breast man.

One thing I did like though was Mince 'n' Mash which I still love, though is essentially a pack of mince boiled in the water of tinned carrots and chopped tomato juice. I love it. James can only digest it if it has half a jar of Bisto poured in and half a pack of couscous so the actual meal itself is so diluted he can't taste it. He just doesn't appreciate a bit of povo-grub.

It was during my mid-teens that I learnt that too much of a good thing can actually start to get on your wick. Ma offered me once a 'Freschetta' pizza that was on offer at the local Spar – you remember it – the four cheese (and it was only ever the four-cheese one I was given. Pepperoni was 10p more) – where the crust rose in the oven. It was DELICIOUS. But, of course, once I said that it was like a red rag to a lazy bull. The very next day I counted and I swear this is all completely true) SIX of the bloody things piled on top of each other, a pile that never, ever seemed to go down no matter how hard I tried (and by God, did I try). To begin with I was in absolute heaven – I even managed to figure out the best way to eat it – use the crust to squeeze out the sauce from under the cheese and mop it up, so that it doesn't spoil the true heaven that is frozen four-cheese gooiness on a frozen yeasty-floury slab. Lahhhvely. Soon though I started to miss actually going to the bog and the Freschetta love affair was over. "But you said you liked 'em!", she said, dodgy tab hanging off her bottom lip that she bought from some gypo at Whittlesey market. "I did! But after three weeks I could really do with some bloody vitamins!". My protestations fell on deaf ears and I had to wait until the offer at Spar ended before I could once again actually have a crap and eat something else. A similar crisis of the bowel nearly erupted a few weeks later when a delivery of water-damaged Findus Crispy Pancakes filled up the freezer but I knew I had to act fast and feigned an allergic reaction to the breadcrumbs. I cried in relief when I saw those yellow fingers reach into a plastic bag and put that jar of "Uncle Den's" (times were hard) into the cupboard and calm was restored.

That's probably why I got so fat. Not that I was ever that skinny before the pizzas came along, heavens no, but I certainly didn't learn how to eat anything remote healthy. Couple all of that along with some knock-off sweets (Twax, Bouncy, Sprinters...) and it was a recipe for juvenile diabetes and a future shopping for clothes in the 'husky' sections at out-of-town garden centres.

This sort of thing pretty much carried on into my late-teens and didn't end even after I left home. I soon went off to University and my bad eating habits carried on there. This time, however, with even less cooking as I realised my mother's ability to switch the oven past 180 degrees made her look like Raymond Blanc next to my paltry skills and inability to even know how to chop an onion. I also had to get by on a paltry budget – £400 a month was my bursary and a good £370 of that was earmarked for fags, Lambrini and the monthly mince along to the Dot Cotton club (a gem on an otherwise clap-riddled, drab East Anglian gay scene. RIP Dot!). I also had to buy all my shopping in one go (immediately after that payment went into my account) before I pissed it all up the wall at the on-site Burger King, so it almost entirely went on crisps, chocolate and Diet Coke (gotta watch that figure, after all!) and for some reason no end of sauces. I remember coming home with bags and bags but having nothing that I could throw together into a proper meal, but you could have an absolute fiesta if you came to Room 231 armed with a battalion of breadsticks. This carried on and on and on and eventually I reached the whopping weight of 28 stone. There's a picture of me somewhere where I'm standing against a wall, but my head is miles away from the wall itself. It's awful. A combination of bad food and bad habits meant that any sort of weight-loss was going to be impossible (not that I was even trying). I became responsible mostly too for preparing the meals at the place I worked (hospital) which meant easy access to an endless supply of biscuits and other tidbits. No end was in sight, but, I was young and I didn't really care and I never really felt that 'fat' so had no intention of stopping.

Not long after that I landed in Portsmouth. Despite living in a gorgeous house it was also stuffed with two 60-year old, orgy-loving, dungeon dwelling S&M queens (really gross, believe me), it was handily located on top of a massive hill which meant that every day I had to walk up the bastard thing to get home from the train station (getting down was alright, I just rolled). Couple that with having even less money to spend on food meant that I was pretty quickly shedding weight and lost nearly half of it in all the time I was there. I even skirted XL at one point. My diet though was still pretty bad – the first meal I made James when he came to see me was a cheese sandwich made on stale bread and stale cheese (y'know, when it looks like a cracked heel) and a stolen Petit Filous yoghurt from my housemate Fabian. He still wolfed it down though, the little trooper. It was the exercise, though, and the fact I HAD to do it (I couldn't afford a bus!) that meant the weight had no choice really but to go down. It was quite nice at times. The hill was still knackering but it did become easier, and I was still eating all the things I loved. I started to notice though that I'd get very dizzy and when I played around with the blood glucose meter at work it was always a little too high for my liking. I tried to eat more healthily although I didn't really know how to cook anything, but I could never last long because I just didn't have the money in the first place to buy healthy things, nor have the foresight to actually plan things in advance to see things through the whole month (I was still having to buy food at the first opportunity, before my money went on debts!).

And so it pretty much just carried on like that until we finally moved in together Oop North. Our financial situation was much better meaning we could buy stuff that wasn't convenience or just pure crap, and James was quite adept at throwing together a few different meals. We managed quite well, losing a little bit of weight here and there, before we finally joined Slimming World a few years later and wanted to do things properly. I started giving a few simple recipes a go, like the good ol' Mince 'n' Mash (with real round potatoes!) and branching out into other things. I still remember the feeling of pride I had when I made my first ever spaghetti bolognese and served it up to an equally impressed James. I started experimenting even more with different things, still keeping it simple though, and relying on the Slimming World books like the One Pot ones and the 'Extra Easy Express' that nearly always meant that quick equalled easy.

We then moved into our current, gorgeous house, The Sticky Patch and with it came a new kitchen that we were able to design (with the help of the Ikea man, natch) that we could make our own, and weed out those little annoyances we'd had in our old places, like no worktop space or a sink that was too small. We stuffed it full of no-end of gadgets (like the ones here and a load of books so that cooking could actually be fun. Armed with some pretty decent equipment (for once!) and no end of room I really started to branch out and develop my skills, something which I'm still doing even now! I still struggle with anything too complex but at least now I'll give it a go and most of the time it works out alright. And that's probably the best bit of advice I could give anyone – just try it! If you take the time and able to learn from your mistakes, just try it. Nothing bad can really happen if you get it wrong (except setting yourself on fire and getting salmonella, I suppose...) and if you get it right it means that you'll become even more confident and competent. Looking back over some of the recipes I've cooked I really am quite surprised at how they've come out, given that a few years ago I couldn't work a George Foreman grill.

Next, I'd really like to take a catering course. Not that I see myself becoming a professional chef in the future (Christ no, I couldn't contain myself) but really just for fun and to develop my skills even more. Who knows, maybe we'll end up on the telly. Hopefully thinner and more photogenic by that point, mind. And I wouldn't mind more hair. Perhaps a boob lift too. Oh the possibilities are endless!

twochubbycubs on: shopping

Christ almighty. We've had the plasterers in (it's like having the painters in, only I'm not getting all hysterical and crying into a box of Milk Tray) (I'm kidding, jeez) and the house is an absolute and utter bomb-site. He's expertly taken all of the Artex off the ceiling and made it smoother than a silk worm's diarrheah. Which is apt, given it's an awful brown colour. However, the dust. Good LORD the dust. It's literally everywhere imaginable. We've had the Dyson out all day – which is a feat in itself, given it's one of those fancy digital cordless ones that powers down after twenty minutes – but I'm still finding pockets of orange dust everywhere. I swear I farted on the sofa earlier and it looked like a little firework going off behind me. Awful.

Just awful. Speaking of farts (as you know it's one of our favourite topics), I need to confess something dreadful. See we had those chicken gyros on Friday night and all day yesterday, our farts smelt like a tramp's sock boiled in death itself. They were dreadful – intensely potent and incredibly wide-ranging. Of course, being us, this was just hilarious, and we were farting and pooting and trumpeting all the way around Tesco, beside ourselves with laughter and merriment.

But then, when we got to IKEA, I topped them all. We were there to look at possible storage solutions for our fitted wardrobe (oh the decadence) when I had a faint rumbling in my nethers. I say a faint rumbling, it was like someone testing a speedboat engine. So, sensing an opportunity for mischief, I ducked around a corner, opened one of the doors on the showroom wardrobe, and let out a guff. It was tiny, like I'd startled a duck, but I knew it would be concentrated. I hastily shut the door and called Paul over, on the pretence that I wanted him to check what type of hinge it was on the bottom of the door. He came lumbering over in his own special way, knelt down and opened the door, only to be hit full in the face with the contained fart. I almost saw the skin on his nose blacken. Honestly, you could see the fugitive zephyr as it bounced around the interior. He immediately turned around and called me a filthy see-you-next-Tuesday and I almost broke my back bent over laughing.

Mind, at least we have fun. We might not have the most exciting lives but we're always laughing. We came away from IKEA the same way we normally do, with absolutely nothing in our trolley but our pockets bulging with a quarter-tonne of IKEA pencils, ready to be shoved into the same kitchen drawer as the other 323,537 IKEA pencils we've stolen. Perhaps we should get a log burner after all, we could keep it going for a good few months on nicked stationery alone!

Because the plasterer was going to be in our house all day, we had to fill up the time 'out of the house', so we thought we'd spend a gay few hours tripping around the Metrocentre, which, if you've never heard of it, is the North's answer to an American shopping mall from the nineties. It has everything! Closed clothes shops, closed food quarters, closed gadget shops, a plethora of e-cigarette and mobile phone cover stands AND any amount of imbecilic fuckknuckles walking around getting IN MY BLOODY WAY. I remember when the Metrocentre was worth going to – namely when it had Metroland, where the thrill of going on an indoor rollercoaster totally made-up for the risk of getting inappropriately touched-up behind the ferris wheel. It was a haven for nonces, apparently, though I never experienced that. Must have been my ungainly weight and C&A haircut that put them off.

We did spend half an hour in the Namco Games bit, which is full of those totally rigged but faintly fun arcade machines where you win tickets that you can redeem for lead-covered tat later on. We played a giant version of Monopoly, we did some virtual fishing and, I shit you not, I managed to win a proper licenced Flappy Bird toy from one of those claw machines that usually have all the grip of Jeremy Beadle. I couldn't quite believe it. We did nip next door to the 'adults only' bit where the proper slot machines were but fucking hell, it's just too depressing watching adults feed money into the slots at 10am in the morning. Nobody wins.

twochubbycubs on: more builder shenanigans

Before we get started – I heard an expression yesterday which had me clutching my sides with laughter, and I've tried and tried to work it naturally into my normal dialogue but haven't been able to, so I'm just going to chuck it here at the start of the blog and let it set the tone:

..."she had a fanny like a butcher shop with blown-in windows"...

Seriously, how can I get that into normal conversation? I can't exactly chuck it across to the man who has been round to size up my blinds, can I?

Yes yes, I know, I said I'd update, but then I also said it would just be chaotic with all the decorating and people being in the house, so we took some time off instead. Listen I thought this blog would fizzle out like a disappointing fart after a week or two when we started, so the fact we're here almost a year later is good enough! So shut yer hole. Even getting to the computer to type up this blog has been like a thrown-out round of Gladiators, climbing over paint-pots and sanders and forty inches of dust just to get to the keyboard. Christ knows what my name would be if I had been a Gladiator...'GELATINE' perhaps, or 'SWEAT RASH'. You would have had to slightly de-tune the TV to soften the image of me in a lycra unitard too, with my tits jiggling about like duelling jellyfish and my cock-and-balls smeared across my front like a run-over weasel.

Of course we've had the natural gaggle of people in the house, quoting for work, looking disdainfully at our paint colours and over-egging their quotes and then backtracking so fast their shoes smoke when I start haggling. Case in point – we had a local company come out to quote for installing an alarm system a couple of days ago. He turns up, starts rattling our windows and doors and telling us that 'given the fucking area youse (wince) live in, you really need to improve your security'. The area we live in! The cheeky little muckspout.

Anyway we have security – we have a good alarm system, we just fancy getting CCTV cameras because it'll annoy the neighbours who'll automatically assume that they're pointed directly into their living room and that we'll be sitting tutting at them sweating and fretting over their Prima 'Easy' sudoku. Can you still get Prima? I have a faint recollection of reading it in a dentist surgery a few years ago and them not needing to anaesthetise me because I'd actually died of boredom.

We've had a painter in the house all week and he's been brilliant – meticulously clean, efficient, turning up on time and doing a cracking job. But CHRIST has it been stressful – each morning before work I'm having to run around the house removing anything indecent and/or smutty. The normal products that help a happy homo-marriage, but not something I want my painter to have to move with a gloved hand. We'll be finding bottles of lube, douching bulbs and fetishwear stuffed down the cracks in the settee and behind the towels until at least 2018.

Hell we had to stop the TV from syncing with the computer and displaying the contents of our photo slideshow just in case he was busy glossing the skirting boards, flicked on the telly for a bit of Jeremy Kyle and was confronted by a 55" LED display of a hardcore bukkake session. Nothing matt about that, mate. He probably already thinks the house is haunted by the gayest ghost imaginable given I'd forgotten that when I show people at work how our fancy lights work where you can control the colour and brightness from the iPad, it'll be changing them at home as it's all connected via WiFi – imagine trying to paint when the lights keep flashing and changing from Hussy Red to Septic Green.

It doesn't help matters that Paul seems to think it's entirely appropriate to 'drop the kids off' first thing in the morning before his steamy shower, meaning the bathroom smells like an animal rendering plant for at least three hours. I wouldn't care so much but the painter was recommended by someone whose opinion I actually welcome and I don't want him going back and telling them that our house smells like a sewage outlet.

My haggling has also been coming along wonderfully – after making a new enemy at the sofa shop by taking £700 off her commission, I managed to haggle 50% of the cost of our blinds. I say I haggled, but really, he told me it would cost £900, I said no and that I'd pay £450 and not a penny more. He immediately said that was fine. I'm fairly sure it wasn't because he was swooning at the sight of me stood in front of him in my vest looking to the world like a hot-water tank spoiling for a fight, so it just shows how much these companies try and screw out of you.

Now before some clever-dick points out that we could buy them online and fit them ourselves and save so much more money, well yes, that's true, but you don't know us. We'd install the blinds upside-down and on fire. It's like the motto that I really should have tattooed on the lower of my back – 'I prefer to get a man in'.

twochubbycubs on: recycling

I can't begin to tell you the satisfaction saying that brings me, not least because the house no longer looks like a knockoff Dignitas clinic. I've never known someone match their carpet to the interior of a used commode before. The carpet was fitted by a pair of carpet fitters who had clearly just finished a shift as runway models for Abercrombie and Fitch – one was so good-looking I almost told him to go outside as he was smoking inside the house. **Boom**. Not our type – Paul and I prefer a more rugged/lazy look, but Christ it must be nice to be blessed with natural good looks. That's definitely not me, I've got a face that would make an onion cry, but eh, I get along in life.

Part of preparing the house ready for the carpet involved moving all of our furniture into the bathroom, like a game of Hoarders: Tetris Addition. I took the opportunity to get rid of the giant media unit we have which holds the TV and Sky box and all the usual technological accoutrements that litter a living room. Bear in mind that wasn't some fag-burned bit of Formica, it was a decent, solid piece of furniture in excellent condition – well, one of the little knobs was a bit loose, but what more would you expect in our house? Overcome with a pique of philanthropy (and partly because there was no way we were going to get it into the DS3), I rang a local 'community charity' company who collect secondhand furniture to furnish the houses of the disadvantaged – people who've been smacked about or smacked up. Great cause.

They promptly turned up, ran their fingers over the wood and told me 'it wasn't appropriate for their clientele'. Seriously now, I'd understand if it had a giant plastic cock stuck on the side or spent condoms plastered on the underside like smutty papier-mâché, but no!

I asked him why and he wheezed out that 'it would just sit in the shop collecting dust'. Well heaven forbid! I feel it had more to do with the fact he couldn't be arsed to lift it. I sent him away with a flea in his ear, and, in a proper huff, took it outside and smashed it into matchsticks with a sledgehammer. I know I could have stuck it on freecycle but I find that whole business very stressful – I once put an advert in there for a Nintendo 64 to take away and I got so many illiterate emails in barely-legible English that I thought I'd been hacked by a Russian Johnny 5. The art of please and thank you are seemingly lost on those who are desperate for stuff to fill up their car-boot sale table for furniture. I did, somewhat meanly, follow that up with an advert for a spare Xbox 360 and then replied to each email who didn't say thank you or please with a 'you were the first to reply, but your lack of manners have cost you dear'. Oooh, what a sanctimonious arse. But I do so hate bad manners.

We once used freecycle to pick up a landline phone a few years ago – we went (on the bus, those were the days) to pick up a little answerphone machine only to find that when we got there that a) the tattooed wardrobe (who had clearly never used the phone to book a dentist appointment) who answered the door wanted twenty quid for it and b) it was so lacquered with years and years of nicotine that I didn't dare dial a number longer than the speaking clock for fear of contracting emphysema.

Anyway, back to the carpet. It's marvellous – the last big bit of DIY that we needed to do before we buy lots of nice things to fill the house up with. However, it's not without problems. See, a new carpet needs a bloody good vacuum (yes it does, it's an old myth that you don't hoover a carpet) to get all the fluff off it. Grand, no problem, we've got a fancy Dyson Digital. Problem is, the Dyson Digital only lasts about six minutes on full suck (just like Paul) and needs emptying out after two minutes of vigorous vacuuming. I'd no sooner hoover one third of a room when it would turn off, needs emptying, switched back on and then beep – out of battery. You've never seen anyone hoover so fucking quickly – all I needed was Philip Schofield bellowing at me from behind a sheet of plexiglass and it would have felt like I was on The Cube.

But the carpet still looks lovely so it was worth it, right?

twochubbycubs on: x-rays

I'm in a huff. I left work at 5pm and it took me two hours to get home, saying as every single person in the world decided in unison to drive towards Alnwick on the A1. Bumper to bumper traffic and even though I took a diversion seemingly via Northern Ireland, it was still all very stressful. I've mentioned so many times about poor drivers that this barely needs a mention but a big FUCK YOU to the tagnut in the Audi behind me all the down the A1, who despite being stuck in EXACTLY the same traffic-jam as I was, spent most of the time bellowing at me in the mirror like he was trying to put out a fire with swearwords. Apologies that my DS3 doesn't come with a fucking flight pack, you stupid sunset-coloured packet of shit. Oh and whaddya know, when he DID manage to get past, did he indicate? Did he buggery! Audi drivers: you DO have indicators in your car – there's a big knob in the car to operate them.

AND BREATHE.

At least when I managed to turn off and the traffic calmed down I was able to take in a bit of scenery and stop for one of those fantastically freeing extravagant pisses that only men can have by the side of a road or tucked down a layby. Admittedly my knowledge of foofs isn't exactly shit-hot but it's my understanding that it's far more difficult for ladies to have a quick tinkle without having to take everything off or risking falling into a nettle patch with a froth of piss around your ankles. Here's a fun fact for you though – it doesn't matter how discreet a bloke is, no matter how carefully he parks his car and how far into a bush he goes to have a wee, the very second urine leaves his helmet a car will promptly appear full of children and nuns, leaving him with the unenviable choice of carrying on and causing offence or having to reverse the flow, which let me tell you now, BLOODY HURTS. It's like trying to fit a washer to a gushing tap. I bet even Neil Armstrong up on the moon nipped behind the lander for a quick Jimmy Riddle only to be met with a rocket full of Russians gazing balefully at him the moment he 'pulled the cord'. Anyway, it seems fair that men have the upper hand when it comes to weeing, given ladies can have so much fun with their bajingo. If I was a lady, anything I owned that was even slightly cylindrical would have a very glossy patina to it, let me tell you.

I had to go for an x-ray this morning on my shoulder. Nothing exciting I assure you – I've got a trapped nerve or something which is making my neck ache and my fingers tingle unnecessarily. Explain to me this – how comes I arrived at 9am for a 9.30am drop-in session only to be met with a veritable sea of lightly shaking old ladies all ahead of me. How? What time did they turn up for that to happen? I mean I appreciate getting an x-ray might be a day out but if they were anything like my nana, you could hold her up to a bright light and see Mint Imperials through her papery skin rattling around her body at the best of times. Ah nana. I tutted and moaned and then remembered they'd fought in the war for me. So I upped the volume of my tutting knowing the shellshocked amongst them wouldn't be able to hear for their ringing ears.

Actually, it was a very pleasant experience – pulled into a room, told to remove my shirt, complimented on my beard and then blasted with radiation, which before I met Paul was pretty much my average night out. They did give me two heavy bags to hold to 'pull my shoulder into the correct position' which, judging by the fucking weight of the bags, was somewhere in Aberdeen. Of course because it was a big brute of a bloke talking to me, I didn't want to lose face and drop the bags so I had to stand still, grimacing and squinching my eyes together in pain. I bet he told everyone when I left that I was absolutely dying for a shite. Can't fault the NHS though – doctor told me I needed an x-ray yesterday and it was done by this morning. That's almost as good as when I went for a private MRI a few years back, where I paid a billion pounds just to leaf through a copy of Home & Country in the waiting room and be called Sir by the receptionist. Actually, thinking about it, two MRIs and two x-rays in however many years...that surely means I'm overdue a superpower or something? I'd be a crap superhero. Captain Mince. The Anal Intruder. Barry Beige. All possible names.

I've got to be careful when I'm visiting the doctors or

having anything done, because invariably my anxious mind tries to default to the worst case scenario. I was sitting cross-legged watching the TV before and when I got up to discover my left leg had gone to sleep, well, that was it, I'd diagnosed myself with motor neurone disease (and please, I know it's an awful disease, that's why I'm scared of it). I've already resigned myself to the fact I've probably got a spine like a packet of Ritz crackers that someone's kicked up a flight of stairs, but really, realistically, I'll have just pinched a nerve swimming and my body is acting accordingly. Oh it is awful being neurotic.

Anyway, only a little entry tonight because it's time for The Apprentice. I know, I know. I don't know why I watch it either. I don't like Karen Brady, I don't like Alan Sugar and Charles Littner may as well come out in a cape twiddling a moustache to complete the 'villian' role. At least Nick was gentle in his absolutely devastating, soul-destroying cutdowns. Charlie Brooker said it best when he described Alan Sugar as looking like a water-buffalo straining to shit in a lake. I still watch it though, so really, who's the mug?

twochubbycubs on: Paul's holidays

So, we finally managed to track down an Iceland in the local area today that still had some ready meals in stock. I went to the one in Gateshead which fortunately was stocked all the way to the top, even though someone who looked like a post-menstrual imagining of Pauline Quirke was circling nearby like a stinking, shuffling Belgrano. Not a bad selection either, so I got plenty of sausages and meatballs and a few tikka masalas. In a strange coincidence, James did exactly the same thing and flounced into the Cramlington one on his way home, so now our freezer is dangerously overstocked and I daren't open the door because it feels like I'm stuck in a hall of mirrors with Wor Margaret.

But anyway, I digress. Tonight – Tikka Masala and Rice. I'm rather looking forward to it, I don't mind a good curry and the spicier the better. I was going to make a 'Grecian Pizza' – I called it Grecian because it had Feta and Olives on it and that's all I know about Greek cuisine. It was going to be the 'ring' pizza you see in the Fakeaways book with a fancy salad in the middle, but could I hell get it to roll right. I tried everything but it was just wasn't going to happen. A shame, really, because I was an absolute natural when I worked at Domino's Pizza in my teen years (best job in the world. No, really) and could whip up a thick, thirteen incher in seconds (still can on a good day and with a good breeze behind me). But because I was in a huff I just rolled out a misshapen slab and flung it into the bin when I couldn't get the shape right.

I absolutely love Greek cuisine, and anything Mediterranean. I'm trying hard to convince James that we need a holiday around there, just so I can vacuum up my own bodyweight in Feta. Travelling is one thing that we absolutely love doing. It's only really been in the last few years that we've gone anywhere that exciting, mostly due to a lack of money or something coming along that is more important (we had to cancel a trip to Iceland to buy a new kitchen instead. Booo!) so a holiday in the sun is well overdue. I still get like a giddy schoolboy at holiday time. I'm sure James slipped me a wobbly egg or two (a la Shannon Matthews) when we went to Germany because I just couldn't stop flapping my hands like a kid with ADHD. I always had crap holidays as a kid. We once went to Benidorm in the early 90's which was absolutely fantastic but since then they were just dreadful. You know it's bad when a few wet weekends at Butlin's Skegness is a highlight.

The worse one though was to Ireland. No rolling hills, leprechauns or culture for us. Oh no. We went to stay with my then stepfather's family in a run-down part of Downpatrick where the spirit of The Troubles was still well and truly alive. There were no fewer than eight of us crammed into a tiny two bedroomed house, and the kids were all bundled two-a-piece into three-storey bunkbeds made from pallets and chickenwire. You think I'm joking – I'm really not. The house was wall-to-wall Virgin Mary and that bloody awful picture of Jesus doing a Goatse to his chest. You know the one I mean. I was handed a rosary by an elderly woman and had no idea what to do with it, so I wore it round my neck for the whole weekend. I thought I looked fabulous, personally and never resisted an opportunity to strut around with it.

In the evenings we had to secure the house against the IRA (or was it the Police? I can't remember what side they were on). It meant some elaborate traps had to be set by the front door in case it was kicked in. It looked like a fancy laser matrix but out of skipping rope. I got a smack across the head from someone who earlier had pissed against the bedroom wall because when I went to get some squash during the night I set off some trap that meant a radio fell into the hallway and set some picture frames cascading down the stairs like a paramilitarian game of Mouse Trap. It was all so surreal! Fortunately we never went back. I think if it had been suggested I would have seriously considered putting myself into care.

The worst part of the whole time we were there was the food – not that it was that bad, but because we were only fed once a day. ONCE. And it was at some weird time like 3pm. Not quite lunch, not quite dinner, but far too far away from what would be breakfast. A nightmare for a fatty like me. Give me waterboarding any day over that absolute horror.

And, for some reason, I came away with ABBA Gold on tape.

I'm glad to say that was a definite low point and they only ever got better since then. To be honest I don't think I could have tolerated anything worse without doing some sort of spazz-out on the whole lot of them and that most certainly wouldn't be pretty.

One place I'd really love to go though is the Far East. I'd love it! I love the whole culture and Western mysticism about it all. China, Japan, Singapore – I'd do all of it, and chow down every last crumb of chow mein I could find. I'd probably whinge that it wasn't like a 'proper Chinese' you get from some foul-smelling grotty shop in Blyth like I'm used to. Top of the list is North Korea but the food there is shit so I might not bother unless I can get away with smuggling in a Matheson's sausage.

twochubbycubs on: our German holiday: part one

Well, that's me and the husband back from the land of sausage and beer and hyper-efficiency. Germany was amazing, there's really no two ways about it – and I'd heartily recommend anyone sitting on the fence to climb on down and give it a go. Now, whenever I go away, I always end up prattling on about things way too much – but I like to write, so here is part one of our trip. There's a lot more to come...recipes/weight loss is coming back online next week, as this is my holiday time! So imagine us, bleary-eyed and staggering out of bed last Wednesday morning and on our way to Germany!

We did all the usual pre-holiday activities – giving the cats strict orders not to crap on the living room carpet but to go outside and somehow smear it under Neighbour Number 2's door handle, turning off all electrical sockets because everyone knows that the electricity will leak out and start a fire, and blowing a few air kisses at Number 2 who I know will be devastated not seeing our giant bodies sashaying down the front garden. Luggage into our old car (Black Betty – I wouldn't take the new car because I'm super-paranoid about it getting scratched by some blind old duffer getting out of her car), house locked up, cats giving us fuck-you-looks in the window, and we were away. Almost immediately I'm tutting and sighing like I'm on a respirator because Paul wanted to drive. I'll admit it –

I'm a terrible passenger when I'm being driven – I spend most of the journey plucking fitfully at my seatbelt and hanging onto the roof handle like I'm on a rollercoaster, wincing and sucking air through my teeth every time a car appears on the horizon three miles ahead. Paul's actually a really good driver – I just like to be in control of the car. I wouldn't care, I drive like I've got a bomb stuck up my arse but what's good for the goose...

We arrived at the Holiday Inn Airport only to note that we were actually next door to Edinburgh Zoo and there was the small matter of no airport being in sight. Upon wheeling our fey little cabin-suitable suitcase/rucksacks into reception, we were told (somewhat icily, for a bloody Holiday Inn) that we were in completely the wrong hotel. Paul dropped the rucksack down the steps of the hotel with an almighty bang as he left. The temperature in the car dropped a mere five degrees afterwards. After a short diversion over the tram lines, we checked in, promptly fell asleep, and woke up refreshed and ready to go early Thursday morning. We nipped down for the all-you-can-eat breakfast expecting to fill our bellies with half a pig and a billion eggs, only to be met with a lacklustre continental offering and pursed lips from the Breakfast Manager (!) because I couldn't use the rotary toaster. You know, that's one thing I can't stand from hotel staff – attitude. It's entirely pointless, because all it does is put me off returning and creates a bad atmosphere. Plus his badge said BREAKFAST MANAGER, for fucks sake. What do you do to become a breakfast manager, a training course in arranging Weetos? A day course on the importance of correct grapefruit juice presentation? The knobber. We departed, left poor old Black Betty in the long-stay carpark and headed into the airport.

Edinburgh Airport isn't the most thrilling place we've ever been, but we managed to pass the time by having to rearrange our hand luggage to comply with Easyjet's admittedly fairly generous cabin policy. We didn't bother taking a suitcase but instead packed six days worth of clothes (each) and a change of shoes into our rucksacks. As it happens, a call went out for bags to be put in the hold in exchange for speedy boarding, so we took full advantage of that, giving pitying looks as we were whisked onto the plane ahead of everyone else. I don't see the point of speedy boarding – all it actually means is that you can sit and nurture your deep vein thrombosis ahead of everyone else. After all, everyone will get a seat on the plane – it's not as if you're going to be turned away at the door or blocked getting on by a stewardess brandishing a metre long Toblerone like a bizarro version of Gladiators.

I do have a weird relationship with flying. I'm not scared that we're going to crash – I rationalise in my head that if the plane does decide to smash into the ground at 600mph, I'm not going to have too much time to consider my options. So if it crashes, it'll be quick. Instead, I spend the few hours before my flight worrying that I'll have a panic attack on board and need to be strapped into my seat with a couple of belts from other passengers and a sock in my mouth, or that I'm going to have a picture of my jeans-clad arse lumbering down the aisle used in a 'TOO FAT TO FLY' farticle on Buzzfeed. The flight is always fine, although I usually spend a good hour or so desperate for a piss but stricken with the knowledge that as soon as I squeeze into that tiny metal coffin/toilet and set him away, the plane will immediately nosedive and I'll come tumbling acrobatically out of the netty with my cock flapping about and piss in my hair. As it happens, the flight was smooth as brushed silk and the only downside was Paul having to sit next to someone who smelled like she'd brushed her hair with the toilet brush. The flight took an hour and a half and it felt like we were no sooner in the air than back on the ground. I can't fault easyJet – the flights were cheap, the cabin was clean and the staff were marvellous (same coming back, too). Despite it feeling a bit like I was flying inside a tangerine, it was a perfect flight. We were in Germany in no time at all!

After a quick mince through border control (where the lady in the passport booth looked at my passport, then at me, then at my passport, then at me again, then showed it to her colleague, who then looked at me – all that was missing was for my moon face to be projected on a screen behind her and an applause-a-meter set up to gauge reaction) we were down into the underground/overground rail system of Berlin, called the U-Bahn and S-Bahn respectively. Despite the fact that the underground map looks like a lunatic has used every crayon in his box to draw an approximation of an cockfight and then chucked a bag of Scrabble tiles at it, we were on our way in no time at all. Costs are very reasonable, around €7 for an all-day pass for both systems, although we ended up buying five tickets after I lost the original two in my coat, pressed the wrong button the third time and had to buy ticket 4 and 5 as replacement. No accounting for dimness.

Our hotel was near the Zoologischer Garten metro stop, a mere five minutes away through a very pleasant but entirely too hipster shopping mall. The hotel itself – 25Hours Bikini – was more of the same – very cool, exceptionally unique, but a bit too 'trying too hard to be zany' for my taste. But that's because I'm not cool, never have been, never will be. We were checked into our Jungle XL room (so-called because it overlooked Berlin Zoo) and whisked up in the speedy little lift, which rather cleverly had video panels in the wall which displayed random bits and pieces like a cat in a hat and David Bowie. Delightful. The corridor, with the room numbers suspended from the ceiling in bright neon and padded walls, made it feel a bit like a knocking shop, but it was unusual enough to be fun rather than intimidating.

The room itself was a treasure, though – spacious, clean and full of little secrets and toys, like a suitcase nailed to the wall with a hole on the side which, when peeked through, had a load of tiny German models queuing up for bread. The bath had one of those fancydan electrical systems which fills and heats the bath to the correct temperature, but I'm always slightly concerned that it'll protest under my weight and electrocute me as punishment for me straining the metalwork. There was the usual flatscreen TV, which displayed a disappointing lack of blisteringly hardcore German pornography, but it was only 3pm so they had to get the kids TV scheduling out of the way first. A powerful shower, comfortable bed and a free bike in the room (which it may amaze you to know did not get used) completed the setup. Everything looked high-end but kitsch, and it worked well. Paul sandblasted the toilet, I took off my flight socks, and out we went to make the most of the evening.

twochubbycubs on: our German holiday: part two

My last entry stopped as we ventured out into Berlin, and right outside of our hotel was a Christmas market, one of many we'd end up visiting. Christmas markets in the UK don't compare – full of tat, tarpaulin and crap food. In Germany, the stalls are wooden, heavily decorated and full of nice trinkets. It was here that we tried our first currywurst, which everyone raves about. Meh – it's sausage, chips and tomato sauce with curry sprinkled on the top! Delicious yes, but not as exciting as I was expecting! We kept seeing stalls selling Glühwein and, not knowing what it was, we ordered some.

Fucking vile. It was mulled wine, and I can't bear red wine at the best of time, but this felt like I was drinking warmed through Radox. We took a polite sip in front of her, went round the back of the stall and dropped the rest down the drain, where I can only imagine it's burnt its way through the sewage pipes and caused an incident. We couldn't face going back and giving back our empty cups, so that mistake cost €12! BOO! She did give us a smirk on the way back around too, the cow.

Looming large over Alexanderplatz was Berlin's TV Tower, so we wandered over to that. A few Euros later and we were speeding in a fantastic quick lift up to the panaroma view floor, 666ft in the air, allowing you to look over Berlin. Here we did experience a bit of an odd thing – the terse German! He asked if we were English and when we confirmed, he looked at us as though I'd broken into his house on Christmas day and shit on the turkey. At least the lift was fast and we were at the top in no time. Naturally, we immediately ordered the gayest possible drinks we possibly could – when the barman takes ten minutes to make a cocktail and it has three seperate fruits adorning it (and two fruits drinking it), you know it's camp. It was beautiful at the top of the tower – Berlin bustling below, all the Christmas lights and decorations twinkling away and spreading out for miles. It was like the Blackpool tower, only you're not looking out over a vista of tattooed seacows playing bingo and a sewage pipe pouring into the Irish Sea. Thanks to the sheer amount of alcohol in our drinks, the view got a bit wobbly, so we dashed back out.

Another Christmas market followed – lovely yes, but it caused a bit of a row. Well row is a strong word. We spotted an animal being led around a little paddock, and I was adamant that it was a horse. Paul said a donkey. We didn't know the German for either.

The bloody thing had horse ears! I took a picture but apparently this isn't the beast that caused an argument. I did exclaim loudly that THERE MIGHT NOT BE A DONKEY BUT THERE'S CERTAINLY A FAT ASS, but, having realised I'd gone too far, I spotted a ferris wheel and whisked Paul onto it as a distraction.

I have no fear of heights, but I'm not particularly keen on fairground rides – for example, I'll happily ride any rollercoaster until I stroke-out and have to be carried out the park on a stretcher, but I don't trust anything that can be assembled overnight from inside of a truck by someone with yellow fingers and a breezy understanding of basic health and safety. Nevertheless, I duly climbed on board, all the way focussing on the rusty bolts, creaking metal and peeling paint like I was about to have some sort of Final Destination episode. Would that bolt come loose, fall 70ft, strike the horse-donkey, who would then kick the ride operator spark out, who'd fall on the safety console, somehow disengaging the wheel lock and send us freewheeling merrily down the Alexanderplatz, culminating with me being wedged in a chestnut warmer where my previously inhaled sip of Glühwein would ignite inside of me, blowing me up like an especially Christmassy suicide bomber?

No.

But we DID ruin some poor lad's date, I reckon. He clearly thought he and his little slip of a girlfriend were going to get a ferris capsule all to themselves and was in for a good few minutes of 'checking the depth', as it were, until us fatties bailed into the capsule shouting about bloody horse-donkeys and making the whole thing shake like the Apollo Service Module coming back to Earth. He spent the ten minutes of the ride giving us shitty looks. I don't know what the Latvian is for 'SILLY FAT BASTARD' but he clearly didn't know what eyebrow-threading was so I reckon that puts us about even.

After the ferris wheel, we had to make our way over to something called Exit Game Berlin, which we had prebooked before we set off on holiday. Essentially, this was a live version of those 'Escape the Room' games you get on the Internet (or, fact-fans, those early 'Mental' games on The Crystal Maze) where you solve clues hidden the room and work out how to escape (or in our case, how to stop a crazy Berliner poisoning the water supply – gasp!). We confidently set out, armed with a map on how to get there and the correct underground lines. Well goodness me if we didn't end up in a rough part of Berlin. I'm terrible on holiday – I'm so fearful of having my wallet/phone/bits and pieces stolen that I'm on a constant cycle of checking my trouser pockets, coat pockets, shirt pockets – and I'm not exactly subtle about it – I end up walking down the street like I'm doing the world's slowest Macarena. Nevertheless, we eventually found the place – it was a tiny, tiny little door in the middle of the street which we promptly knocked on.

No answer. Knocked again. No answer. So, thinking it was part of the 'clue', we spent a good five minutes checking for hidden buttons, cameras, knockers...until the guy came to the door, asked who we were, and told us we were in entirely the wrong place and that we needed to be on the other side of town at a different escape game. A fifteen minute taxi ride later, during which I felt like Princess Diana getting sped through tunnels and through traffic (I winced when I saw a Fiat Uno – I thought it was the end), we were there.

And, forgive me, it was FUCKING amazing. A proper room set up like a kitchen, but with crazy pipes everywhere, chains, hidden boxes, UV writing, secret codes, a telephone. You're locked in (well not locked in, but that's part of the game) and there's a big clock in the corner counting down from 60 minutes. You have an hour to complete the task. Someone is watching you and can give you clues if you get stuck, but, although it's difficult, you can just about do it in an hour – we did! We came away from the experience thinking it was bloody fantastic, and it truly was – worth going to Berlin just for that! There's one opened up in Newcastle which we're looking into, but it costs £60! Christ.

Given it was knocking on to midnight at this point, we made our way back to the hotel, stopping only for a quick glass of schwipp-schwapp (Coke with Orange, who knew) and another currywurst.

twochubbycubs on: our German holiday: part three

There's a bit in an old episode of Absolutely Fabulous where Edina goes into her kitchen and selects a bottle of champagne from a chiller cabinet, only for it to be replenished like the machine that replaces the pins in a bowling alley. It's pretty much like that with our freezer and Ben and Jerry's at the moment. I get rid of one, only to find Paul has managed to go to ASDA, restock and be sat back down on the settee without me blinking. Peculiar. Well it is Christmas...back to Germany!

We woke up the next morning with a tightly packed schedule and we were mincing down Karl Marx Allee in no time at all with a view to visiting the Videogame Museum. Paul tried to engage me with tales of socialist architecture and other nonsense but he possibly assumed from my glazed over eyes, deep sighs and putting a hand over his mouth, that I wasn't interested. We had an agonising problem of where to have breakfast, given there was only a McDonalds (reasons to decline: not on holiday! Never on holiday! We have to eat somewhere local, we're on holiday and we're not that type of tourist!) or an art gallery café (we're not hipster enough! I don't have pieces of lace in my beard! They're going to serve our coffee with a side of scorn and the toast will be organic carpet-toast spread with derision!) – we settled on the café. Breakfast in Germany is amazing – you essentially get all of the fat-bastard level of the food pyramid in one go – bread, meat, jam and cheese. She did put a token bit of rocket on the side but we ignored that – we're on holiday, if I'm not having mild palpitations by 11am then something is wrong.

The Videogame Museum was great fun, full of interactive old computer systems and rare controllers. It will sound as boring as all outdoors to someone who isn't into gaming, but for us two fatties it was smashing. Only thing was, it was overrun with children, which immediately creates two feelings – rage and worry. Rage because I'm a selfish adult who has forgotten he was a child once and immediately starts scowling and hissing at the children pressing the wrong buttons with their sticky hands, and worry because I'm always terrified that the parents will think I'm a nonce if I'm loitering near their children with a barely disguised grimace on my face. On top of that, I have an irrational dislike of anyone playing computer games 'incorrectly' – I once had to go for a lie down after trying to explain Tetris to my nana who was waving around the DS like she trying to land a failing Messerschmitt at sea.

At the videogame museum was something called the Painstation. Essentially, it's a two player game of Pong, where you hold a knob (steady) and keep your other hand on a small metal plate. If you lose a ball on Pong, your other hand either gets an electrical shock, a small burn (the plate heats up) or whipped by a strap of elastic. It's sadistic, cruel, unusual and, worse than that

– it was out of bloody order! I was gutted. Paul wasn't, because he knew I'd kick his arse at Pong and he'd end up with a Jeremy Beadle hand through all the whipping. Ah that's cruel, I always liked Jeremy Beadle – and say what you like, at least he could always get the last few Pringles out of the tube. So who had the last laugh?

After the museum it was a short hop, skip and a jump – well, meander, struggle and chafe – to the DDR museum, where we spent an hour or so examining the exhibits and pondering thoughtfully on the challenging existence in East Germany. Paul did, at least. I spent an hour picking up the big black phone on the desk and pretending I was on Deal or no Deal and then tutting at people for climbing inside the model Trabant they had on show. Honestly have these people got no respect?

A donut and coffee followed then we were off to the Sealife centre and in particular, the giant Aquadom nearby. We spent a good ten minutes being complimented on our English by the German lady on the counter and then forty minutes or so trying to get a good picture of a stingray. Are we the only people who come back from these places with hundreds of shite photos of fish that get deleted on the plane home? I'm not sure what makes me think I'll need an encyclopaedic collection of blurred photos of marine life on my phone but I'm always compelled to snap away whenever I'm somewhere like that. My photography skills are shit – it looks like Ray Charles has been on photographic duty. I might take a course – but I probably won't, I'm lazy. Anyway, the Aquadom is a giant aquarium in the shape of a tube, and you get in a great glass lift and travel up the middle.

I was a bit disappointed, I'm not going to lie. It sounds great fun, but in reality, you're looking at about two thousand fish in a tank whilst riding a lift. Meh. We almost booked the hotel surrounding the aquarium but I'm glad we didn't – the last thing I want is someone peering out the glass lift and seeing me drying my arse in my hotel room, the size of which is all distorted thanks to being viewed through water.

We broke our rule of eating 'local' afterwards, taking a late lunch in a place called Andy's nearby, which promised German/American food at decent prices. It was packed, and at least I had a German beer and sauerkraut with my meal – Paul inexplicably ended up having an entirely not German nor American pork gyros with fried onions. Delicious meal and thanks to the pickled cabbage I barely had to walk to our next destination, instead choosing to hover gently down the street.

Next, the Berlin Dungeon. I was expecting little, but it was actually pretty decent, as long as you like seeing rough looking women pitching around in the dark with blood on their face and sores on their legs, with the scent of faeces and death in the air. Well, I'm from

Newcastle, it was just like being at home. The whole experience was made brilliant by the Scottish women who were with us, who, when the lights dipped, shouted loudly 'AH'MA GONNA SHITE MYSELF'. Even the actors cracked up at that one. Also, I'm not sure 'YOU'LL CUM BLOOD' was supposed to be on the script during the plague section, but everyone's eyebrows raised in a very British unison. Actually, that's an aside – I've always associated Germany with sheer, unadulterated filth – it was always the German couple who used to get their hairy tackle out on Eurotrash back in the day, for example – but there was zero hardcore pornography on their TV channels after 10pm. I was very surprised!

We finished off the night by enjoying a meal in Nocti Vagus – a completely dark restaurant – you eat in the pitch black and are waited upon by blind or almost blind waiting staff. It was...unique! You choose your menu in the bar upstairs, do a veritable conga down into the dark, and then spend two hours enjoying your meal in the dark. I'm far too suspicious that people were pinching my food in the dark, and the temptation to hurl a meatball in the dark was strong, but we were on our best behaviour and came out of it feeling slightly dizzy (because you have nothing to focus on for two hours) and satisfied we'd enjoyed ourselves. The show that comes after the meal was a bit ropey, but...you've had a meal in a pitch black restaurant! At least that's cool.

twochubbycubs on: our German holiday: part four

We woke on our last day in Berlin with a heavy heart, and only a small part of that was down to the amount of cholesterol and fats we had taken on during our short stay. Berlin was amazing – something happening on every corner, history all over the place, fantastic mix of people. Having all of the Christmas markets on only added to the atmosphere and neither of us would hesitate in going back. Heartily recommend. Nevertheless, we traipsed down to the checkout, gave our luggage to some hipster fucknugget who had left his little afro-comb in his afro (argh!) and wandered out to kill the time before we were to get our overnight train to Munich.

First, Checkpoint Charlie, which took us about forty minutes to find. It shouldn't have – if we'd just turned left instead of right as we breathlessly climbed out of the underground station, we'd have been there, but instead we walked for forever in a massive circle until we found it. Meh. I know it's historically very important but I felt its impact was lessened somewhat by the McDonalds just to the side of it. Plus, they had a really ropey statue of a soldier with a bit of tinsel on his head. How respectful!

Afterwards, we spotted the Ritter chocolate museum on a map, and headed there. Again our sense of direction failed us, and we wandered and wandered and wandered, all passive-aggressive sighing and bitchy looks at everyone else who were clearly going exactly where they wanted to go and knew exactly how to get there. The smug twats. After gradually turning our feet to corned-beef in our shoes, and with the blood pouring out over the top of our socks, we FINALLY found Ritter World. Well, honestly, I was expecting Willy Wonka's Chocolate Factory, I got Billy Vanker's Chocolate Camp. It was full of tourists and fat children jiggling about with sticky hands and gleeful expressions.

Paul immediately managed to cause international offence by declaring loudly 'well you'd know all about that' in response to young slave workers picking cocoa beans along the chocolate highway – he was actually talking to me in response to eating chocolate but the young Puerto-Rican couple in front of us looked pretty crestfallen. I'm surprised he manages to brush his teeth in the morning – whenever he opens his mouth his boot automatically falls in. We loaded ourselves up with 24 bars of Ritter chocolate, ostensibly to give to co-workers – we had the box open by the time I'd put my wallet back in my pocket.

A trip to an experimental computer art-gallery followed next – yet again our normally faultless navigation failing us, leading us into a proper run-down sink estate where I started my 'protect everything in my pockets' Macarena dance that I mentioned in a previous entry. In our defence, the art-gallery was tucked away down a side street full of chavs smoking weed. I felt like I was in a Paddy Considine movie.

The art gallery was, as you may expect, full of experimental videogames and controllers, and we had a whale of a time geeking out. It was smashing but the best part was the virtual reality headset at the end. Paul normally can't manage anything like virtual reality – he gets dizzy looking at a magic eye puzzle due to his boss-eyes. Ah bless. He's got lovely blue eyes – one blew to the East, one blew to the West. Kaboomtish.

We did stop for something called 'Knoblauchbaguette'. My reflex action already had me on my knees until Paul pointed out it meant garlic bread.

Anyway, you think me writing about videogames is exciting? Well you haven't heard anything yet, because after the videogame museum came the...font museum! That's right! We saw this on tripadvisor and thought it would be right up our street, and indeed it was, being only a mile or so mince from the videogame museum. We're sticklers for the right font – it really makes my face itch when I see screenshots that people have put on from their phone and they've chosen to use Comic Sans as their display font. Comics Sans should only be used in care homes to illustrate which tap is hot and which is cold, and nothing more. The museum was full of 'letters' – random letters from hotel signs, train stations, massive installations – some old, some new, some neon, some metal – it was really quite interesting! I don't know if I'd pay the amount we paid to go around but I still got to crack a joke as I left and they shook the 'suggested donations' box at me – I said 'Are you taking the P'. Well, as you can well imagine, how we all laughed – we were still chuckling and shaking our heads whimsically as Paul pulled me out by my fagbag. Spoilsport.

By this time the night was cutting in, so we wandered back to the hotel, picked up our suitcases and nipped into the closest restaurant for a last-minute meal before we got on the train. Well fuck me. We couldn't have picked a more German looking place, it was like being in a themed restaurant. The waitress was wearing lederhosen, there was oompah-oompah music playing, the menu was full of words longer than this bloody blog post...you get the picture. I ordered something that sounded like a bad hand at Scrabble and received a pile of meat and potatoes which was absolutely bloody delicious. I washed it all down with a bathtub sized glass of German beer and suddenly the restaurant seemed like the finest on Earth. Paul had duck and a fizzy water, the great big puff. We settled the bill and waddled, clutching our stomachs full of fermenting beast, to the train station.

We were planning on driving to Munich but I've always fancied an overnight train journey, and it was around £200 for the both of us to have a private cabin. That makes it sound infinitely more grand than it was, but it was surprisingly roomy, with two bunkbeds, your own netty, a table to rest at and even a shower! A shower! On a train! The only time I've ever managed to get wet on a train is when I'm sitting next to the toilet on a Pendolino and it lurches around a particularly sharp corner.. Once the train pulled in, we were escorted to our 'room' by the train conductor, yet another officious looking man with a face full of woe who looked as though he'd push you under the train if you asked him anything. He assured us he'd 'look after us through the night' like some creepy fez-wearing Harold Shipman. I was left more than a little terrified. He shut the door and Paul immediately dashed to the toilet 'to try it out'.

I optimistically hoped that this meant testing out the flush or, at a push, having a tinkle, but no, it meant hearing the world fall out of his arse, punctuated by 'OOOH THAT'LL BE THE CURRYWURST' and 'I'M NEVER HAVING SAUERKRAUT AGAIN'. Just once I'd like to be able to relax in a new environment for longer than ten minutes without having to hear my other half straining out a poo. It's not too much to ask. Course, it gets worse – no sooner had he pressed 'flush' then the train conductor clicked the door open and asked whether or not we wanted food. Fuck food, all I wanted was a tank of oxygen, and he totally knew what Paul had just done because I saw his nose wrinkle. Frankly, I'm surprised his nose didn't burn up like a dry leaf in a bushfire. He didn't come back until the morning.

Mind you, it wasn't just Paul causing embarrassment – about half an hour into the journey I remembered that we had a shower in the tiny bathroom and immediately undressed. The shower cubicle was approximately 80% the size of me but by gaw, I was determined. Through the human equivalent of pushing a beachball into a postbox, we managed to get me in, but I literally didn't have space to move, so it was a case of standing there letting the water pool around my shoulders as Paul lathered shampoo into my scalp. Finally, there was a loud sucking noise and the water found a way through the dam of my back fat and down my bumcrack and disappeared. I win again! After ten minutes, Paul pulled me back out of the shower and back into the little living room area. Now this is where it gets embarrassing – in all the excitement of working the shower, we hadn't realised that the train had stopped at a rural passenger station and was obviously taking on a few more people – us looking out the window could barely make anything out because our room was bright and it was night outside. This situation wouldn't have been so bad had I been dressed, but I'm ashamed to say that at least six good, honest German folk on the platform opposite were treated to the sight of Paul changing into his nightwear and my hairy arse pressed up against the glass like two paint-filled balloons. We only realised our error as the train pulled away – probably ahead of schedule to save my blushes. Wars have started over less than my arse in a window, trust me.

The rest of the journey passed without incident, although I had trouble sleeping through the rocking of the train. Paul was out like a light, but I remained fitful on the bottom bunk, sure that every creak and groan of the metal bed above was a sure sign that he was going to come crashing down on top of me and that I'd be smeared up the side of the train like a fly on a windscreen. I kept myself amused by writing up the first few days of the holiday and looking wistfully out of the window as the night turned black. Oh, saying as I indulged in some toilet talk before, I'll add a bit more – the combination of good, rich German food and the rocking of the train meant that we were both full of wind – and when one wasn't farting, wafting and laughing, the other one was taking up position. The poor bastards in the room next door must have thought a brass band was tuning up before a key performance. When we awoke in the morning, the air was so thick I almost swam to the toilet. Even putting on my glasses didn't remove my blurred vision. I'm only thankful it was a no-smoking train else it would have been like the Paddington Rail Disaster all over again.

At six there was a sharp little tap on the door and the conductor, barely hiding his wince, set down a tray of breakfast goodies on the table. It was the usual German fare – apple juice, jams, bread (the bread was fresh when brought in but after two minutes in the fetid air of our room, had gone a lovely toasted colour) and minced animal. They love their indistinct pâté, that's for sure. Still, it was free food and I couldn't waste a crumb, so I didn't, and it was delicious.

The train pulled into Munich at around seven and we were unceremoniously dumped on the platform as the train hastened away, probably to be burnt to ashes thanks to our almost inhuman farting. We jumped onto the underground and after a short ride, we were at our hotel. The guy checking us in clearly thought we were checking him out, and he was posing and fluttering his eyes and being all coquettish. He didn't have a fucking chance, he had more make-up on than Dame Barbara Cartland for one thing, and he gave us a proper 'knowing' leer when he realised that we were a married couple with a king-sized bed. I really hate that! He might as well offered us an upgrade, rimjob or felch for the amount of subtlety he was displaying.

We gave him fairly short shrift and were allowed up to our room, where I'm disappointed to say we stayed for the rest of the day. Actually – disappointed is the wrong word, a holiday is for resting, and we had a lovely day in the room, ordering room service, watching the German version of Air Crash Investigation and sleeping. No word of a lie – we pretty much slept from 8am to 8am the next day. The room service was extortionate – €60 for two burgers, although they were the size of footballs and delivered with the usual German élan (i.e. no care at all – they crashed the tray down like they were delivering a verdict on England itself).

Mind you, that's not surprising, given our hotel room probably smelled like the countryside of England did when we had the foot and mouth crisis and all the cows were being burnt. Fact: the foot and mouth outbreak started less than a mile from my house. I still blame my mother for feeding the dog Aldi stewing steak and starting it all off.

twochubbycubs on: our German holiday: part five

How's this for a twist? After our day of sleeping and eating burgers, we both woke up around 11pm and decided on a whim to visit an underground salt mine in Austria, which was only a two hour train ride away. The tickets were booked and the alarms set before the half cows in our bellies started turning into poo.

We awoke bright and breezy – well, as bright and breeze as you can be getting woken up at 4.45am by eight separate alarms. I feel bad for our room neighbours, they probably thought the sky was falling in although, if the apocalypse comes, I don't think it'll be heralded by a calypso version of Ode to Joy. After a quick ride on the U-Bahn, we were at the München Hauptbahnhof by six just ahead of our early train to Salzburg. Munich, so early in the morning, was gorgeous, but there was no time to admire it as we were whisked to our first class seats where there is nothing more eventful to report other than we slept most of the way, with me only waking up whenever I heard the buffet trolley coming. I swear I can hear a Kitkat being snapped from over 300 yards – I was like the world's most corpulent meerkat peering over the seats. I like to get the full benefit any time I travel first class – if there's a little lamp, I'll flick it on and off, if there's a doily on the back of the seat I'll be sure to rub my forehead with it. Although, given how excellent standard class is in Germany, first class was an unnecessary frippery. Still, it did extend me the chance to say 'Well, it doesn't look any bigger than the Mauritania' when I stepped aboard. The train sped us into Austria and we were in Salzburg in no time at all.

Our first impressions? Not great. Salzburg had a curious bland square when you stepped off the train, full of people begging for money and smoking cigarettes that smelt like burning hair. We slipped into a McDonalds (so cultural – but it was the only place open) for a bit of breakfast and I thoroughly enjoyed my crappy croissant – the stress of having my wallet stolen and my pockets pinched only adding to the flavour. We decamped to the bus-stop to wait forty minutes before the bus to the salt mines rolled in. I barely had enough time to admire the fact someone had taken a shit into a tuna can and left it on the bus-stop seat. Disgusting, but I couldn't help but admire his technical prowess. It's the little things you remember.

The bus ride was just lovely – rolling forest hills on one side, crystal clear blue streams on the other. It felt like I was in an advert for aftershave. The illusion was only spoiled by a little old lady next to me who seemed to have packed enough food and snacks for a bus journey to Krakatoa. She just didn't stop eating, smacking her lips together and fishing around in her endless bag of treats – she was like Mary Poppins but with saturated fats. First there were sandwiches, then biscuits, then crisps, then boiled sweets, then a banana – it was a shame we had to get off the bus when we did because I was sure she was about to pull out a pan and a cylinder of Calor gas and rustle up some bacon sandwiches. Ah well.

Naturally, being us, we managed to get to the salt-mine precisely one hour before it opened, and, being in the middle of Nowhere, Austria, there was nothing to do or look at. Indeed, the only movement was me doing the hop-back-and-forth piss dance. Paul is like a feral cat, he'll happily piss anywhere and everywhere, but I'm very British and like to do things properly. Alas, with the sound of the babbling brook and Paul's impressions of a waterfall ringing in my ears, I could hold it in no longer and had to nip to the side of a service road for a tinkle. Of course, no sooner had I got my cock out than a coach full of French school-children came barrelling around the corner like the bus from Speed. I almost re-circumcised myself in my haste to put it away and not be arrested for indecent exposure. I wish I knew what the French for Gary Glitter is. Well actually, it would be Gary Scintillement, and that sounds quite charming and non-threatening to children.

The hour passed by in no time at all – nothing makes time pass quicker than being surrounded by a litter of French schoolchildren, all screaming and shouting in French and smoking Gauloises. Thankfully, the doors crashed open at 11am and we were in. First task? Change into the type of jumpsuit last seen on Sue,

Computer Analyst from Burton-on-Trent on The Crystal Maze. Thankfully, I was given the correct size and was straight into it, but Paul was handed an M. There are no conceivable circumstances where Paul could be considered an M unless that M stood for 'Muffintopped'. He had to go back to the stern, moustachioed lady on the front desk and explain, with him speaking no German and her speaking no English, that he was altogether too fat for an M. She gave him an L and a sneer. It was still like trying to stuff a settee into a bin-liner so, exasperated, he went back and she finally threw an XL at him with a loud 'Mmmff' sound. Bless him, it was tight, but he managed to get in, even through the denim was see-through across his arse where it was stretched so tight. She was horrible – awfully judgemental for someone who was keeping the backs of her knees warm using her tits.

Dressed to depress, we were herded up into a group by a very stern looking man and taken to a tiny train (it looked like something you'd see in the Borrowers) for our trip into the side of the mountain and into the mine itself. It was brilliant! Despite feeling like I was going to be decapatitated at any given moment by a low beam, the train chugged along in almost pitch black until we were around a mile into the Earth. There, we were given translating tools which we promptly pocketed and forgot about. The leader was the very personification of dourness but he did try to make things interesting. We ignored him entirely and spent the first part of the tour looking around the mine. It was brilliant – but it gets better.

To get to the next part of the tour, we had to descend eight stories. You were given a choice – either walk down a twisty turning path for about ten minutes or slide down on a proper wooden slide! Well look – we're two gay lads, we're not going to turn down a slide down a shaft on a decent sized bit of wood, are we? Oooh nasty!

Now deep into the mine, we spent a while looking at mining equipment and following the story of salt, before the next amazing part – crossing the underground lake which they called a 'mirror' lake, because the water is so clear and undisturbed that it creates a perfect reflection of the ceiling above. Of course, being British and cynical, I spent a good ten minutes telling Paul that it wasn't a lake at all, it was just polished glass and a special effect, until he got tired of my cynicism and splashed his hand in the water. Well honestly. What do you get in terms of special effects here in the UK at outdoor attractions? Impending bankruptcy and Hepatitis B. I was enthralled. As we crossed the lake, they played a tasteful laser show (the first time in history that the word laser has ever been prefixed by 'tasteful' I reckon) and some music. Without wanting to sound cheesy, it was magical. There was a bit more chat and then we were in a funicular back to the surface in no time at all. I can say, with all honesty, no-one has ever had more fun deep underground in Austria since Josef Fritzl got himself a Screwfix catalogue and a tape measure.

You have no idea how long I've been itching to bust that gag out.

Now, I wish I could tell you that after the mine we spent a merry afternoon exploring Salzburg, but we didn't. We're not a fan of Mozart, we're not a fan of being asked for change and the whole town is on a gentle slope, so we were back on the train to Munich quicker than you can say Siebentausendzweihundertvierundfünfzig, which is the German word for 7,254. Obviously. Back in Munich, we were off to bed to sleep off the excitement and ahead of a lovely day exploring Munich the next day...

twochubbycubs on: our German holiday: part six

Alas, I wish I could tell you more about Munich, but I lost my page of notes from that day by sensibly leaving my notebook on a bus. I'm very old school like that – I like to think it adds an air of sophistication to be scribbling notes whilst I'm wandering around, but actually, combined with my big flappy coat, it probably just makes me look like a trainspotter. And that's not fair, I've never masturbated in a train station over a steam engine.

The morning was spent mooching around Munich's city centre, which, as you can imagine, was altogether very beautiful and Christmassy. I confess that Christmas market fatigue was setting in – there's only so many wooden carved dolls of Santa you can gaze at before your smile slips from admiring to rictus, stopping at polite and strained on the way. We spotted that Munich has a giant museum and, after only the smallest of arguments about directions (which, naturally, I won, given Paul couldn't direct a shite out of his own arse), we were on our way.

Well. It was certainly comprehensive in its wares. Like the Christmas market I mentioned before, I started getting fatigued at 'oohing' at things in glass cases around twenty minutes in – and this museum was colossal, with over 25 exhibitions each covering more floor-space than Newcastle devotes to its entire art scene. These covered topics such as glass-blowing, mathematics, oceanography and chronometry, which is the study of time measurement, which seemed apt given how long I spent looking at my watch and tapping it in Paul's direction. Look, I'm not some hairy uncultured philistine who can't focus long enough to appreciate the works around me, but it had been almost three hours and my capacity for feigning interest in how a pill-dispenser works was at an all-time low. I told Paul I'd meet him downstairs and promptly lost him for forty five minutes whilst we chased each other round in ultra slow-motion through the physics department and the planetarium, finally reuniting in the AIDS display. Such is the romance of our existence.

We departed, crying with boredom, and spent a happy hour pootling around from various coffee and doughnut shops until we decided we needed something to fill the afternoon. After much discussion (as much as one can discuss with a mouthful of cream and pastry – Paul spends his entire life wiping crumbs from his face, and they're normally mine) we decided to trundle over to the Tierpark Hellabrunn, Munich's zoo. I'm not normally a fan of zoos – nothing says getting back to nature like watching a gorilla pick his arse amongst a litter of Cornetto wrappers and dying vegetation – but well, it filled an hour. At least that was the plan. It actually ended up taking all afternoon – we massively underestimated the size of the place. You know sometimes when you go for a walk and you forget that you have to walk back to wherever you started? Well that was this afternoon, only with more depressed lions.

Actually, be fair, the zoo was terrific, with large roomy enclosures and lots to see and do, plus we had the added bonus of having it all to ourselves because, frankly, who the fuck goes to a zoo in the middle of winter. We posed with lions, we pointed at bears, we peacocked our way around when we saw another gay couple on the horizon with better shoes, we laughed merrily as we discovered most of the toilets and shops were closed for the season. Who closes a toilet for the season – what is it doing, taking Christmas in the Alps? I'm a geet hard Geordie, I don't care if the seat is cold, and I'll blast through any ice-crust. Honestly.

By the time 4pm rolled around and darkness has closed in, we thought we had reached the exit, only to find we were at entirely the wrong side of the zoo and only halfway around the circular path. I could have cried. My feet were aching from walking, my jaw was aching from complaining and Paul's ears were aching as a direct result of the last two problems. We decided to sit for a moment in the giraffe enclosure – I've never seen a giraffe look so disdainful.

A moment turned into fifteen minutes and became one of those awful situations where you don't want to stand because the very moment you do you're reminded of how painful your feet are and how far you've got to go. Luckily, the giraffe itself hastened our departure by letting rip with a fart that, had I still smoked, could have lit my cigarette. I've still got the scent of warm hay in my hair. We struggled out into the night and, all the while moaning and sobbing and bleeding into our shoes, made it back to the exit just before they closed up. They seemed surprised – well, as surprised as their typically expressionless faces allowed – to see us, and hastened us on our way despite my remonstrations as to why they didn't respond to our distress flares. Sods.

I can't recall how the rest of the evening panned out – I know we are somewhere terribly expensive and got drunk somewhere equally as expensive, but as neither of us managed to make a tit of ourselves, it hasn't been burnt onto my mind like so many other shameful encounters.

Our flight back home was early the next day – and that too passed without incident, alas. I say alas, the last place I want to have "an incident" is 33,000ft in the air, especially if all I have to comfort me is a tangerine headrest and a steward so camp he farted glitter. We were home in no time at all, welcomed by the indifferent stares of our cats and a few couldn't-care-less Christmas cards.

Isn't it funny – whenever I'm on holiday I'm always excited to get back home – to sleep in my own bed and to crap on my own toilet. But the second I'm over the doorstep I've got wanderlust and I'm looking into the next holiday, cursing the life choices that meant I'm not a billionaire with the world at his feet. It was marrying Paul that did it – see never marry for love, folks, always marry for money. You might need to wince your way through lovemaking but think of all the pretty stuff you could have. I jest I jest.

Germany, then. Amazing. Everyone always speaks highly of a German holiday and I can see why – everyone was unceasingly friendly, the cities are packed with stuff to do and I've never devoured so many delicious snacks as I did in those few days. The Christmas markets are wonderful, invoking a proper sense of traditional Christmas, and the cities themselves could not be easier to get around, served as they are by efficient and comprehensive public transport systems. It's fairly cheap – certainly the flights and hotel can be sourced for a very reasonable price and eating out and shopping doesn't break the bank. Food was tremendous, lots of sausage, which is perfect for a sausage-botherer like me. Go!

We flew with Easyjet from Edinburgh to Berlin and whilst there, stayed at the 25 Hours Bikini Berlin hotel, which overlooks the Berlin Zoo. We took an overnight train with Bahn on their City Night Service, departing late in the evening from Berlin and arriving early in the morning in Munich, staying in a private cabin. Finally, we stayed at the Pullman Munich in a deluxe room.

It was all very civilised.

twochubbycubs on: taxis

Can we talk about this stupid voice that young ladies seem to have decided is just right-and-dandy for this modern world? I know it's been discussed to death but it drives me so far up the wall I have to stop and fill up at Vertical Petrol on the way. I'll give you an example. Tonight in Tesco I was in that unhappy situation where everywhere I went, the same shopper and her melt of a boyfriend went. I had to buy peas, there she was, I had to buy KY jelly, there she was again, speaking like *thiiiiiiiiisssss* and *draaaaaawing* out *raaaaaandaaaam syllaaaaables* for god knows why. I just can't bear it. Things came to a head, as they so often do, in the reduced vegetables bit, where she picked up every fucking item and croaked what she thought was a witty rejoinder to everything – 'OMG who even (EVAN) needs a baaaaaaay-bee sweet potaaaaahto' 'OMG look at these taaaaaaaaaaaaaaaaaaaaaaaaaaaangerines they're like 8p' 'jeeeeesus what's a squaaash LOL' (and she SAID LOL) – to which I threw down the peas that had been turning into puree in my hands and stalked off with a loud OH FOR FUCK'S SAKE.

I know, not big nor clever, and probably made me look like an arse on reflection, but I think I'd genuinely rather have my ears pissed in by a horse than have to deal with that. Not everything needs schtick. Why do people pretend so? You're from Kingston Park lover, not Sweet Valley fucking High. It did cross my mind that her cotton-bud shaped boyfriend might have caught up with me to rough me up in the yoghurt aisle but frankly he looked the sort who couldn't direct a shit into a toilet bowl, so my fears were groundless.

To be honest, I was just in a huff because yet again it took me an interminable amount of time getting home for the third night in a row. At least tonight I got a bit of satisfaction from sending some douchebag in an Audi down onto the Central Motorway rather than letting him cut in at the lights. I was late yesterday due to someone breaking down right in front of me and blocking the way (fair enough, not like I could help, I know less about mechanics than I do about the female orgasm) and I was late getting home on Monday due to being caught up in a protest by our local taxi drivers. They had decided to go on a 'go-slow' protest of driving their cars very carefully around Newcastle, blocking the roads and delaying people in protest of Newcastle City Council scrapping the 'knowledge' test that's usually mandatory for taxi drivers up here. I hadn't realised anything was different with cars going around Newcastle at 3mph until I heard Carol on Look North explain it whilst I scraped yesterday's dinner out of the slow cooker. They've got a point, though. I hate taxis at the best of time because I like driving and don't enjoy strained conversation about football and tits, but I can tolerate them if the driver is decent and they know where they're going. But, more often than not, they don't – and it's not like I live in some far-off utopia, I'm just off the A1. I recently had a taxi driver who not only wanted me to instruct him, he also made me sit in the front because he was a 'bit muff and jeff'. I almost asked if he didn't just want to go the whole hog and have us switch seats and for me to drive him home, bit was dark and there are a lot of country fields that I could be rolled into a carpet and dumped into, so I didn't.

There was a taxi driver in Orlando who comes to mind – he took us from Disney to Orlando International Airport. All very pleasant, bar for the fact he was a) off his face and b) on the game. He kept turning around to talk to us, letting his car veer across the road whilst he did so, and went from gentle conversation about Cher to offering us hardcore gay sex and free crystal meth. You don't get that offer with Blueline Taxis. I remember him tossing us a cigar tube and telling us to take a sniff, which naively I did, before realising it was weed, which pretty much guaranteed me getting fingered for drugs by a swarthy security guard later at the airport. Ah fun times. He did tell us he was going to take his mother to see Cher before she died (his mother, not Cher, I♫ BE-LEE-IEVE ♫ she died many years ago and is just a corpse on strings now) (ah that's mean, I like Cher)...I wonder if he ever got there. Probably not. He looked like he lived the type of life which ends up with you motionless in a pool with a bumhole like a yawning dog.

I'd love to be a taxi driver, although I reckon most of my

passengers would be putting in claims for tinnitus because I'm always shouting and bawling away inside my car. It's stress relief. I can talk to people quite freely when I'm in control of the situation so the social side of things would be fine – essentially if they ever started a sentence with 'I'M NOT RACIST BUT' I could just speed round a corner, open their door and tumble them out under a passing lorry. I'd struggle with people who smell like sour milk or those people who put out their cigarette and stick the remainder back in the packet because you have no idea how bad that makes you smell, but generally, I'd be good.

twochubbycubs on: the cinema

But before we get started, I come bearing good news. I'm sorry, that never normally happens, I've been under pressure, it's that time of the month, I'm just keen etc. No, remember our bathroom problem where Paul and I were down to one tiny bulb in our bathroom, turning every trip to brush our teeth or wipe our bum into a perilous adventure fraught with tension that we'd be plunged into absolute darkness mid-pinch? Well worry no more! Our wonderful, marvellous and above all else hella-manly plumber/electrician has saved the day! But mind it took something else breaking before we called him in. Our extractor fan has clearly become so affronted and overworked trying to waft away the smell of so many rich Slimming World infused motions that it went into overdrive and refused to turn off – not even using the switch would stop it – we had to take out the fuse for the lights throughout the house before it finally shut off. Which wasn't ideal. A plea was made to the chap who originally did our bathroom and he has been this morning and not only replaced the fan, he's only gone and replaced all the lightbulbs! Best part is, I wasn't even there when he did it so I didn't need to feel all emasculated and embarrassed that we had let ourselves down so badly.

One thing I'm a smidge alarmed about is that we've gone from one 30w bulb in the bathroom to six 50w beauties – if I happen to find an interesting magazine article whilst I'm on the netty I'll probably come out with a tan. It'll make brushing my teeth like being on a mediocre game-show – I'll just need Dale Winton mincing around behind me explaining my brushing technique to an imagined audience. Perhaps I've thought too much about this. Let's move on.

It was only a short post yesterday as I was at the cinema seeing Kingsman: The Secret Service, with Phillipa who you may know from the poorly-spelled insults she occasionally leaves on the blog. Great film and heartily recommended – we laughed, we cried, she spilt her popcorn – the usual, and that was before we'd even sat down. Colin Firth plays an absolute blinder, really branching out from his upper-class-English-fop role that was all I associated him with. I admit to being distracted nearly all the way through by the girl in front of me and her shovel-faced boyfriend. She'd clearly come dressed for a bet but that's by the by – it was her haircut which was distressing me. She'd tried to fashion it into a bun but instead ended up with this weird bowl, where, if I had been feeling bitchy enough, I could have easily have parked my 35-gallon-Diet Pepsi there to prove a point. It was upsetting purely because of my OCD – I hate things being messy. If I didn't think I would have been either stabbed by a needle hidden in her hair or glassed by her dead-eyed lamp-post of a mate I would have reached over and tidied it up. To make things worse, the popcorn was disgusting – it tasted like they'd washed it alternately in Charlie Red and the North Sea.

Didn't stop either of us eating it though, though I had to stop once my lips started turning inside out like a slug. Luckily, Phillipa had her hunger satisfied by the ice-cream, pick and mix and salty popcorn and I wasn't sent out to get a pig on a spit for afterwards. I do love going to the cinema and now that I can't have my usual settee-cushion of popcorn and binbag of pick-and-mix, I don't even need to fret about taking out a mortgage to cover it.

So: where are we on the Two Chubby Cubs European Tour, eh? Somewhere exotic, warm and unusual? No. We're in France. I half-toyed with taking a picture of a crepe with a Gauloise stubbed out in the middle of it, but that's not embracing our trip. It's not like I don't care for France, I've been many times and always enjoyed myself, but I once got ripped off outside the Eiffel Tower by a caricaturist and I've never quite forgiven the country for that. It wasn't so much that I paid a ridiculous amount for the drawing, it was the fact that the drawing made me look like John Prescott examining his pores in a Christmas bauble.

twochubbycubs on: fireworks night

Fireworks night. Yak. I'm a right miserable sod, because I don't enjoy fireworks night. It's not that the colours don't amaze me or the bangs excite me, it's just I spend the whole time wincing and thinking 'oooh but what could you have bought with that money?'. It's the Geordie in me. Plus, everyone else's fireworks displays are always a bit crap, aren't they? They certainly are around here – the sky being full of Aldi bangers that pop apologetically 12ft off the ground with less bang and smoke than what my thighs make when I move quickly. We go to the Hexham display, and that's alright, but I find it's invariably full of children getting in the way and crying. Honestly, why people don't just shut them away in a cupboard is beyond me. Perhaps that's why I can't have children (well, ethically I shouldn't, but biologically I can – nothing wrong with my gentleman's relish, thank you very much). Perhaps we've been spoilt – we've experienced the fireworks at Disney Orlando, where you experience such a visual and aural overload that you don't even notice them dipping their hands in your pockets to make absolutely sure you have zero money left. It's certainly the first and only time I've developed sunburn from a fireworks display.

Mind, not that I'd see much now – my eyesight is dreadful. Don't get me wrong, I can still see Paul if he so much as ventures anywhere near my wallet, even when I'm at work and he's at home* – but I've been finding that my eyes are just getting worse. Nothing exciting, don't worry, I just use a computer a lot and I've been putting off going for an eye-test for ages. See, any kind of test is a minefield when you have health anxiety because an anxious person makes all kind of crazy medical leaps. Eyesight getting worse? That's because there's a tumour the size of a rugby ball pressing my eyes flat. Tickly cough? That'll be polycystic ovaries. Since I've adopted a mantra of 'only worry if it gets worse', I've put off the eye-test for long enough.

* funny fact for you. I have a lovely picture of Paul and I lying on a bed together when we first started 'going out' (oh how I hate that term, but see it's more polite than putting 'rutting like dying pigs'). We both look content. My eyes are fixed on the camera I'm holding in front of us. Paul's eyes are very pointedly and determinedly staring at my wallet, just on show on the table. How I tease him about this even now – if he married me for the money then he's really done quite poorly.

Anyway, on Monday, I bit the bullet. I actually went for an eye-test. That might not seem like a lot, but you have to remember how much I hate eye-tests because I've had nothing but terrible experiences with them. Take my last one at Boots Opticians, where the whole test was done almost in silence save for the sound of the skin on my cheek blistering under the assault of the ophthalmologist's stinky breath. I'm sorry, but if I had a job that routinely involved me getting so close to people that I could give them stubble burn, I'd make damn sure my breath didn't smell like an sewage outlet. Hell, it's one thing I'm genuinely paranoid about – I hate the thought of having the type of breath that makes people audibly wince when I yawn or ask me if I had enjoyed the faeces I'd clearly had for dinner. If I know I'm going to the dentist or for an eye-test I spend a good three days beforehand brushing my teeth, swishing mouthwash and sucking menthol mints until it gets to the point where I can't have a glass of water without my breath freezing it solid like that shrill tart from Frozen.

I have to say though, for once, it was altogether very pleasant, with the good staff at The Big Opticians in Byker putting me at ease. Can't recommend them enough, and not just because I told the lovely lady serving me all about the blog. I've come away with a new pair of Paul Smith that are slightly more rounder than normal (I asked what was suitable for a "fat face", and such bluntness seems to have worked wonders) and I'm not half as poor as I thought I'd be. Excellent. I asked Paul what he thought and he said I looked like Dame Edna, then immediately backtracked and said they were lovely. That was lucky, because how I would have been chuckling over the divorce papers later on. So that's my eyes sorted, now I just need to do my hair.

I'm at that difficult stage now where I have to either commit to shaving off all my hair or going for a haircut.

And I hate haircuts. It amazes me that they can actually cut my hair given I retreat my head back below my shoulders like a shy tortoise. I can't stand people touching me, I can't stand small-talk and I have as much style as a troubling fart, so going to a hairdressers is just awful. I'd sooner get a colonic in the middle of Boots with a group of students grading the look of my bumhole. I get asked what I want 'doing with my hair' and I struggle to reply with anything other than 'cut'. It doesn't help that I always look great when they whip off the blanket and show me the back of my head, then I blink and my hair immediately looks like something someone's used to shift a particularly difficult scuff mark off a strip of lino. But I do need to do something with it, given I've been told I look like Donald Trump. From a loved one, no less. I know someone who's not getting anal for at least two weeks. I sometimes wish I had that slightly stereotypical gay trait of being able to look good in any old outfit, but honestly, the only thing that looks put-together and stylish in my wardrobe are the built-in shelves.

twochubbycubs on: mechanics

We were supposed to be going to Hexham to see the fireworks but see it's been raining like a pissing cow, so we didn't bother. I can tolerate sliding around in the mud with a group of men waiting for a banger to explode behind me and a large rocket to go off in my face – hell, that's 3am on a Sunday morning for Paul and I – but the thought of having to drive along the country roads in this weather, invariably stuck behind Arthur and Martha Pissknickers in their 40mph-at-all-costs Astra…well that was just too much to bear. Luckily, if I gaze left out of my window I'm treated to a wonderful audio-visual display anyway, as my neighbour who can barely drive struggles to reverse off her driveway. Honestly, her reverse light flickers off and on so much I'm not entirely convinced that she hasn't slumped over the controls clutching her heart and she's morse-coding CALL AN AMBULANCE at me. Ah well, it's a cold night, she'll be someone else's stiff problem in the morning.

I'm kidding I'm kidding.

It's actually quite warm.

We didn't get a chance to lie in this morning, saying as Paul had helpfully booked his little Micra in to have a tyre changed at 9am in the bloody morning. On a Saturday! I was calm and collected when he told me the news and then asked me to take the car – I left him with two working teeth, so all was well. Paul goes through car tyres like most of us go through excuses as to why we've put on weight. I swear Paul's car spends more time up on the ramp than it does on our drive, blocking the neighbour's view of the road (eee, no wonder she struggles so much). Nevertheless, I forced myself out of bed at 8am, had a half-hearted shower and a twenty minute morning piss, and I was on my way. I said goodbye to Paul the only way I could, by silently creeping into our bedroom, pulling down my trousers and letting out a particularly noxious fart out a millimetre away from his face. Still didn't wake him mind, though his tongue died.

I drove to Ashington (oh the glamour) in the pissing rain, eyes full of sleep and mind full of cotton-wool. I don't wake up in the morning until I've had at least three cups of coffee and a Double Decker. The trip was as uneventful as driving with about 5% of your brain awake normally is – red lights missed, cyclists to prise off the bonnet, the usual (**OK, I really AM joking on that one**). At one point I felt a rumble in my nethers and, forgetting my destination, I let rip with a fart that could have parted the sea. Even the car sped up of its own accord. Of course, I hadn't remembered where I was going – a garage where doubtless some fancy-dan in overalls would want to clamber around in my car – and as it turned out, I was only 600 yards from arriving. This led to me having to do several extra laps of the estate with the windows down and me tilting my bulk to one side each time I went around a corner to try and displace any remaining air-pockets of stink. Paul's Yankee Candle air-freshener did nothing, though I'd genuinely rather smell what billows out of my arse of a morning than the insipid sickliness of 'A Child's Wish'.

Realising that I'd done all I can to dissipate the smell other than calling in an exorcist, I confidently turned into the garage, and ignoring the street-long garage forecourt, promptly drove down someone's drive just to the left. Realising my mistake and forgetting how shit the gearbox was on the Micra, I spent a minute or so doing a tiny 533-point-turn and turning around, the mechanics in the garage giving me eye as I did so. Having parked, the mistakes continued to pile up – I walked into the back office and announced myself as the Micra driver only to be told to go to the reception and that 'this was a staff room' (which is a rather extravagant thing to call somewhere consisting of a settee and copies of the Daily Sport). Signing the car over, I was told to take a seat – I demurred, saying I'd never fit it in the boot* – and went to get myself a coffee from the machine.

Irma Grese behind the reception counter looked at me like I was muck on her shoe and waited until I'd upended all the Splenda and taken a stirrer to tell me that 'coffee was a pound'. I looked down at the watery brown liquid I had in my hand and had to bite my tongue not to reply 'how much for this stool sample?'. I explained I didn't carry cash (I really don't) and she, after quickly checking with Google as to the legality of having me taken out and shot behind the tyres, 'let me off'. By god though, did she let me know she'd done me a favour – she spent the next forty minutes sighing and snorting so much that I almost called for oxygen.

Aside from her theatrics, the time passed quickly enough, with me alternating between cursing myself for leaving my phone at home and finally catching up on Jordan's love life via the various Heat magazines littered around. I do hope her and that varnished walnut who "sang" Mysterious Girl make a go of it. I did half expect to see at least one mechanic being taken away on a stretcher after venturing into the car's Cloud of Death', but no, all was well, and the mechanic ushered me over to 'take a look'. Take a look? At what? Unless he'd accidentally fitted a Domino's pizza or a ship's wheel instead of a tyre, what could I say? Nevertheless, because he was manly and I'm not, I pointed at the tyre and made appropriately straight-man remarks, like 'cracking job' and 'ah yes it looks so much better now', until he pointed out that it was the back tyre on the other side of the car.

For fuck's sake. If I can find a way to make a tit of myself, I'll do it, I really will. I paid up, left with a flounce of my coat, and promptly climbed into the passenger side of the car. I wish I could say I'm exaggerating, but I'm genuinely not. When I realised my mistake I tried to make it look like I was just getting something but they knew – you don't put your foot in when reaching for the glove compartment, do you? And so with all that over I finally managed to get myself into the right seat – and then stalled it, because I'm not used to Paul's car.

SO, I won't be going back there.

As an aside, our local KFC is a hovel, no fibbing. We went through the drive-through (I'm sorry, but I'm not putting thru, I'm just not) once and had to wait by the intercom whilst the chickenkicker finished her rollie **in front of us** before lumbering back into the shop (I'm sorry, but I'm not putting restaurant, I'm just not) and phlegming her way through our order. Bah!

twochubbycubs on: being grateful

We've went and bought a new gadget – it's a NEST smoke alarm. We need a new smoke alarm – we've been using our old one to prop the dishwasher up, and given the amount of vodka and aftershave in our house, it's too risky not to have a working system. Now, this isn't just a smoke alarm. It's fancy. Real fancy. Our house is becoming the gadget city we always wanted, see. This smoke alarm hooks into my WiFi and will alert me if the batteries are low or if it detects smoke. And how does it do this? IT BLOODY WELL TALKS. Admittedly it's in a plummy 'don't be scared, but you're about to be cremated' voice, whereas if I'm about to die, I want a fucking air-raid siren, not Joanna Lumley whispering me to the grave. If I'm honest, we only bought it because it a) works with our thermostat (it'll thoughtfully turn the boiler off if it's pumping out more poisonous smoke than the shelter outside a Mecca Bingo at the interlude) and b) it glows. It will momentarily glow green when you shut all the lights off so you know it works. It'll glow red if you're on fire. It'll even glow white for 20 seconds in the hallway if you get up for a piss, which is handy if you're like us and your bathroom lights are so intense that your helmet blisters as you urinate.

Speaking of bright, they say you should always look on the bright side of life. I generally do. My days aren't often filled with wonder and drama but they're always littered with tiny moments of joy or laughter, and that's a nice way to live. For example, I take great solace in, every day at one attosecond past five'o'clock, I hurtle out of my work office, straight to my car on the 11th floor of the car-park, throw 'The Final Countdown' onto Spotify and hurtle down the ramps as fast I can so that as my car pulls out of the car-park, 'IT'S THE FINAL COUNTDOWN' plays. There's just enough time to do it as long as no-one gets in my way. That said, more often than enough, I'll get stuck behind someone who's as thick as a submarine door and is trying to operate the barrier by inserting her Boots Advantage card and calling for help on a box of Lillets. But it's still good fun – a simple pleasure, but a pleasure none the less. I mean, that happiness normally dissipates a second later as I'm stuck behind some numpty in a BMW who thinks the indicator stalks are somewhere to rest her ankles when she's got a client in the back-seat.

The reason I mentioned happiness is because I actually got myself upset earlier – and you need to realise, I have a heart of solid black granite. The only time I get upset is when Paul eats more than half of the Ben and Jerry's. GOD-DAMN IT. No, I was reading an article on the BBC News (link) about a young Iraqi gay lad who was forced to leave his country simply because he was gay. His own dad told him that he would be happy for ISIS to chuck him off a tall building to his death, or burn him alive, simply because of his biological leanings. I couldn't comprehend it. Men are being sent into the desert with their arseholes glued shut so that they die an incredibly painful death just because they like a bit of cock. All very distressing and we shouldn't linger on the details.

What it did make me think though was how bloody lucky I am / we are to live in a country where being gay just isn't a problem. Not really, not on the scale it once was. The fact that I can live with my husband in the middle of Menopauseville, Northumberland and no-one really bats an eye is testament to how far we've come. My nana, god bless her, told all the old wrinklies at the WI about my wedding and challenged anyone who had a problem with it. She literally took all comments on her whiskery chin. I can't personally remember the last time I experienced any sort of homophobia.

Sure, there's the well-meant but incredibly offensive comments – I was told once by a colleague that 'my religion doesn't agree with gays, but don't worry, I can tolerate you' – like I was a bad smell, or an ingrown toenail. I resisted the urge to snip back that I don't agree with grown men in frocks putting their holy willies into little boy's bottoms, but what's the use. You also get a lot of people asking 'how it works', like there is a hidden user guide (a gayde?) that explains all the mechanics (when he pushes, so do you), but that's fair enough. I don't mind answering questions as long as you're comfortable with vivid descriptions and use of the term santorum. It's a given now that if I'm filling out a form, I'll be able to choose 'Civil Partnered' or

'Married' as opposed to 'Living with Partner', which was simply a euphemism for being a chutney-ferret.

Actually, the most devastating thing about filling out forms these days is that I've gone up an age-bracket – I now fall into the 30-34 category. Sniff. Might as well order myself some piss-knickers now. Sigh.

twochubbycubs on: annoyances

I'm in an awful mood because it took me ninety minutes to get home instead of the usual twenty-five, thanks to all the braying hoo-rays spilling out of Newcastle Racecourse and blocking the road with their shitty Audis. So, instead of my usual pleasantries, I'm going to rattle off a list of random things that piss me off. WARNING: COARSE LANGUAGE. Of course!

sour sweets – they're never quite sour enough for me. Seriously – if I buy a packet of sour sweets, I want my mouth to resemble the arsehole of someone who's trying to hold back a fart at a funeral. I want to wince and tremble every time I put one on my tongue, not crash my car because my eyes have rolled to the back of my head with disappointment. Take a note Haribo, you lying bastards;

hun – I know it's an obvious one but it drives me up the fucking wall quicker than Princess Di's driver. Out of all the facebook platitudes, this has to be the most vapid and inane – there's simply no excuse;

hairflickers – I went four years with hair past my shoulderblades and at no point did I feel the need to swoosh my hair like a horse being bothered by a fly – it's an affected, fey little move and I don't think I'm especially irrational for hoping it snaps your spinal cord;

bingo websites – since I signed up to a few bingo sites a while back (read here for my guide to making some easy money from them), we have been inundated with shitty little pieces of junk-mail through our letterbox, and they're all the same – horrible balloon font (the type of font you'd use for warning signs in a special school), some actress who was last seen in Crossroads with badly whitened teeth, a few rainbows and a shit name – rehabbingo.com, spunkgarglerbingo.com, punchmyclitbingo.com and so on;

mincers – that stupid affected little mince that certain ladies do on the way to the car at the supermarket, with their knock-off handbag in the crook of an elbow and a bunch of keys to the other. We get it, you can drive, but I'd bet my house you've got 'SPEED BITCH' on your bumper and think your indicators are for resting your ankles on during coitus;

scratchers – people who buy scratchcards and can't even wait until they're out of the shop before losing all dignity and going at them – there's someone in our local newsagent who is a bugger for this – he's got a permanently silver fingertip. Use a coin, you sweaty-faced titrash;

straight men – well, not all straight men, only those who think that because I love a bit of cock that I must want theirs. I don't. And just as an aside, if you're a straight man who enjoys a bit of lavender action behind your wife's back, then YOU'RE NOT FUCKING 100% STRAIGHT. The whole thing about it 'not being gay if you don't push back' definitely, absolutely does not apply. There's a simple enough test for blokes: if you have a cock between your legs, that's reasonable. But if you have one pistoning away between your bumcheeks, then you're not straight – and that's cool, everyone has different degrees of sexuality, but stop with the 100% bollocks;

readers – people who read communal newspapers and don't put them back in any sensible order, instead leaving all the pages out of sync and the entire paper looking like it's blown down the street by a force 9 gale;

Paul – that I can't find a good word to describe Paul – I don't like husband because it sounds like I'm trying to make a political point, I don't like partner because it makes it sound like we've only been together for a few months and are just testing the water, I don't like 'boyfriend' because I actually have hair on my arse and my voice is broken so it's not relevant, I don't like life partner because just fuck off, I don't like other half because that's how thick chancers on game shows refer to their wives and apparently referring to him as Fatty or Shitty McGee is insulting;

's – it's **Tesco**, not Tescos. It's **ASDA**, not ASDAs. It's especially NOT Marks and fucking Spencers;

drawn on eyebrows – why lighten your hair and then shave off your eyebrows and then draw them on with a Midnight Black Crayola? It's even worse when they use a tin of Impulse as a drawing guide and put those half-moon shapes on above their eyes, giving them the look of someone who's just been shot right on the sphincter with a pellet gun;

my face – I don't like being told to cheer up. Look, I'm a genuinely cheerful guy most of the time, it just so happens that years of being cripplingly obese has left my face looking like an elderly pug being given bad news. I appreciate the concern, but equally, fuck off; and

phantom shitters – I'm not coy about dropping the kids off as and when I need to, so public toilets hold no fear for me. That said, it absolutely boils my piss when I nip into the gents only to find someone has sand-blasted the bowl or left something that could resink the Titanic floating around for everyone to look at. It's not that bloody hard to flush a toilet and, if you've left the pan looking like someone wearing heavy boots has stepped on a Reese's Peanut Butter Cup, fucking clean it up! The brush next to the toilet isn't a bloody ornament.

CHRIST.

twochubbycubs on: my enemy

Gosh! Remember yesterday I was blathering on about my lights being fixed in the bathroom? Well, excitedly, I drove home like I'd spilt acid in my lap just to get home and try them out – and they're great! Perhaps a bit too bright – I tried to read Bill Bryson in the bath but the top of the book started smoking after ten minutes. I could open a Stand 'n' Tan, although I don't want old orange women with necks like crinkle-cut crisps stubbing out their rollies on my nice carpet. Still, at least I can see where I've dropped the soap after I've been singing 'Just Call Me Angel In The Morning' into it to get Paul out of bed.

Anyway, I'm a terrible person – I have a new enemy, and he's a Big Issue seller.. He's not the same tramp who hustled me for a fiver a few months ago, but instead he's a Big Issue seller and I find him absolutely revolting. I know that makes me an awful person with a lack of compassion but I can't help it – humans take an instant dislike to each other sometimes. Anyway, I see him whenever I'm mincing to Marks and Spencers in Newcastle – he stands in the middle of the path with his magazines and annoying face and jabs you with the magazine, all the while saying the same thing over and over in a voice that cuts me like a knife – BIG ISSUE PLEASE. Except it's BAAAAG ISSHOOO PLEEEURGHASE. He doesn't say the words, he throttles the fucking life out of them. When he's not smoking and thrusting a magazine at you, he's coughing up big old balls of phlegm and spitting them on the pavement, second only to seeing people smoke near babies, is something I loathe. And the noises! He doesn't so much bring up his phlegm as fucking mine it. I know I should be sympathetic but as I said, I'm dubious of his intent and let's not pretend we are all holier than thou, anyway.

Anyway, my new phleghnemy aside, I gave into considerable temptation today. Well yesterday, but I couldn't post yesterday as some people from work read the blog and I didn't want to give away the surprise. Part of my job at work is to think of events and ideas that'll make everyone else happy, and it was my idea to buy everyone a £1 mix-up. Because everyone loves sweeties, right? So, I picked up £165 worth of pic-n-mix and had to spend an afternoon decanting them into colourful little bags and adding even more sweets from the leftover bit of budget. I'm sorry, being surrounded by that many sweets, I couldn't help myself and the diet was forgotten – to be honest, everyone ought to be grateful they didn't find me rolling around on the floor covered in jazzies and cola cubes, laughing hysterically from all the sugar.

twochubbycubs on: a bit of everything

Here, can we all agree that the silly woman in that bloody Oral B advert can fuck right off with her 'go pro with my toothpaste' schtick? It's been a long time since an advert annoyed me so. I can't decide if it's because of the way she delivers her lines like one of those gap-yah knobbers who inflect every syllable upwards like they're asking questions, or whether it's because we're supposed to give the shiniest of shites about her dentist appointment? Perhaps it's the fact SHE HAS NO FUCKING TOOTHPASTE ON HER BRUSH WHEN SHE'S BRUSHING HER TEETH. Plus the toothpaste must have one hell of an anaesthetic in it given she seems to paralyse one side of her face after brushing, the smug twatapotamus that she is. Anyway.

Today's been the first quiet day in a long while, hence you're getting a blog post. Yesterday we had to have our electrician around as an emergency because the bathroom lights (installed three years ago) had been merrily trying to set the house on fire. Drama! That's all fixed, but I could have done without him knocking on the door at 9am (instead of the agreed 10.30am) as it meant I had to go from fast-asleep to fresh-faced within twenty seconds. Those days are behind me – I look like I've fallen face-first into a fire for a good half hour in the morning until I've freshened up with a shower and four tankards of coffee.

Lucky I didn't have morning glory, though I suppose could have given him somewhere to hang his cabling. He barrelled into the bathroom before I had a chance to check whether Paul had left one of his trademark 'freshly-ploughed field' skidders on the toilet, so I just went back to bed and left Paul to deal with any potential embarrassment. The electrician is cracking anyway, I reckon he'd have just made an off-taste gag about Aberfan and got on with it. We've had top luck with all of our 'tradespeople' so far, luckily. Certainly no-one has felt they've needed to do the whole 'TITS AND FOOTBALL' chatter that never washes with us, although I did manage to embarrass myself with the joiner who has been fitting out our wardrobes by asking him if he had wood. I should have just committed and leered at him instead of letting the tops of my ears go red.

So today we've had a lie-in – well, Paul did, I got woken up by one of the cats who, yet again, decided that the very first thing I needed to see when I woke up was her puckered bumhole glaring at me as she fussed about on the duvet. It's not fair, Paul would sleep through a gas explosion whereas I wake up if someone sighs in Darlington. I reckon Sola knows that and decided that 9am was when she wanted her food, so I needed to be up. Ah well. After two hours of me making increasingly loud noises in the kitchen, Paul rolled out of bed and we were on our way to the cat and dog shelter.

Regular readers will know that Paul and I regularly walk dogs at our local cat and dog shelter, Brysons. It's an easy way to get a bit of body magic and the dogs bloody love it. Brysons do amazing work with so little funding so we're happy to help, plus we had a bucketload of extra donated food that my work had put in for, so all was great. We were given a little beauty of a Jack Russell crossed with something else. I'm not a fan of small dogs – especially yappy breeds – but she was adorable, even if I did pick her up for a photo only for her to lick so excitedly at my face that her tongue actually went into my mouth. I don't know who came off worse in that situation frankly, but if the bitch doesn't buy me some flowers and arrange a second date I'll be fizzing.

After the dog was walked, we decided (against better judgement) to have a spin out in the car and go to Dalton Park, which is a local outlet centre. We apparently didn't learn our lesson from our jaunt to Royal Quays, which was incredibly disappointing (link opens in a new window). We need some new shoes, shorts and shirts before we go to Corsica, and apparently there is a Cotton Traders there which is suitable for our vast frames.

Well, honestly. What a heap of shite. For one thing, it was absolutely rammed to the point where we were struggling to park – and this was at 3.30pm on a Sunday afternoon. Who the hell wakes up on a Sunday and decides that what they really want to do on their day off is look around an M&S outlet centre, buy a factory-seconds bag of Turkish Delight and enjoy a sun-warmed fly-buzzed potato in Spud-u-Like? I was immediately seething at the temerity of everyone else for bringing their bloody children along. Shopping should be a pleasurable experience and not feel like I'm on Total Wipeout trying to reach the tills with screaming children snottily orbiting my ankles. BAH. Still, I spotted a 'The Works'.

I love The Works, it's like someone created a load of nonsense books for a bet and put them out to see if they'd sell. Crotcheting the Norfolk Broads with Wincey Willis? The Better Sex Guide with the late Wendy Richards? Painting with Mist? Absolute tut! That said, we somehow managed to spend £50 on yet more cookbooks that will languish on our shelves unread and unloved until we have a fit and decide to donate them to charity. I swear we keep our local Scope exceptionally well-stocked for books, no wonder the lady who runs the shop drives a Mercedes and has a Radley bag which I BET someone donated. Scandal!

The lady behind the counter at The Works decided that no, putting eight hardback books into seperate bags was an entirely silly idea and really we would best be able to manage by putting all the books into one carrier bag and then quadruple-bagging it, meaning I had to struggle around the bloody shopping arcade like

Sisyphus, trying desperately to mask my hard breathing and tomato face. Great fun.

We did pop into Sports Direct for roughly fifteen seconds which was fourteen seconds longer than we needed to be reminded of why we never venture in there. It was awash – nay, it was crawling – with the slackjawed masses you see in the paper for shoplifting buying themselves new accessories to match their grey sweatpants. Men shouldn't be allowed to wear those grey sweatpants that hug every wrinkle and vein, it removes all the mystery for Paul and I as gay men, like knowing your Christmas present in advance.

We ducked next door into the Adidas outlet and asked (well, no, interrupted the chat about football between him and a co-worker) the first member of staff we saw whether they had any size 12 trainers in stock. Well jesus, you'd think we'd asked him why sheep don't shrink in the rain, he looked so dumbfounded. It's not the most unusual of questions to ask in a fucking shoe-shop but hey, clearly when God was handing out brains he was off getting a second helping of mouth, so that was that. We gave up at this point and went home, stopping for a consolation McDonalds on the way home. I know I know, but if you won't tell Margaret, nor will we.

twochubbycubs on: Valentines Day

Paul broke The Rule today. We both agreed that we wouldn't buy each other a Valentines gift because we're saving up for something big, and for once in my life I decided to stick to it. Normally I roll my eyes and buy a gift anyway whenever people do that — my nana is a particular bugger for it — 'OOOH DON'T MAKE A FUSS ETC' but if you turned up on Christmas Day with a card, well-wishes and lack of present, she'd sit there like you'd swapped her sherbet lemons for hard-boiled piss. But no, this year I stuck to the rules, and Paul promptly presented me with a new bottle of Tom Ford's Grey Vetiver — my favourite scent in the whole world. He'd done well, soaked in all my hints in the car journey on the way home from work, gone to John Lewis and promptly forgot the name and scent — managed to find it by describing it to the perfume lady and through scent alone! Normally I smell like chips and shame, so it'll make a change to smell all classy like. In my defence, I did ask him whether he'd want a Vivienne Westwood necklace that I'd seen, but he replied by saying that it was a bit too gay. It's as if the last eight years of sodomy and frotting never happened.

Nevertheless, I had a trick up my sleeve. I've secured a white t-shirt out of the wardrobe, hastily printed a picture of Barack Obama on it and turned it into my 'YES, WE CAN' shirt, meaning that if he asks me to do something, the answer will automatically be yes. It's fun and it's free – what price dignity? I'm glad we don't own a pool though, a day like this can easily end up turning sour (the "Barrymore Effect") and the last thing I want is to be found face-down in a swimming pool with a bumhole like a windsock and 'anal trauma' on my death certificate. So lord knows what I'll end up doing today, but at least I'm not The Worst Husband in the World anymore.

Mine was printed on recycled ice-lolly sticks, meaning I'd already given Paul wood by the time we had got out of bed this morning, which I'm sure you'll agree is incredibly efficient. I only noticed one of the whales had lipstick and mascara on when I got the card home, but that's alright, we're both confident young men who are at ease with our roles.

twochubbycubs on: TV

I am gutted that, yet again, we're sending a load of dross to Eurovision! Have you heard it?

It sounds like the type of ditty that would play out over a Buy as you View advert. I'm not one of these tubthumpers who claim we'll never win Eurovision because if we sent a decent act, pumped a lot of amyl nitrates into the air and actually spent some money on publicity, we'd do well! Paul and I will still be watching it, eating our Austrian food (that'll be our European tour country for that week) and screaming at the telly, but just once I'd like to see us succeed. Still, it'll be a good night in front of the TV regardless.

We don't watch a lot of TV – at least, not British TV. We used to be well into Coronation Street (rock and roll lifestyle) but that went dull, fast – and Eastenders is only decent when something big is happening, otherwise I end up trying to cut my wrists with the butter knife by the time it's over. We'll take in the odd documentary and we do love a good drama (for good drama, I'm talking about stuff like Lost over crap like Broadchurch – if you want to see Olivia Colman cry, watch a film called Tyrannosaurus, she's brilliant in that). If you like reality TV but with decent production values, download a programme called The Amazing Race – UK TV doesn't show it because we'd sooner watch tone-deaf bumholes singing on a talent show.

Doctor Who is a guilty pleasure as is popcorn fodder like 24. What we DO enjoy is a good quiz show, not least because we like shouting at thick people on TV.

That said, I'd be shit on that new show, 1000 Heartbeats, where your heartbeat is monitored as you answer questions and your clock counts down faster the quicker your heart beats – I'd be so out of breath climbing the three steps up to the podium that I'd only have four seconds to answer fourteen general knowledge questions whilst getting shouted at by besuited Yorkshire lamp-post Vernon Kaye. I'd love to have a go in The Cube, but I know for an absolute fact that when they did that swooshy camera movement where it spins 360 degrees around The Cube in slow-motion, my arse-crack would be hanging out of my George boxer shorts and I'd be pulling that cum-face I usually pull when I'm concentrating – tongue half out, brow furrowed like a crinkle-cut crisp. I've mentioned before that Paul and I would adore the chance to go on Coach Trip, and indeed we auditioned successfully for the show, but then they took it off air for three years, perhaps hoping our clogged-up arteries would kill us off before we had a chance to get on the bus, call someone a jumped up shitbag and get asked to leave Lithuania in an armoured car.

I'd have been absolutely top at The Crystal Maze though. I say that from the comfort of my living room, admittedly, but I would have been a guaranteed two-crystal winner and that weekend canoeing in Middlesex could have been mine. Of course, no sooner was I old enough to apply, they took it off the bloody air. There's been talk of bringing it back time and time again, including, horrifically, the idea of having Amanda Holden present in the Richard O'Brian role. Amanda Holden! A woman so pointless and personality-free that you could put a privet hedge with a crow stuck in it where she sat on Britain's Got Talent and people would be hard-pressed to tell the difference. That's what ruins TV – 'celebrities' famous for fuck all (in her case, having the dubious honour of turning down Les Dennis' cock in favour of the unfunny one from Men Behaving Badly) taking part in shows and quizzes in lieu of decent folk from Ordinary World. Even if they somehow resist the urge to throw celebrities into the mix at every opportunity, they try and turn the ordinary folk into celebrities instead – like the gay couple from Gogglebox for example. Yep, they're funny, but why are they in an advert with Kevin Bacon for bloody mobile phone services? Actually, why the hell is Kevin bloody Bacon in an advert for a mobile phone service? Kev, I've seen Footloose, you're worth so much more!

Gosh, that was a bit of a rant. See that's probably why they didn't come back to us re: Coach Trip.

twochubbycubs on: garden centres

I managed to make a tit of myself today in a garden centre, and not just because I'm a 30 year old lad who'll actively choose to go to a garden centre on a Sunday afternoon. What can I say, I like the variety – where else can you go and buy a new connector for a hosepipe, a double DVD box set of Das Boot and Last of the Summer Wine and a white chocolate florentine? Years ago I would have rather ran a power-sander over the tip of my cock than schlep around sniffing flowers and Yankee Candles, but I'm getting old now.

Can we take a moment to discuss Yankee Candles? Now, and this will come as no surprise to anyone, I don't mind a scented candle, but can someone explain to me how they come up with the names for their 'scents'? Red Raspberry I can understand, but who decides what a 'Wedding Day' smells like (disappointing sausage rolls and regretful sex?) or indeed, what the hell 'New Born' is? To me a 'New Born' candle should smell like placenta, chyme and the crushing realisation you'll never have your life to yourself again, but the good folk at Yankee Candle seem to think it smells like a urinal cake. Ah well.

We were there trying to find some suitable garden furniture for the new patio we've had built in the back garden. This is proving tricky in itself. All we want is a decent hardwood table and chairs. There's no point in getting anything that needs to be brought in over the winter because we're simply far too lazy and it'll just to be left to rot. We had three pairs of boxer shorts hanging on our rotary drier all though Christmas last year because we kept meaning to bring them in. It was only when a particularly strong January wind blew one pair onto next door's greenhouse roof that we took action.

There's no point in getting anything plastic either, because it looks absolutely awful, and you just know the very second our arse touches the seat it'll splinter into individual atoms with a loud enough crack to blow the windows in over the road and rattan isn't going to work either because it'll give too much under our weight and end up looking like a knackered shopping bag after three or four lazy Sundays.

So yes: hardwood, oak preferably. The garden centre didn't cater for such a ridiculous notion as decent garden furniture but it did have a very comfortable little fabric sun-lounger on show. Of course, me being me, I had to have a go, and I poured myself in like one might tip a jelly out of a mould. It was grand, save for the fact that, thanks to my weight, the fabric pretty much ensconced me like a venus-fly-trap and it soon became clear that I wasn't going to be able to get back out unassisted. Bearing in mind it was fairly busy and Paul was busy in the candles bit trying to figure out what the fuck 'A Child's Wish' smells like, I had to free myself using only my own steam, especially as I couldn't swing my legs out as the crotch on the jeans I was wearing had split a few weeks ago and I wasn't entirely confident I was wearing underwear that wouldn't have shown my balls to the world.

So – turns out the easiest way is simply to swing to one side and tip the whole lounger over until I was wearing it on my back like a turtle and then throw it off. The whole process was over in less than ten seconds but my face was burning so brightly that I'm surprised Paul's 'Felching Remains' Yankle Candle didn't set itself away and take out his nosehair. We left immediately, hurtling out of the entrance hiding our faces like a disgraced politician entering court. So that was that.

twochubbycubs on: buying a sofa

They say that moving house is one of the most stressful things a couple can do – well, that's bullshit. Listen, we moved the entire contents of our flat to our new home in a Citreon C2. You've never lived until you've hurtled down the A1 with the threat of a chest of drawers tumbling off the roof of the car and littering the road with boxer shorts and buttplugs. Actually, moving was quite a charming experience, especially once we had a bonfire of all the old biddy furniture in the back garden – who would have thought that ulcer dressings and boxes upon boxes upon boxes of expired Solpadeine would go up like Piper Alpha? Not me!

In retrospect, I wish we had kept the commode – given the way our neighbours are, I would have cheerfully and lovingly sat it right in front of our living room window and had a shite whilst staring icily at them eating their cereal of a morning (and I bet it's boring, 'help-you-shit' cereal, like All Bran or Start). That would give them something to talk about other than the colour of our fence and the fucking clover in our garden.

No, moving house was easy. It's decorating that's really turning my teeth to dust as I grind them with impatience and anger. Today Paul and I went sofa shopping, see, and quite genuinely I'd rather spend the afternoon having various items of kitchenware roughly inserted into my anus in a display window in House of

Fraser rather than repeat it. It was just awful, with each shop bringing a fresh horror.

We made the mistake of starting in DFS, where we were immediately accosted by someone fresh out of nappies and with more product in his hair than there is on our freshly plastered ceilings. I reckon he took longer on his hair that morning than I've spent cumulatively on mine my entire life. And I used to have long, luscious hair, like a fruity Meat Loaf. His opening gambit was 'So are you thinking of buying a sofa?'. I resisted the urge to throw my hand to my mouth in mock surprise and go 'Heavens no, I've come to have the car's tyres realigned and my brake fluid changed, how DID I end up in here?'.

I can't bear nonsense questions like that (and I'm never rude to shopworkers, mind, they're just doing what they're told) – I'm hardly going to be renting a sofa for a weekend, am I? We shuffled around the store until his Lynx Africa got too much for my sensitive nose and we bid him goodbye, promising to 'come back later'. Honestly there's more chance of Princess Diana 'coming back later' than me.

Next was Barker and Stonehouse, which is pretty much the antithesis of DFS in terms of 'style' but I found it ghastly, not least because I immediately felt incredibly out of place in my George jeans and painting hoodie. There are some beautiful pieces of furniture to be had, but it all felt a little bit overpriced, and the only assistance offered amounted to nothing more than such an angry glare from an bumptious oil-slick of a man that I actually thought I'd trod muck in on my shoes. Perhaps he was looking disdainfully at our B&M carrier bag full of hot chocolates, but what can I say, I like a bargain. I got a quick snipe in as I left that 'perhaps if I was opening an upper-class brothel, I'd consider it', but it fell a little flat.

The next shop was some 'Sofa Warehouse' or suchlike – the only thing I remember about it was that, when I enquired about leather sofas, he immediately showed us to this god-awful brown number that looked like the first turd after a bout of severe constipation...and had cupholders in it. I'm sorry but no, cupholders in a sofa is strictly the domain of people who put tomato ketchup on everything they eat and who breathe loudly through their mouth. I mean honestly, I don't even have a tattoo of a loved one's name in copperplate on my neck. I bet the same people who leave comments like 'RESIPEE PLZ K THX HUN' under my food pictures have cupholders. Is it so difficult to strain forward and pop your can of Monster down on a coffee table? We made our excuses there and then.

And so it went on. We visited almost ten different places and each one was absolutely rammed full of awful shapes, awful textures, awful colours and awful people. There was one settee that looked like it had been stitched together by Stevie Wonder at gunpoint –

about eighty different textures and patterns all stretched horrendously over some cheap metal legs. It looked like a corrupted MPEG of a colonoscopy. Who buys stuff like that, seriously? I wouldn't burn that in my garden.

We did eventually find a settee we like, but then being tight-arsed Geordies, we dashed home to see if we could find it cheaper online and via Quidco, which we've dutifully done, but no – it's cheaper in store! So that means tomorrow we're going to go back and haggle like we've never done before. The sales assistant looked hard-faced (although it was hard to tell under her fifteen inches of Max Factor – she sneezed at one point and I swear half her cheek fell onto her blazer) but I reckon I'll be able to get £200 off the asking price and free delivery. That's my goal.

Tell you what though, you couldn't pay me to deal with the general public – we witnessed some appalling behaviour from families with children today, including one set of parents who let their litter tip a fucking settee over and ignored the somewhat plaintive cries of the poor assistant who clearly knew that a call to a claims solicitors was mere moments away. You also get arseholes coming in like me who fake-smile at you, take a free cup of coffee and then spend thirty minutes clumsily pawing their way through the fabric selection book before hurtling home to order it online and put a hammer in the nail of the coffin of your job security. In my defence: I'm always super-polite and I'm never, ever rude. Plus anyway, I'm going back tomorrow so she'll be getting her commission.

Christ though, it'll be ten weeks before delivery. Ten weeks! What are they doing, pulling it with their hair from Penzance? Bah! That leaves nearly no time at all for the cats to completely destroy it before Christmas comes and we have to host family.

twochubbycubs on: B&Bs

I'm spending the evening looking at hotels and bits and bobs to do in Iceland. We've decided to give Air B&B a go.

I know, I know. We're asking for trouble.

I've always wanted to stay at a B&B, because they're usually somewhere beautiful and it doesn't quite feel like you're sleeping in the jizz-dust of 1,000 businessmen that have literally come before you. But I just can't. For one, I have a shit poker face, and if I was shown into a room and I didn't like it, the disappointment avalanching across my ashen face would immediately make me an enemy of the host and she'd spit in my breakfast. I can't bear chintz and flimflam and unnecessary accessories (although that would make a good band name, no?) either, so unless it was a perfectly sterile room decorated in tiny nice things, I'd feel uncomfortable. Then there's the small talk – I don't want to be fussed over as I try not to die in my morning coffee or asked where I'm going / how I'm getting there or tutted at when I don't take my boots off. I'd spend the entire time away agonising over any little offence I may have caused that I'd simply need another holiday afterwards to relax.

That said, I did once see a B&B on Four in a Bed where about two hundred cats roamed the property and it was pretty much a guarantee that you'd end up in bed with a hairy Persian sitting on your face – and well, that sounds good to me.

Speaking of cats, we took ourselves off to Mog on the Tyne (what can I say, I'm a sucker for puns – I'd eat my dinner in a clap clinic if it was given a pun for a name…something like Spotted Dicks or The Leaky Bucket) a couple of weeks ago. Mog on the Tyne is Newcastle's first cat café and, with a rare afternoon off, Paul and I decided to try it.

It's brilliant. The food is basic café food – paninis, quiche, brownies et al – but the focus lies squarely on the ten or so cats that mill around the place, fighting, purring or – as is always the case with me – showing their bumholes as you try to finish your brownie. The café is fitted out with all sorts of toys, climbing frames and beds and the cats seem perfectly content – of course they are, they're getting made a fuss of. You have to pay a fiver each for entry (which is unusual, because in the Bigg Market, usually it only takes a Blue WKD and a ten-deck of Lambert and Butler to be guaranteed entry) (sorry) which pays towards the upkeep of the cats, and the food is reasonable quality. It was a charming way to spend an hour and I'd heartily recommend it if you're a cat fan. Of course, if you're not a cat fan, then you have other options available, such as having a quiet word with yourself regarding the direction your life has taken. Our favourite cat was seemingly everyone else's – a beast of a pussy called Stan who had suffered a nasty road accident. Aye, he took the bend at Billy Mill roundabout at 50mph in a Ford Capri and lost control.

No, he got run over and although he's fine now, he's unable to put his tongue in his mouth, meaning he has a permanently dopey expression.

You can find more details on Mog on the Tyne at their website – www.mogonthetyne.com – give them a go!

Of course, the bonus of visiting Mog on the Tyne was that as soon as we got back, our cats were all over us like flies on muck. I felt like a husband cheating on his missus, especially as the cats kept sniffing the end of my fingers and recoiling (which to be fair, I do myself). *Awkward*.

twochubbycubs on: anxiety

Serious post tonight, folks, though I'll chuck in a few jokes because why the hell not. I received an email from wordpress (the guys who host my blog) saying happy anniversary – it's been three years since you set up your blog. My first thought was that I had clearly stroked out for a few months because I was sure twochubbycubs had only been going for a few months, but then I twigged it was actually my first blog where I documented my 'battle' with health anxiety. I was so proud of that blog's name – I called it shakerattleanddroll because of my obsession with my shaking (Parkinsons), rattling (tablets) and droll (the sparkling wit you all know and love). Mulling on it a moment or two, I thought it might be a decent thing to talk about anxiety to give some hope to anyone out there suffering with it.

I suffer from health anxiety – I'd go so far to say that it doesn't affect me so much anymore and that I have a handle on it, but I'll still have the occasional wobble (the wobble being a clear sign that I've got vertigo, or balance problems, or seasickness, or a brain tumour). Anxiety is an awful, awful thing and those who dismiss it as anything other than a serious illness can kiss my arse. I'm a strong-minded, confident bloke and I was brought to my knees through health anxiety – quite genuinely the worst three months of my life. I became hyper-sensitive to every little thing that my body did and what it meant – always the worst case scenario, and was completely unable to relax or think straight for months. Imagine always fearing you were about to die.

My obsession became multiple sclerosis – I became genuinely quite convinced that I had MS simply because my eyes were aching and I had perceived weakness in my right leg. I had, quite innocently, typed those symptoms into Dr Google and of course, the worst case scenario came up. I knew nothing about MS at the time (I could write a fucking book on it now) but everything 'clicked' in such a way that I started experiencing other common symptoms – balance problems, forgetfulness, more vision problems, which only reinforced my belief. I spoke to doctors who ruled it out but I knew that MS is an incredibly hard thing to actually diagnose because there isn't a concrete test for it, so I ignored them. It's actually a very common disease for those with health anxiety to latch onto for this very reason – plus a lot of the symptoms of anxiety and MS match up, and the more you worry about having MS, the more your anxiety grows, the worse the symptoms get...

Then, because I saw an article on Parkinsons, I became convinced that I was suffering from that purely because my hands were shaking a little. Just like that, MS was forgotten (and it seems ridiculous to me now) and Parkinsons became the focus. Pick up a piece of paper by the corner and hold it in front of you – watch the edges shake a little. It's perfectly normal. But to me that was a sign I was going to spend my life unable to type and never eating peas again. Eventually, I pretty much snapped through all of the worry and went to talk to my doctor, who god bless her, went through each and every one of my 'symptoms' and told me it was anxiety.

I was put onto an anti-depressant called citalopram for six months – only a small dose, but enough to 'take the edge off' my worries. It worked to some extent because it dulled my senses and stopped me thinking about every little thing, but I was cynical about it working. Then it happened – a few peaceful hours became a full day, one day became two, two days became a week, and I just stopped worrying, and I stopped taking the tablets and felt fine. Paul was an absolute wonder through all of this, being my constant rock, as always, and I do try and tell him how thankful I am.

It's not perfect – even now I catastrophise – if I have a headache, I'll immediately start running through my mind the possibilities: brain tumour (unlikely, I'm not seeing blue flashes), mad cow disease (possibly, I grew up on cheap beef), stroke (touch each tooth with the tip of your tongue, if you can do that, you're not having a stroke). Crazy. But, I know how to deal with it – I take solace in statistics. The same logic and rationale that gets me onto an aeroplane keeps me from flipping out over health worries. I've had a weird tic in my left eye for a good few weeks now but I don't care, and that feels good.

I'm not posting all of this for attention or for people to say 'Oooh, haven't you done well' – in fact, no comments wanted, I know I've got it licked. No, I'm posting this because if anyone is reading this and going through anxiety themselves – whether health anxiety, general anxiety or just a period of depression, know that it does, and will, get better. At my darkest I thought I'd suffer for the rest of my life and to be quite honest, it's probably always going to be a small part of me, but I go weeks without thinking about it and I can't, genuinely, remember the last time it was a problem. It might feel neverending or that there's no hope, but there's always something positive to cling to, and things always get better in the end. I did...!

twochubbycubs on: visiting a sex shop

Today, we ended up in a sex shop, thanks in no small part to my dear mother. If you're prudish, scroll down to the recipe.

See, you may recall me whingeing that our ongoing hunt for garden furniture was bearing no fruit? The situation remains the same, so my mum helpfully pointed out a place she'd found in an industrial estate by the banks of the Tyne which 'might have' sold charming garden furniture. Paul and I duly set off after a quick stop to IKEA to have an argument and walk around in a HÜFF like 95% of the other couples there. Hell, we didn't even stop to buy a hotdog, that's how severe the argument was. All was forgotten by the time we got back to the car, of course. I reckon they pump testosterone through the vents at IKEA to cause all the discord. So off we went to find the garden furniture place.

Well honestly. We ended up on a bleak, wind-swept, pretty much derelict industrial estate – the very type of place where someone is taken on TV to get shot in the back of the head by a bent copper. I didn't dare stop the car in case a load of chavs came dashing out of the river to steal my tyres. We drove around and around until we eventually found the place but given a) it was closed and b) there were three balding, shirtless old men smacking an old fridge with a wrench in the courtyard, we sharp left. It was only after four or so miles of air-conditioning and Radio 4 that I stopped talking like I was an extra from Kes.

But listen, we at twochubbycubs don't like to miss an opportunity for shenanigans, and we soon spotted a way to liven up our afternoon – a visit to a sex-shop. Yes, this dystopian wilderness offered up the opportunity to peruse all sorts of erotica and, following the tasteful roadsign signs promising cocktails and sex-toys, we were in. Previous visits to sex shops have always been awful – Paul was once served (not serviced) by someone who had his cock slapped on the counter like a discarded buffet sausage roll the whole time, and I got stuck behind someone roughly the size and shape of a reversing coach loudly bellowing about her desire for a 'clit ring'. I almost blurted out 'have you tried a hula-hoop, you brash beast' but instead chewed my lips in restraint.

Now, neither of us are prudish about sex. I think it's absolutely smashing and can heartily recommend it. But some of the things on show in there made my eyes water (and only the top two, mind). A 20" latex fist to pop up your bottom? 20"! What are you hoping to do, scratch the back of your teeth with the fucker? What if you're too rough and a giant black rubber cock comes bursting out of your stomach like that scene with John Hurt in Alien? There was also the terrifying named 'arse-lock' which was essentially something that looked like a trainspotter's flask made out of rubber combined with a stretchy rubber hoop, the idea being that it keeps 'everything locked down from bumhole to ballsack. SOME MIGHT CALL THAT MARRIAGE, AM I RIGHT? I spent a couple of minutes trying to figure it out until I realised how pervy it looked and quickly backed away to look at mouth-gags.

The whole experience wasn't helped by being stared at the whole time by two middle-aged ladies who I thought I faintly recognised from my school-dinner days. What did they think I was going to steal? It's not like you can make a quick getaway with a dildo the size of a roll of carpet hidden in/on your person, is it? I did try cracking a joke – pointing to a fire extinguisher on the wall and asking how much it would be for that model – but their stony faces sharp put paid to my ribald humour.

Tell you what hasn't changed a bit though – pornography, though I was somewhat startled to see so many erect cocks winking at me from the shelves – I felt like I was operating a gloryhole in a hall of mirrors. It's all so hilariously naff, especially the attempts at gay porn where the 'lads' are supposed to be straight / butch. I've certainly never known many 'scallies fresh out of borstal' who wear lipliner and purse their mouths whilst they're getting bummed. And I've known a fair few.

However, the award for most awkward went to the DVD of porn that catered for those with a wheelchair fetish. Let me make something clear – I'm not ripping the piss out of the fact that disabled folk have sex, not one bit – it's the fact that this DVD was so, so, so, so distasteful. The DVD had a big 'blue badge' on it like the one that gives you free parking and plastered on the middle was a randy old bugger who was the absolute double of the caretaker from the Harry Potter movies, with a full bonk-on and his hand on some passing girl's clapper. It gets better – they'd mapped flames on the wheels of his wheelchair. But even that's not it – it was the fact it was called The Handi Man. I love a bit of wordplay but I'm not convinced I'll be sending that in to I'm Sorry I Haven't A Clue. Good lord.

We didn't buy anything, by the way. Again, not because we're prudish, but rather sensible folk buy their toys and kit from places like lovehoney.com. Honestly, the things that have come through our letterbox...

twochubbycubs on: taking a bus

I've never felt older than I did this morning, when, standing at a bus-stop surrounded by screaming kids effing and jeffing, I tutted to myself and thought 'kids these days'. Well actually, what I thought was 'kids these days...if I kicked the littlest one under the wheels of a bus would I REALLY be in the wrong?'. Which is a trifle worrying but honestly, they were so loud. All the conversation was happening at twice the speed I'd expect, like someone leaning on the BPM slider on an old record-player. At one point I thought they were speaking Gujarati until I made the words 'here-man-ye-FUCKING-DONKEY' explode through all the vocal drawls and tics. Plus half of the little scrotes were smoking, albeit they were doing that affected 'suck in a tiny bit and exhale like you're trying to blow out a chip pan fire' smoking. I mean if you're GOING to smoke do it properly, I didn't hear one lung-rattling cough amongst them. Amateurs. I was on half a tin of Peterson Old Dublin at their age.

You may wonder why someone as sociopathic as me was on a bus – well, I had to take my dear little car in for a service. It's a brand new car so there should be no problems and it could have waited but see, my windscreen wipers were leaving an annoying smear on the window and rather than just clean them myself, I just took the car in for a full service and asked for a new set. We're terrible with money, what can I say. But we've got no debt so we're doing something right! I had to sit outside the dealership for twenty minutes waiting for someone to open up, and then I was immediately cut up in the queue by someone with a nicotine fringe and Build-a-Bear shoes. It's OK, I'm British, I'll queue politely and stare at the back of your greasy head with such unimaginable fury that I'm surprised the word KNOBJOCKEY didn't burn across your ears.

He was booking in his bellendmobile for a service too and I almost ground my teeth into diamonds at his excruciating exchange with the receptionist. See, she asked him what time he wanted to pick up the car, he replied 'Whatever time is good for you, I'm easy'. That made me vomit gently against the back of my teeth but I held it back. She then suggested 4pm – nope, no good, he was picking the kids up. 5pm? No, he was taking his mother to hospital. 3pm? He'd be at work. Tomorrow morning? He drives a lorry for a living, he'd be away. I mean HAWAY MAN, it's not bloody hard to give HER a time instead of trying to be a smooth bastard with your plaitable earhair and chip-fat musk. After what felt like enough time to the rubber on my tyres to perish in the sun, he fucked off, it was my turn, I signed the car over and was away before she could click her pen.

The bus, then. Awful. For so many reasons. Firstly, I like my own personal space. I don't like sharing that personal space with someone for whom deodorant and mouthwash are part of an "alternative lifestyle". I

273

immediately tune into their every defect – the way their nostrils whistle when they breathe out, the way they click their teeth over every speedbump, the way they lean against me as the bus turns a corner. I hate it. I'm not perfect by any stretch but see that's why I contain myself in a car. People don't respect personal space but I probably take it to the other extreme – I wince like a beaten dog if someone so much as gets in the lift with me.

Plus, the journey cost me £2.20. For a distance no greater than two miles, all downhill. Had I not been worried about my lovely shirt, I could have laid on my back and barrelled down the hill like a roll of carpet. I could even have walked (shock, I know, but even I'm not fat enough to decline a walk downhill) but I would have been late for my dentist and he's the last guy I want to piss off. That's extortionate, and it took almost half an hour because the bus stopped quite literally every 100 yards or so to let someone off and on, with all their bloody questions taking another five minutes. The driver had all the charisma of a roadside piss and snatched tickets and cash like he was on the Crystal Maze. I don't doubt there are exceptions but do they make all bus drivers go to a training camp to thrash all the human decency out of them? Or is it dealing with rotten human beings all day that turn them into such miserable buggers? I saw someone stumble over the word Megarider and I honestly thought the driver was going to punch her on the tit.

Ah well. The dentist went very well – I'm not even going to write a sarcastic recount of that, because I just can't fault my dentist. He's lovely. He takes the time to tell me what he's going to do and I think he must minimise anything that 'hurts' because I rarely feel a thing. Apparently I have animal teeth AND naturally white. Not surprised, what with all the "whitening solution" I've had cascaded over them over the years, am I right? If I was richer, I'd have every last tooth torn out and replaced with big fake white teeth. I know it looks unnatural but it's the one thing about me that I'm genuinely shy about – even though my teeth are pretty decent. Paul hides his teeth all the time too, despite having a lovely smile – but in the nine years we've been together I've never been allowed to look at the back of his mouth. The guy is happy enough texting me a picture of his balloon knot with an 'URGENT: OPEN THIS' caption, but his teeth? No. Weird.

Anyway, as it happens, the car came back completely free of any worries and they replaced the blades for nowt because they should have lasted longer! RESULT.

twochubbycubs on: Amazon Prime

I managed to get into a proper argument with some pallid-faced swamp donkey on facebook who tried to peddle her Juice Plus shite in my group. She private messaged me to tell me that the fact I'd deleted her snake-oil post told her that I hate women and people who try to make a go of themselves. Honestly – I could eat a tin of alphabet spaghetti and shit out a better argument than that. I don't hate women (except Mylenne Klass...and I don't hate her, she just makes my skin shiver) and I'm all for entrepreneurship, but as well you all know, I can't bear the idea of vulnerable folk being duped into buying worthless, untested medicines on the scientific advice of a hairdresser from Worksop.

What I can't get my head around is the fact PEOPLE FALL FOR IT. Why?! I can understand folks who are seriously ill buying a pill in the vain hope of it helping, but spending hundreds of pounds just to shift a bit of weight? Bah! Are these the same people who buy laptops from a car boot sale and get them home to unwrap a cardboard box full of bricks? Or the people who get an unsolicited phone-call from Microsoft telling them they need to buy antivirus software at a cost of two bajillion pounds? Honestly. How do these people sleep at night? Penniless, I presume. Anyway, the argument rumbled on for ages, with Juice Plus curing her of depression, suicidal thoughts, liver disease, tennis elbow, easy living and fast cars (apparently it didn't cure her of her verbal diarrhoea or dirty mouth), until I copied our chat in with the Juice Plus representatives and left it at that. I know nothing will come of it because Juice Plus is a dishonest pyramid scheme sold by numpties and dolts, but meh, made me feel better.

Now, my next piece is going to feel like an advert for Amazon Prime, and well, although I'm going to stick a link on the bottom, this isn't really an advert at all. Just an observation. Paul and I are members of Amazon Prime, and have been for a very long while. I can't remember the last time I paid for it because every time something is late, they stick an extra month on the membership. We've become accustomed to ordering something on a whim and having it turn up the next day, which is handy as it gives us no time for buyer's remorse. Hence the cat tower. Hence the all-in-one breakfast sandwich maker. Hence the shit-you-not Teasmade. A bloody Teasmade, I ask you – I don't even drink tea in the morning. I don't get out of bed unless I'm having a palpitation just from smelling my morning coffee. Anyway, we got a little email the other day with the news that Amazon Prime Now has launched in Newcastle. What is it? You order something on Amazon, and it's delivered within two hours for free.

Well fuck me. The only thing from turning Paul and I into perfect spheres with weak ankles is our inability to muster up the energy to drive to ASDA of an evening to buy ice-cream. Now it's delivered by Amazon within enough time for Paul and I to have quick marriage-friendly nookie, make tea and watch Emmerdale. It's too convenient. It's not without flaws, though. You can only select from a range of groceries and flimflam via their App, which is proper hokey. I put 'dip' into the search box and it suggested some taramasalata, tzatziki and er, industrial strength cat-nip. One whole kilogram of the stuff. A kilo of cat-nip delivered within two hours! Unless you're fighting a fucking tiger in your box-room, who the hell needs that? Nevertheless, we persevered and placed an order full of Slimming World friendly things – the usual Haagen Daaz, Goodfellas pizza and bags of Skittles. Look, we had to spend thirty quid, and I wasn't going to spend it on bloody quinoa. I bet Mags is sucking on a Bensons and Hedges quite furiously with the thought but you know, I've got to let my (apparently Geography-teacher-esque) hair down.

What followed was a tense 80 minutes where we watched, in real-time, our order being picked from somewhere on an industrial estate in Gateshead (hey, we didn't order a bag of ket and mild domestic battery, did we?) – all terribly exciting. When the screen updated to show 'MARK' had picked up our order and was beetling up the A1 to our house, well, we were agog. It's a bloody miracle, technology. We had it on the big TV in our living room like the shittest, cheapest version of 24 you can imagine. The whole process fell down at the end though, because the driver turned onto our street and spent five minutes trying to find our house. I'll give you a clue, mate – it's the only one that's not attached to any others, plus we were flashing the lights from green to red whenever he backed his van out of sight. The groceries were all nicely chilled and the ice-cream was spot-on. It took eighty eight minutes from beginning to end, and that includes 5 minutes of the driver being unable to find the only house in the street to be named after a sexual consequence.

Would I recommend it? Yes. Amazon Prime is amazing, anyway, if you're a big Amazon shopper. Yes it costs £79 a year but you get plenty of perks with it. Plus, you can always sign up for a trial and then cancel. But don't forget to actually cancel. Otherwise you'll be one of those turds who complain about getting money taken out of your bank account for something you've asked for. This two hour thing is dangerous for Paul and I though – we already dish out way too much of our monthly pink-pound disposable income to Amazon – I can't help feeling that eventually I'm going to be paying them my wages direct and they'll be sending a box van of goodies every month, probably branded Amazon Instant, with a picture of a smiling man sucking the pound coins from my pocket on the side. Ah well. If you did want to try it, you can do so here.

I still can't believe it. I'm easily impressed, but jesus, Amazon stuff delivered within two hours for nowt. I remember ordering pornography online back when we first got the internet and actually taking time off from school just to sit by the letterbox for about two weeks in case my father accidentally opened my post and wondered who the hell had sent him RUGBY CUM BATH 2: SCRUM, BUM AND ORAL FUN on DVD. I might have made that title up but you get the drift. I feel I should hasten to say that my parents weren't lax when it came to supervising my internet security...I was just better at it. Honestly, you parents out there who think the kids can't access what they want on the internet, you're so wrong.

Finally, Paul, being a sod and knowing I didn't have the iPad with me on my commute into work on Friday, started streaming Enya's new album through the car speakers. Yes, I could have turned it off, but then I have to listen to myself swearing at people and I shame myself, so I left it on. Jesus, how does she do it? It's like she records one song and then changes the key, layers it on top of another song, and plays it backwards. She's the aural equivalent of a malfunctioning self-checkout. An ex of mine used to be absolutely obsessed with her, almost to the point of being unable to come without me whispering LET THE ORINOCO FLOW in his ear as we made love. I say made love, he was a means to an end, so let's not romanticise it too much. Anyway, I spent most evenings at the age of seventeen being forced to smile politely as he showed me the Irish tinker caterwauling her way through videos that looked like something even a gap-yah student would deem too pretentious. Christ it's no wonder I'm so mentally fragile.

twochubbycubs on: cliques

I can't begin to describe the absolute cuntnugget that I happened across yesterday. I was queued up in Subway awaiting my usual lunchtime trough of food (plain chicken, all the salad bar onion, double gherkin, double pickle, honey and mustard, no drink, cheers yes, haha) when in walks some twat wearing a top-hat. In Newcastle, in Subway, with a waxed pointy moustache to boot. It gets worse – when he got to the counter, he actually came out with 'So how on Earth does this work, then'. I was filled with irrational hatred. All I could think about was dashing back to the counter, pushing his face through the glass sneeze-guard and holding his head down in the pickles container until he stopped struggling for life and the police arrived to take me away. He was singularly the most achingly try-hard hipster twat that I've ever had the absolute displeasure to orbit.

It is, without doubt, the worst 'subculture' that exists right now. Zip backwards fifteen years ago and it was easy (at our school at least) – you had normal kids, then on either side of those you had chavs or Goths. And mind, these Goths were the starter Goths – none of this professional goth/emo whatever you see around town. They all had knock-off coats like Neo from the Matrix and a Livejournal account for photos of their self-harming. I had long, black hair for a good portion of my later school years but I was never a goth, not least because I was too fat – there's nowt worse than a tiny muffin-top popping out over a pair of New-Rock boots. One of my exes told me he was a goth before we met up but that only extended to have long hair – I'm not sure how gothic giving someone Enya's A Box Of Dreams on a first date is.

Chavs on the other hand are less tolerable but I just put most of that down to being thick. It was the time of coke-can fringes and Kappa tracksuit and for the most part, given it was a fairly posh school I went to, we'd only really see them out and about in the wild, their tracksuits rustling in the breeze. As I get older I find myself growing more contemptuous of a subculture that seems to revel in stupidity and an ability not to throw a trampoline on any square of dog-shit littered grass bigger than a postage stamp, but that's by the by – it's hipster that draws my true ire.

It's just so loathsome, so affected, so nonsensical. Every year – including going backwards and forward through time, no doubt – it's the same. Newcastle becomes awash with students all trying to outdo each other on the poncy twat stage. Instead of the booming Geordie dialect ricocheting around the streets of the city centre, you'll hear trust-fund rah-rah knobheads, whose idea of living dangerously is a quinoa salad on a terrace in Jesmond, stumbling around in their lollipop trousers and 1920s make-up. We have bars opening up all over the town catering to such predilections, all copying the 'trends' that London washed its hands off three years earlier – a drink served in a jam-jar? Oh outrageous. And I fucking hate it.

twochubbycubs on: 'gay'

We've been looking at holidays and have discovered that Thomson have a specialised 'side business' selling 'gay holidays', called Freedom Holidays. It seems like a load of patronising guff but they're well-meaning so I'll forgive them. Being gay is becoming less and less of an 'issue' now. Indeed, Newcastle is such a liberal, progressive city that I actually forget how lucky I am sometimes. I'd feel comfortable walking around holding hands with Paul, or buying rings together, or discussing frotting and cottaging over a frothy cappuccino on The Green. I don't even think about it. I'm sure that's partly because of the thriving and varied gay scene. which is littered with lots of different bars catering to all sorts of happy, cheerful people whose only common thread is that they enjoy a bit of cock. Or indeed, a bit of quim if they're a lady. That said, we tend not to venture out on the scene – not least because we both feel old and our knees hurt and neither of us can dance. Camp shrieking is heavy on the ears and well, music isn't what it used to be. That said, back in my youth (fucking hell you'd think I was 70, not coming up to thirty) I had some good times on there, dancing (well, more 'fitting' in tune to the music) and trying to hide my man-tits.

This sounds like stereotypical fiction but I can assure you, on the life of my poor old nana, that it's true – I once got in a fight with a lesbian over whose turn it was to use the pool table. It gets better – there was previous bad blood between us because I interrupted her Anastasia marathon to put the Grease megamix on the 'Choose Your Own Music' jukebox. The whole situation couldn't have been more stereotypical unless I had thrown my campari over her and she'd come at me with a powertool and dungarees before we settled it with a dance-off. Along very similar lines, my ex-boyfriend once had a chair thrown at him by a raging lady who (genuinely mistakenly) thought he was taking a picture of her across the pub. He was actually taking a picture of me trying to carry drinks whilst pissed, not her – he didn't have his wide angle lens for one thing.

The Eagle is about the only bar where we'd be welcomed with something other than a pair of pursed lips and a snide comment about our attire, but it's not really for us. Admittedly, we both go for the more 'manly' type (hence we found each other) (because I'm so masculine it hurts, naturally) and we'd be in our element in a bar like that, but of course, because it's a manly bar, it's instantly all about sex and it is incredibly seedy. There's a gloryhole in the gents, for goodness sake. For those unfamiliar with what a gloryhole is, it's essentially a hole drilled into the side of a cubicle wall where someone might pop their dingaling through in the vain hope of satisfaction. Well honestly. The only thing I want popping into my peripheral vision when I'm using the lavatory is a fresh, cooled roll of Quilted Velvet for my nipsy, not some angry looking willy with its owner hidden from sight. I'd be tempted to stick the toilet roll on it and use it as a dispenser. Still, each to their own. There was a tale that used to go round that some vengeful ex took a knife in there and sliced off his partner's schlong as he popped it through. It all goes on!

twochubbycubs on: hairstyles

Want to know something embarrassing?

The first MP3 I ever downloaded was The Boy Is Mine by Brandy and Monica. Good lord! I was a country boy growing up in a council house in BHS adult-sized trousers, I don't think I was ready for all that ghettofabulousness. I'm surprised the download made it past all the porn, mind, though I don't doubt it took twenty minutes to download. Kids these day don't know how lucky they are. Could have been worse – one of the first CDs I owned by Doesn't Really Matter by Janet Jackson. Argh, I really had a thing for a marimba and sass.

The reason I am rambling on about music is because it's an integral part of writing this blog – I can't write unless I have music playing and no distractions, and even then I'll spend forty minutes trying to find something I want to listen to on Spotify. It's very distressing – a whole world of music and I always end up coming back to the same twenty or so songs. Paul hates it, because I always end up singing along and my voice sounds like a cat being pushed through a mangle, plus I add new notes and words into the lyrics, so a simple beautiful verse becomes peppered with falling scales and swearwords.

Anyway. I'm a bit pushed for time tonight so instead of words, I'm going to show you something. Something

AWFUL. You may remember from my About Me page that it's always been a hope and a dream of mine to get into the newspapers holding out my fat-bloke trousers after I'd lost so much weight? Well, when I was 18 I managed it! My hair though, seriously. I used to have hair like Enya in her Orinoco Flow video.

I'd give anything for a chance at that long hair again, though I wouldn't have it quite such a sex-offender colour. Plus those trousers! 46". Christ. Plus, white jeans. Never give a fat bloke white jeans, they'll always have chocolate in their pockets and it'll look like they've shit themselves when they stand up. What I didn't mention in that article is how seething I was about losing out at the Slimmer of the Year finals to some black-footed leviathan who was too fat to get on an operating table. I didn't have a sob story.

Ah well. It's not like the haircuts ever got worse. Well, save for the Myra Hindley...

twochubbycubs on: neighbours

I can't quite believe Neighbours is still going, let alone celebrating 30 years on the air. I was always a Home and Away man myself, partly because as a fat child I couldn't be bothered getting up to turn the channel over after Fun House. I remember the great disasters like it was yesterday – the big flood, the earthquake, Evil Ailsa, telling my mum she looked like Irene who used to run the diner. Good times! I spotted the 30th anniversary trailer for Neighbours before on TV and I'm happy to confirm that yes, I DO still look like Harold. Mind, that would make Paul Madge, so that really quite tickles me.

Oh, speaking of being tickled, I've had a great ten minutes. See, we use something called Spotify which allows you to listen to thousands and thousands of different music tracks. All very exciting. We've got Premium which means you can access your playlists on the move and Paul's phone syncs his music through his car. However, I've learned that I can log in from home and change the music playing in his car whilst he's out and about. Anyway, he's out driving people to a young Marxist meeting, and I've been making all sorts play in the car (Heaven Must Be Missing An Angel by Tavares, Lovin' You by Minnie Ripperton and my personal favourite, Can You Feel The Love Tonight from The Lion King). His response was a smidge curt.

I hope he doesn't kiss his mother with that mouth. Although that would explain his stubble burn.

Anyway, yes, Neighbours – or indeed neighbours, was what has been on my mind.

When Paul and I first started shagging 'going steady', we moved into a flat on Newcastle's Quayside, seduced by the fabulous views of a concrete factory and the Millennium bridge. It was lovely but the entire block of flats were taken up by the kind of pretentious, rah-rah-rah knobheads who we both loathe with a passion. We had a homeless man living in the bin store, shitting everywhere, and someone set up a 'collection point' for him. Now, I'm a liberal guy, I really am, but I don't want to tread in human shit every time I put my bins out. It's not a lot to ask. Our neighbour downstairs used to have cracking arguments with his girlfriend mind which provided much hilarity until we thought he had belted her and so we called the police. They never talked to us again after that. Well, briefly – Paul had been drying some boxer shorts on the balcony when the wind caught a particularly well-worn pair and blew them over the edge and sadly, because the girlfriend of the lad downstairs was out smoking on her balcony, they landed right on the top of her head. She thought we had done it deliberately and launched an absolute torrent of abuse, we probably didn't help by shutting the balcony door and screaming with laughter. Oh dear. We only lasted two years there before moving out, with the prevalent memory of the place being the black suede headboard in the master bedroom. Well, it wasn't black when we left, let me tell you. It looked like a Jackson Pollock painting – what can I say, we were young and keen in those days, and who the fuck chooses black suede as a headboard? Frankly, we needed something laminated.

We then moved to Gosforth into a Tyneside flat, which was slightly less salubrious but a lot more homely. The only problem was our neighbour upstairs, who came down for a vodka when we moved in and then turned completely mad. She was the type who'd happily clatter around on her cheap lino in her best Primarni heels when she rolled in at 3am with that night's bus-stop encounter gelling on her thigh, but would hammer on the floor and yell about the noise if I so much as yawned. For a good few weeks we crept about underneath like the fucking Borrowers, which was incredibly difficult for two twenty stone blokes to do, before realising that we weren't being unreasonably noisy, she was, and that we should really get our revenge. Luckily, that was fairly easy.

In our bedroom was a grand, open fireplace which had been somewhat shoddily sealed off by someone putting a slab of stone just above the grate. Her bedroom, immediately above ours, shared the same chimney. Sound was usually muffled thanks to the stone but, after we moved it slightly, we were able to get up to all sorts of mischief. We'd wait until we knew she was in bed, move the stone a tiny bit, and fart up the chimney. As I said before, we are big blokes, and frankly, we fart like bulls at the best of times, but we used to store them up to the point of stomach pains just so we could blow them up the chimney. It must have sounded like someone was practicising the tuba in the chimney stack, especially given how the sound would amplify. We'd also make off-putting sex noises if she had anyone round and, in what I think was the most inspired move, we played a load of Roy Walker sound-clips (like Chris Moyles' Car Park Catchphrase) when she had her mother around. She moved out about a month afterwards and silence fell. When she left, we felt able to tidy up the patch outside the house, and planted lots of nice flowers which was grand until the snooty moo to the left of us came downstairs and criticised our cheap pots. Cheap! We were on a budget back then, and anyway, it was the rougher end of Gosforth, not bloody somewhere posh. Our retaliation was swift – we went to Poundland, bought all manner of garish gnomes, plastic frogs, tatty windmills and other such flimflam until our garden looks like a roadside memorial to a boy-racer. She never talked to us after that, although I drove past the flat the other day and there's still a god-awful, sun-bleached frog in the front garden so whoever has the house now must have THE worst taste ever.

Finally, we moved to our current house, and it's perfect – why? Because we have no immediate neighbours.

We're a detached bungalow!

twochubbycubs on: wealth

There was a TV programme smeared on BBC One called Britain's Spending Secrets? Did anyone catch it? It was presented by Anne Robinson, who, despite being only one facelift from having a second pair of lips to talk through, I rather like. She's disarming yet dangerous – I always feel that if I was to talk to her I'd start off joking about boobs and end up confessing to being making super speed soup out of Shergar. I love how that sounds as a sentence. All those S's. Ssss.

Anyway the reason I bring up Wednesday's TV like it's even slightly relevant is because of how angry it made me. The show itself was the usual bit of evening fluff where some people talk about having money, some talk about not having money, the presenter (attempts to) smiles her way through having to sit on someone's Perfect Home settee and disguise the fact she wants to go home and boil wash her Etro blazer. And of course, being the BBC, it's all done without the malice that would have accompanied it if the show had been on Channel 5, which seems to have morphed into the 'Benefits' channel, where even the most mundane activity has been turned into an excuse to film fat people struggling off the sofa whilst that fucking annoying pizzicato violin music plays.

Fact for you: it's called Dance of the Woodland Pixies. Youtube it and you'll feel like Alex Polizzi, checking hotel toilets for pubes and looking disdainful.

Part of the show involved swapping two mothers over – one from a 'buy buy buy' family, the other from a 'save save save' lot. Predictable snipping. You can expect that. No, what made my blood turn to piss was the sight of the 'rich' family sneering at the 'poor family'. The mother of the rich family made a big point about how she bought her daughters anything they wanted, that it is better to live for today and enjoy your money rather than worry what is coming (not completely untrue) and that labels made her happy. That's fine, save for the fact she was instilling the same virtue in her daughter, who stood laughing at the 'poor' mother because she had the temerity to buy her stuff from a car boot sale. If I had been so openly disrespectful when I was little the skin on my arse would have looked like a slab of beef.

I could vaguely understand her reasoning if she had a gorgeous house and enough money in the bank to wipe her arse with £50 notes, but she actually had quite a run-down looking home, an average salary and a husband who walked behind her at all times. There was such an air of undeserved condescension about her that I almost bit clean through my cocoa cup. I can't work my head around those who live their lives through what the label on their handbag says or what the tags on the back of their coats read. The only label I ever take notice of on a person is if they have 'CAUTION: BITES' pinned to their shirt. There's no shame in having nice things but to use your shitty labels to pour scorn on others? Harumph.

Of course, if we're going to be mean about the whole thing, she was prattling on in Debenhams (where all the well-to-do folk shop, naturally) about how she doesn't blink twice about paying for a label because it's the first thing people notice about her...well it wasn't for Paul and me. We noticed her bad hair-dye job (sweetcorn yellow) and the fact that she thought a Radley handbag was the height of sophistication far quicker than we did notice her fanciness. Inner ugliness always shows, no matter how much 'expensive' make-up you trowel on.

Rest assured, if Paul and I had money, we wouldn't be spending it on expensive clothes. I don't see the point. Frankly, as long as my cock isn't hanging out (which thanks to most of my jeans having a split in them, it normally is) and my tits aren't on show, I'm fine and dandy in cheap clothes. Let's all go to Tesco, where Jaymes buys his best clothes, la-la-la-la.

No, if we won the lottery, especially if we won one of those ridiculous figures where your brain really has to think to work out exactly what the zeroes mean, we'd spend it having a bloody great whale of a time. I don't think I'd ever move again, for one thing. We'd have a chef, a driver, a decent PA, someone to come in and wash my belly-shelf. I'd like to think I'd be generous but I reckon we'd turn into evil rich people within approximately 30 minutes – paying Disney for the sole use of their parks and then sitting at the gates turning kids away, that kind of thing. I'd go round to all my exes with a car made of gold coins and jeer at them from the window. There'd be so many holidays that coming home would be having a rest.

Would I work? Would I fuckity. I must write my resignation letter in my head at least twice a week, and I actually enjoy my job, so if I had money behind me, I'd never work again. I can't bear that, you know, when some yellow-eyed binman wins a few million and promises to carry on working. No! You don't get to keep working, give your job to someone else and get yourself a new liver, you joyless bugger.

Ah, a boy can dream.

twochubbycubs on: IKEA, again

Blimey. What a day. I knew there was something the matter with us when we starting planning our day at IKEA. ON A BASTARD BANK HOLIDAY. IKEA is pure hell at the best of times – one of these places that makes you think you're going to have a wonderful day bouncing about on sofa cushions and bean bags and being one big giggling family with a hot dog and an ice cream at the end, when the reality is actually you spending one floor staring intensely into the back of someone's head because they're walking far too slowly, and the second floor wanting to just die because you're SICK OF THIS SHIT ALREADY. So, against our better judgement, that's what we did today.

But with a difference.

After having the Ikea experience on multiple occasions for big projects (like the kitchen) we've eventually got this all down to a tee. So, down to the second, we had the whole day planned out that minimised any interaction with slow-walking, gormless members of the public, ordered a new living room set, refunded a dodgy kitchen door (that I accidentally drilled through – eeehwhatamilike) and threw in a breakfast for good measure. Well, you need that energy if you're going to mutter 'FUCKING MOVE' under your breath every ten seconds.

We arrived on the dot, just as the revolving door started to move and slyly minced our way through all the shortcuts to get straight to the restaurant – the most important part of the day. Once James had wiped away his tears after noticing they'd gotten rid of the potato cake (NOOOOOOOOOOOOO) we were straight to the BESTÅ stand to fuck around on some crappy little computer bunging cupboards on walls. If you've ever fancied having a sob into some KUNTÅ sidetable go ahead and try and plan your living room on their online planner. It's what I imagine it'd be like to be Stephen Hawking on speed trying to describe the texture of Quark on that little Atari he's got strapped to his chair. Stressful isn't the word. You might as well etch your design it into your arm with a compass and present it the warehouse staff.

I'd fantasised about at least ten ways of dispatching multiple rough sorts on the way to the lighting section. I can never understand the mentality of people who think it's perfectly acceptable to just stop in the middle of an aisle when there's practically a stampede of guffawing Geordies rampaging towards you (not unlike that scene in the Lion King but with a lot more polyester and teenage pregnancies). I bet those people are also those that pull their trolley across in a supermarket like a barrier. I'm far too polite (cowardly) though to ever say anything. I just stare at them like I'm trying to burn through them with laser-beam eyes. James isn't quite so composed and will just barge through shouting at people to 'MOVE!', like a hairy snow plough. He almost ran someone off the road simply for having the temerity of having a mauve car.

Fortunately though the whole day was a success, despite all the eejits and lack of an ice cream at the end and we got everything sorted. They even managed to refund us the drawer and door that I ballsed up without a receipt. God love 'em. As a thank you I was sure to press the green smiley face button that measures people's happiness as many times as I could. I'd like to think it made a difference.

One way we always make our IKEA experience a little more fun is to watch out for any couples that are eyeing up a particular piece of furniture. If either of them makes a muttering that they quite like it we'll always come up behind them and then start slagging it off. 'Oh that's fucking gopping', or, "Oh lord, I've never seen anything as tacky as THAT in my life'. They'll soon walk off and have a tiff a little further on. Oh we're such terrors.

twochubbycubs on: sausages, naturally

Now look here. I wasn't going to do a post tonight because my eyes hurt and I'm too busy putting together a lamp (so manly) but the word sausagefest came into my mind and I just had to use it. So, with that in mind, I'm going to dash off a very quick review of Slimming World sausages and Musclefood's chicken sausages. We're working with Musclefood to sort out a deal for you lot and I'll post that nearer the time.

Before that, because you know I can't go a day without some toe-curling moment of embarrassment, well, as I've documented a couple of times before, we spend a lot of time hiding away all the sex paraphrenalia in our house whenever a tradesperson comes to visit. I fear there is something off-putting about trying to do some plastering whilst a big black plastic willy winks away at you in the corner like a worm having a stroke. Well see the downside of doing this is that you invariably forget where you've put stuff and then it appears at a dramatic moment. Like today, with our alarm man (who was lovely and very charming) who opened our rarely-opened alarm cupboard, took the latch off the alarm case (which doesn't work, so we just use it to hide stuff) only to be confronted by a black prostate tickler that we had squirreled away many moons ago.

Now he had the good grace not to say anything but given I have a slight ping-ding about the fact he might be travelling on the same bus as Paul and I, he totally knew what it was. What could I do? I couldn't reach across him, grab it and pretend it was a novelty cigarette lighter, because knowing my luck he'd have been a smoker, asked for a light and I'd have to spend five minutes flicking the 'hook' end and lightly buzzing the end of his Silk Cut Ultra.

So that's that. Anyway, back to sausages. We're massive fans of sausages (and I'm not even using sausage as a euphemism for a cock there, because if I WAS trying to come up with a euphemism for a penis, I'd of course use Spurt Reynolds) but they are tricky little things. Most of the low-fat sausages have as much taste as a roll of loft insulation, and anything with a bit of moisture is normally so bad for you that Margaret's blue WKD bottle would shatter in her clenched fist if she so much as heard them sizzle in your pan. So we'll cover two: Slimming World sausages and Musclefood's chicken sausages.

Quorn sausages are a bust as they look and taste like something that's been shat out of a poorly cat, so I'm not even going to mention them. I'd get more taste and enjoyment from sucking my thumb and hell, I know where my thumb has been. No wonder my nails are always filthy.

We cook our sausages in an Actifry. If you're on the fence about one of these, bloody get one. You'll never look back, seriously. Above everything else, it's the thing we love most in the kitchen. Well no, the thing we love most in the kitchen is staring at the neighbour over the road trying to reverse the world's smallest car onto the world's largest driveway and still making a proper bloody fist of it. I reckon Stevie Wonder could comfortably reverse back into the same space in less time. Anyway.

twochubbycubs on: our Irish holiday: part one

You may remember me mentioning that we had no plans and were planning a last-minute holiday away wherever we could find a cheap deal to a decent place? Well let me tell you – don't bother. The only available flights were to places which you just know will be full of bald English men with red shoulders reading The Sun and eating full English breakfasts at 4pm. Bleugh. I don't like flying – the thought of flying somewhere with such little reward just ruled going abroad at last-minute completely out. So, the night before we set off, we booked a holiday cottage in the absolute middle of nowhere in the Ring of Kerry, Ireland, and at 5pm the next day our car was packed, Paul had been picked up and we were on our way in no time at all. I normally hide away the sat-nav for reasons below but intrigue got the better of me as to how far I had to drive and the sat-nav was plugged in and on the dash within ten minutes.

Sat-navs are great in principle but I always end up putting mine sulkily away in the glove box after approximately five minutes. We bought a proper fancydan version in the sales but see, I hate being told what to do when I'm driving and struggle with the authority it commands in the car. I always have good intentions of listening to it and indeed, it's never failed to guide us where we need to go, but I still have an inherent distrust and because Paul always sides with the sat-nav, it causes arguments. Plus, it only has two male voices, Daniel and Kevin. Kevin is a sarcastic knobhead so he immediately gets turned off but Daniel has been upgraded to this weird breathy version who almost whispers the commands at us like some robotic milk-tray man. I don't know how appropriate it is to have a semi whilst driving around the Bangor ring-road but there you have it.

We arrived in Bangor at around ten and, due to being full of wine gums and other sweets, went straight to bed. We'd elected to stay at a Premier Inn but this is always a mistake – not because they're uncomfortable, quite the opposite actually – I've always had a great night's sleep at a Premier Inn – but rather I spend all night scheming and plotting about how I might make my money back under their 'Guaranteed Good Night's Sleep' promise. The problem with that is, I've always found the staff so nice and disarming that I immediately become charming and submissive and don't dare mention any perceived problem with the room. Bah. We sped down towards Holyhead in the morning and we were at the dock in plenty of good time to sit and wait in the gales and mist before it was time to board the ferry.

Oh! Before I carry on with the tale, let me mention Paul's idea of breakfast. As we didn't have time to hoover up an all-you-can-eat-breakfast at the Premier Inn, I bustled him into Holyhead ASDA with the direction of getting a breakfast snack for us. He came back with a knock-off, Iron Curtain version of those awful Lunchable things. Haway. It was a little packet which contained a cheesestring, a wrap so dry I could have shaved my three-day-stubble with it, a sachet of knock-off tomato ketchup and some sliced rolled chicken. It was unspeakably vile.

I opened the packet and I swear it hissed when I pulled the lid back. The car smelt like someone had shit out a corpse on the back seat. We got fifty yards down the road before I pulled over and Paul, now with a considerable flea in his ear, had to dispose of the 'meal' in the nearest bin. Honestly Holyhead, get your act together. I had tears in my eyes as we drove past McDonalds to the ferry port, let me tell you. Anyway...

You know what I love about the English? The very second they perceive anyone to be at any sort of advantage to them, they start bitching – and this is compounded if they've paid extra. Let me explain. Paul and I paid an extra £10 each way on the ferry to be given priority boarding, disembarkation (is that a needlessly clumsy word or what) and access to the Stena lounge. It is the ferry equivalent of first class and we only bought it because the seats in the lounge looked moderately comfortable and there was promise of free snacks. Accordingly, when we drove into the port, we were asked to drive into one of two 'Premium' lanes. We parked up and had the windows down only to hear the whisker-faced woman, putting the Tena in Stena Line, in the Audi (shock! horror!) to my right immediately start bitching to her husband that 'they had paid extra' and 'why where we in the second premium lane and they weren't' blah blah. He looked amazingly henpecked. She went on and on and on about the perceived injustice of people boarding ahead of her and only stopped when I put my window back up and we both started laughing at her. I think her mood soured further when we did indeed board first – a whole lane ahead of her – and I gave her and her watery-eyed husband a dainty handwave as we drove past. Stupid old mare that she was – it's not as if those in Premium were going to sailing over on the fucking QE2 and the rest of the passengers were sailing on a floating door.

Once we were loaded onto the ferry, we dashed up the stairs to be the first couple into the 'Stena Plus' lounge. Part of the 'premium' booking is access to this lounge which is controlled by a surly miss and a set of glass doors. We had to give our surname and were ushered in to avail ourselves of the free snacks, which consisted of those little packet of shortbread that you get in cheap hotels and a few cans of Diet Coke. There were some bottles of wine available for those who were already shaking and slurring at 9am in the morning, plus tea and coffee. Once they had allowed all of the steerage passengers onboard and shut them behind the metal gates, we were on our way.

And good lord, what a crossing. We were warned by the captain (via the ship's loudspeaker, not personally – I mean we'd only paid an extra tenner and that had to cover the forty cans of Pepsi that I'd secreted away into my rucksack) that the crossing was going to be rough due to the strong winds and turbulent seas, and he wasn't kidding. The Stena Plus lounge is situated at the front of the ferry and the waves were cresting over the top of the prow as it bobbed up and down. It was awful – it was all I could do to eat my cooked breakfast and fret about whether I'd put the handbrake on, envisioning my car rolling around on the car deck and the weight of our car-snacks causing a frightful Herald of Free Enterprise incident. It was a long four hours – I spent most of it snaffling snacks and gambling in the arcades. Oh and another moan! If you have kids, you don't automatically have the right to use any machine you want or to have people who are altogether more sensible than you to get out of the way just so your crusty-faced little shitmachine can 'have a go at driving'. I know, awful, but some pompous little knobhead with a bristly-little tache and his child took a look into the arcade, saw Paul and I playing Mario Kart Arcade Edition and said to his child 'DON'T WORRY DARLING, YOU'LL BE ABLE TO HAVE A TURN ON THESE KIDS MACHINES WHEN THESE FULLY GROWN MEN HAVE FINISHED'. Honest to God, fully grown men. It was all I could do not to pick up his child and toss him into the Irish sea. I wouldn't mind but we all know that children don't actually play the machines, they just sit making silly noises and taking up space. Frankly, parents should be made to lock their children in the car and they can spend the ferry crossing on the car-deck, well out of the way. The ferry journey passed, eventually.

Now we managed to get all the way to the Ring of Kerry via Holyhead, a ferry and seemingly eight years of twisty roads absolutely fine and without incident, and we were a mile away from our cottage when it all went wrong. We arrived at the right 'area' and that's where we were told to switch off the sat-nag (typo intended) and open up the owner's own directions which would guide us merrily to our cottage in enough time to get the hot-tub going and allow us an hour to flick disdainfully through her CD collection and make snide comments about her glassware.

Well, did they fuck. For a start, she had worded the directions as though as we were in Lord of the Rings, all 'go over the brow of the hill and make a turn (which direction? which hill?)' and 'drive on until you feel a chill'. They were crap. You need to understand how remote the area was – imagine in the pitch black trying to find a remote cottage with not so much as a blinking light anywhere to be seen. It took us three hours – THREE HOURS – of steaming around the countryside along farm tracks screaming and swearing at the perceived injustice of it all. I like to think what the poor horse in the field nearby thought of it all when he saw our car appearing over the crest of a hill for the eightieth time and the last few syllables of a swearing tirade against the Irish, Tom Tom, cottages, Citroen, Enya and Guinness as we sped past. No wonder he got his revenge later in the holiday (that'll be in part 2).

Completely lost and on the verge of driving the car into a peat bog and setting it on fire, we found an isolated little cottage with a light on and knocked on the door. Now imagine that. You're a lady, alone, cooking your evening meal, when two burly bald blokes come mincing up your track and braying on the door asking for directions to 'Cum Bag' (which was our approximate pronunciation of the name of the cottage, which was in Gaelic). The poor lass probably thought she was starring in her own Vera adventure. She took an age to find directions but eventually, helpfully, she sent us on our way. Buoyed with confidence, we shot off and within five minutes we'd taken another wrong turn, driven the car up a forty-five degree incline into a farmer's field and were left spinning the car around in the mud in the pitch black, with Paul outside of the car bellowing directions on where I should reverse and me unable to hear him as I was revving the engine so hard out of sheer, unadulterated anger. Haha. Just to add a cherry on top of this my reverse sensors were blaring away making out there was an obstacle behind me until we realised it was mud on the sensor.

Aaah. We headed back to the road, sulked for a good

fifteen minutes and then decided to go back to the start and try following her directions one final time. We were at the cottage, parked up and steaming, within ten minutes. God knows how, why or what we were doing wrong, but we managed it without a hitch. I was fizzing.

twochubbycubs on: our Irish holiday: part two

MORE CHUNTERING ABOUT IRELAND.

You left us yesterday as we pulled up outside the cottage, and going forward, I'm not going to talk day to day as a lot of the days were the same (pootle about in the car, eat, eat some more, pootle a bit further, eat, stock up on ice-cream and nip back to the cottage in time for Tipping Point) – instead, I'll just rattle off some incidents, high points and thoughts.

First, we managed to cause major offence within twenty four hours. Frankly, if you're of a nervous disposition or candid talk of sex makes you green, just skip ahead a couple of paragraphs.

See, the cottage came with a hot-tub, and we decided to enjoy dusk in the hot-tub completely nude – pity the poor filters having to work overtime to drain out our back-hair and toenails. But, it was incredibly romantic and we were incredibly isolated, with not a soul around us (to the point where, at night, we could look across the valley and see only one solitary light for miles around), and being young, virile young men, we immediately got up to dickens. Well, it was my birthday after all.

Picture the scene – the bubbling of the steamy water, music playing through the iPad, the rhymthic sound of the jets, the twilit light bouncing off Paul's wobbling buttocks (it would look like the Mitchell brothers were hiding just under the water), me playing a mean tune on the old ham trumpet – perfectly romantic for a married couple. Well yes, until a honking big tractor appeared at the end of the garden less than thirty foot away. How we had missed it was understandable – Paul was facing the other way and I was always told not to talk with my mouth full – but how the hell the farmer didn't see until he was parked up I have no clue. Looking back, there would have been a hedge blocking his view until about 40 foot away, and then he probably just thought he was committed.

Good lord. You've never seen two people spring back as quick as we did – it was like someone had dropped a toaster in the water. Half the water in the hot-tub sloshed over the side exposing even more of our milky-white frames. Mind, he was no better – he looked like your very personification of a hard-bitten farmer – tattered cloth cap, wax jacket from the eighties, face like a drained field, and he ambled over with his hand pulling the brow of his cap over his eyes like he was Icarus approaching the sun. When really, it was the FULL MOON he should have been worried about. He spluttered something about the oil heating and asked if everything was alright – I assume, anyway, because we couldn't hear or understand a word of what he said and I certainly wasn't going to engage him in any chatter whilst my boobs blew around in the hot-tub jets. He sharp got back in his tractor and almost did a donut on the gravel drive way trying to get away.

So that killed the mood. To be honest, I'm not a massive fan of the hot-tub, it's what people with bad taste buy when they win the lottery. What might look glamorous on the deck of a gorgeous chalet in the Alps doesn't look quite so alluring pressed up beside a mouldy shed and the frame of a B&Q value trampoline in a shitpit in Southend. Nothing quite says class like drinking Bellabrusco from a plastic beaker as multi-coloured LEDs illuminate your bumhole. Anyway, that didn't stop us, and despite it being a proper fan-on, we used that hot-tub several more times throughout the holiday.

However, I'm not convinced the filter was working correctly, because towards the end of the holiday, the water became murkier and murkier and started to smell. Not that such trifling matter stopped us – here, we're Geordie, divven't ya knaa – but I don't think you should have to crack the top of the water like a crème brûlée before you get in.

Actually, that's not even the end of the hot-tub tale, and nor was it the only time we were surprised by an unwelcome visitor. See, on one of the nights that we spent in the hot-tub under the stars, the local horse made an appearance, looming out of the dark about 5 foot away from Paul's head and promptly did that noise that horses make when they blow air through their

315

noses. Paul shit himself – no wonder the filters didn't work – but soon calmed down when he realised what it was. All was well until the horse bit him on the head – at that point we called it a night. Ah, nature.

Well now look at that – see this is why I couldn't write for a living, I've spent eight paragraphs talking about hot-tubs!

twochubbycubs on: our Irish holiday: part three

You may remember that I said I wasn't going to talk in a chronological fashion about our trip to Ireland? Well there's a reason – me saying that we went out driving each day doesn't sound alluring, so, here's some more random scattershot thoughts about our holiday, in no particular order.

The first town that we visited was a tiny little village called Waterville, which was actually quite charming. However, it didn't bode especially well given everything was shut bar one fish shop (I don't do fish) and a 'crafts' shop. I can't stand 'crafts'. I just can't. Everything about craft shops wind me up, from the nonsense tat on offer to the twiddley-dee music playing to the judgemental looks that your leather shoes get from Astrid Moonglow behind the counter. But who buys this shit anyway? Who has ever walked into a craft shop and said 'Now that's just what I've been looking for – the entire works of B*Witched played on a pan-pipe and fiddle' or, to that end, what sums up a holiday more than an shamrock-shaped ashtray with 'I ❤ Ireland' emblazoned on it in flaking gold Mistral? I've never felt the need to fragrance my home with incense sticks which smell like lavender and burning hair and nor do I feel the need to dry my dishes with a teatowel with Daniel O'Donnell's slightly warped face on it. Frankly, I wouldn't dry my arse with a picture of Daniel O'Donnell but that's entirely beside the point. We did the very 'us' thing of tutting at the window as we walked past and spent a good five minutes wondering how the hell a craft shop in the arse-end of Ireland stays profitable enough to remain open on a grey, dismal day when suddenly our questions were answered by the sight of an David Urquhart coach straining over the horizon and about 300 Chinese tourists bustling out to take pictures of an inexplicable Charlie Chaplin statue.

As an aside, I had to google David Urquhart there to check the spelling and amongst reviews of his coach company, I found reviews for a Pontins resort which were titled 'NOT AS BAD AS IT COULD HAV BEEN' (spelling hers, not mine). Is there ever a sentence that sums up a shit holiday more than that? And the reviews and photos are ghastly – it looks like a prison camp. That said, Paul and I are definitely going to one of these places, if only so I can practice my 'well isn't that just LOVELY' face for a week'.

We also visited Sneem, which to me sounds like an especially complicated part of the penis – you know, like 'Hannah found Geoffrey would agree to anything, especially when she flicked his sneem and prodded his barse'. It was lovely, although I caused immediate and swift embarrassment to poor Paul when he got out of the car to avail of the public lavatory, as I whirred the window down, shouted 'I HOPE THERE'S NO BLOOD IN YOUR SHIT THIS TIME HUN' and drove off down the street, much to the disgusted and aghasted looks of the nearby tourists. He only started talking to me once I'd bought him a Nutella ice-cream. Paul's easy to win around in an argument (tickle his sneem) – basically, the naughtier I've been, the more saturated fats have got to be pumped into him – like a blood transfusion but with a bag of Starmix hanging on the drip stand. In fact, Sneem had rather a lot of lovely places to eat – we tried The Village Kitchen (twice) and it was amazing – they serve black pudding on the pizza, and what's not to like about that? Mmm. Irontacular.

Fun fact – Sneem's own website actually describes the village as 'The Knot in the Ring of Kerry'. Now come on, someone's having a laugh there, surely? You might as well twin the place with Twatt up in the Shetlands and be done. I'm not even kidding – look for yourself at www.sneem.com. I warn you, the website seems to have been designed on a Game Boy Colour by Stevie Wonder.

We had to leave Sneem as we were told, in hushed, dramatic tones like someone imparting a nuclear code or warning of an oncoming plague, that there was a tractor rally happening and the roads would be chaos. Good heavens – why there wasn't a full BBC News crew there I still don't know. I tease I tease, I know you need to find excitement where you can in a place like that – trust me, I grew up in a tiny village where the only excitement was the fortnightly library and wanking, though not at the same time, and certainly not with the librarian as she had a bigger beard than I did.

Whilst I'm here, driving around Ireland – and in particular, the Ring of Kerry, was an unending joy. The rain (which we love, so didn't bother us) kept most of the other tourists at bay and it felt like we had the place to ourselves. They could do with levelling out some of the roads though because good lord it was bumpy (not helped by the fact that as usual I was driving like I'd stolen the car from the Garda). I was always told to drive like I had a pint of milk on the dashboard and I didn't want to spill it – by the time I'd finished it would have been butter. I did show a little restraint after a particularly pronounced bump in the road where I almost turned the car into a convertible using nought but my own head.

I did manage to get stuck behind a caravan – almost inevitably – and immediately started turning the air blue due to the fact I couldn't get past. I'm not against caravans – it's nice that the happily celibate and doubly incontinent have a place to rest their heads – but I could have parked my car, lay down in the road and farted my way home and it would have been quicker. Every turn in the road required shifting down to first and piloting his Shitbox 3000 round the corner like it was made out of tissue and the branches on the tree were broken glass. I managed to overtake with Paul holding my left hand down so I couldn't stick my fingers up at him as I went past. There's no need to drive so bloody slowly!

That burst of anger seems like a good place to leave it, actually.

twochubbycubs on: our Irish holiday: part four

Anyway, back to Ireland, where you may remember we were spending an awful amount of time driving around and being snotty about craft shops? Well rest assured that this continued unabated. But first, an observation. See, Paul and I have the type of marriage where we can openly discuss other good-looking men without one of us throwing a paddy and waving a pair of blunt scissors at the other's cock, and as a result we were looking forward to seeing plenty of rough-hewn Irish farmer types with bushy beards and big soft eyes strutting around. Well, pfft. For a start, everyone was about 2ft tall. Seriously, they'd have blinded themselves if they'd pulled their socks up. Plus, weedy – apparently despite only having shops that sell Daniel O'Donnell tat and Guinness fiddle-faddle the men have found somewhere that sells those bloody awful Abercrombie and Fitch hoodies and tiny pin-leg jeans. THAT'S NOT MANLY. I even saw a man-bun (and you may remember how I feel about that) on someone serving diesel in the last petrol station before civilisation ended. I bet if we go back in a year there will be burgers in brioche buns and someone drinking out of a watering can. Pissheads. Scotland has the best blokes – then England, then Wales, then Ireland.

We visited a chocolate factory. I say visited, Paul barely had time to register the words coming up on the turn-off sign before I had swerved the car across the road and into the car-park. I swear I was inside at the tasting station before he'd even unsuckered the sat-nav from the windscreen. MIND. It was a bit of a stretch to call it a chocolate factory, given it seemed to consist of a few lovely Irish ladies melting chocolate nips and scattering orange peel into it. That said, we still stocked up, ostensibly on gifts for our co-workers, but I'm not exaggerating when I tell you that we had one of the giant chocolate slabs open before we'd even pulled out of the car park. We rationalised it by thinking that, as we'd seemingly shored up Ireland's deficit by buying so much chocolate, the decent thing to do would be to enjoy it. Plus, they'd been a bit stingy with the 'free tasting' considering the amount of money we'd spent – I can remember even now seeing Paul's watery eyes and downturned mouth when she went to put away the tray of free chocolate.

We also visited the "Most Beautiful Cliffs in Kerry" – which I personally think lived right up to the name. It's a strong, bold claim and we almost didn't get to see it. Not because of bad weather, or the access being closed…no, because we were so full of chocolate that we drove straight past when we saw 'only a five minute walk from the car-park' on the side. Isn't that mortifyingly lazy? But I've been each and every person reading this has done something similar. I mean, it was just so warm in the car, and a cliff is a bloody cliff…right? We drove on for another ten minutes before we had to turn back around and go see the bloody cliffs, so ashamed were we by our own bloody laziness. But we're glad we did, because the view was amazing!

Despite the two minute walk being more like a ten minute gentle stroll up a gradient that a marble would struggle picking up speed rolling down, it was more than worth it, even if Paul did struggle with the defibrillator at the end. My sense of injustice was piqued by the gypsy (genuinely, I'm not just being racist) who charged me €4 to park the car and gave us a ticket to view the cliffs, but I didn't fancy arguing with someone who had colour-ordinated his brown change purse with his nicotine-lacquered teeth.

We visited an immeasurable number of beaches, and by god I'll never forget them, not least because I'm still pouring out a good half of them onto my living room carpet at the end of the day. One afforded us the chance, thanks to a stern warning that we simply mustn't go on the rocks (which we immediately did), to reinact that bit where old Jelly Belly Harold Bishop fell into the sea and Madge was left shouting HAAAAARULD at the crashing waves after she found his glasses in a rockpool.

Seriously, every day with us is full of nonsense like this. If we're not re-enacting famous soap deaths – I've done Jim Robinson before, complete with quacks and a rolling orange, we're yelling Titanic quotes at each other. Plus, we left behind some free advertising by etching our site address in the sand for any passing fatty that might be struggling to use up that tub of quark.

Here, one final thing. The cottage had an amazing cottage but clearly attracted the sort of people who were braggarts and fancydans when it came to their wine, to the point where each person staying had placed an empty bottle of their best wine on top of the kitchen cupboards (quite a task, given how high up they were – I had to really stretch and I'm tall enough to be continued). And oh lord, people had signed them too – and the names read like a Vegan's Anonymous meeting, all Cressy and Johnathanial and suchlike.

So, in the sense of causing mischief, we added our own – the biggest bottle of blue WKD we could get our greasy mitts on. I've never drank blue WKD in my life, I don't think. It's like wearing Lynx, once you've actually had sex, it should be beneath you. Anyway. I tell you what's below me? My feet. My feet which aren't cheesy.

twochubbycubs on: our Irish holiday: part five

The day for us leaving came around quicker than you can say 'hot-tub indiscretion' and we left the cottage at a bright and breezy 7am, taking a long video of the place to show that we'd done do damage. Ever the tightarse, me. We immediately ran into a problem – we had to take our bag of general rubbish down to a waste disposal centre as the bin lorries don't operate up to the cottage. At 7am on a bank holiday weekend in rural Ireland, that's quite hard. We spent thirty minutes driving around, with Paul wedged in the passenger seat with a honking bag of rubbish in between his legs, leaking nasty bin juice in my car. After several attempts at finding somewhere to ditch it (there, of course, being no bins anywhere) we eventually tied a five euro note to one of the handles and left it on someone's drive. Well honestly, I wasn't going to take it home as a bloody souvenir. Sorry Ireland.

Of course, thanks to my keen-as-mustard driving (plus the 85mph speed limit – so that's 95mph in real money) and excellent navigation skills, we arrived at the port a good ninety minutes before we were allowed to board. Ninety minutes isn't long enough to go anywhere and do anything so we ended up having a morose coffee in a service station served by someone who clearly used the same cloth for cleaning both his armpits and the grill-pan. Every time he leant over our table to pour a coffee I felt the skin on my face tighten like I was looking into a bonfire. There's no excuse for body odour at all – a bottle of Mum can be picked up for a matter of pennies. Excessive sweating is fair enough – we're all fat here – and it's something I used to get so worried about that I'd barely put my arm up at school in case I had a wet-patch under my arms. For three years they thought my mother had been at the thalidomide until they saw my arm at full length reaching for an extra slice of chocolate and orange cornflake-cake at lunch and called off the doctors. We supped our coffee and, noticing that I had a few Euros scratching around in my pockets, I bought a scratchcard for €2. And won €4. So I bought a €4 scratchcard and promptly won €5. I chanced my luck, bought a €5 card and won another fucking €5. So I doubled down and bought a €10 scratchcard, with B.O Bill congratulating my excellent luck. I won fuck all. You may think I'm being melodramatic when I say I left the place in tears but I wasn't upset, my eyes were just streaming from the vinegary heat-haze rippling from his armpit. I've never known the air in a café to shimmer.

The ferry crossing was uneventful – nothing more to report than the hilarity of watching people trying to light a cigarette on the deck when faced with a nice gale and the swell of the sea. By god they were determined, and I know the feeling being an ex-smoker, but it looked bloody hilarious. I swear you could drop a smoker behind the engine of a Boeing 747 going full-pelt and they'd still be tucking their head into their jumper and spinning the wheel on their lighter like a desperate suicide bomber. We tried to gamble but without any pound coins, we couldn't, so we spent three hours playing Peggle and cramming as many free cans of Diet Coke as we could into my suitcase. If the ship had taken a lurch and I'd slipped over on deck I reckon the resulting explosion of fizz on my back would have sent me clear into the Irish sea like the gayest distress flare Holyhead had ever seen. Upon disembarkation (really) it was like we had cataracts – the fog was so heavy and dense that suddenly a 250 mile drive back to Newcastle at 50mph didn't seem so alluring. We tried to book back into the Bangor Premier Inn for another night of unrivalled Welsh glamour only to be told that there was no rooms left. Bah. Obviously everyone had the same idea as us – get to a hotel and sleep out the fog which was blanketing the country. A desperate search on a shite mobile reception told us that there was two rooms left at a Premier Inn in Widnes, but due to us stopping to buy some sour strawberry laces and Paul needing his usual eighty nine pisses, we got there just a moment too late as a family checked in just in front of us. No idea if they'd had a room booked for months and were just there as planned, but I was so put out that I did a silent fart on the way out to foul their reception. And trust me, after a week of rich food and Irish treats, it didn't smell of peaches.

We decided to head for Wakefield. The glitz! The glamour! The incest! I joke. A room was secured and comfort awaited but before we got there, we pulled over for our evening meal at a services. By, was that depressing. At 11pm on a Sunday the only option open to us was a Ginsters pasty, a Kitkat and a bottle of water. Delightful. I did spend a few minutes playing the slots despite knowing it's a mugs game but actually, we won £20. Tell you what though, we left depressed. See, next to us was a middle-aged woman who was feeding £10 notes into the machine and spinning the slots for £2 a time. She was there when we went in, she was there as we played and she was there when we left – if she hadn't spent over £200 I'd eat my hat. Whilst we were in WH Smith I was being nosy and keeping an eye on her (well, truth be told, I was waiting until she fucked off so I could empty the machine myself) and in walks her husband, rolling along like a disgruntled potato. He asked when she was coming out, she said 'I'M ABOUT TO FUCKING WIN'. He had their tiny daughter with him and she looked knackered. Suddenly it wasn't quite so funny. As we left, the mother was still there pumping the notes into the machine, and the dad and daughter were outside sitting in a car. Nearly midnight on a bank holiday. All I could think was what the money now sitting in the machine could buy the kid and how shit her homelife must be. Paul and I are lucky that we can chuck £20 into a slot, have a gamble and walk away if we lose, but this was the ugly side of things. Those machines are nothing other than pure evil – you can gamble £2 every five seconds or so and whilst yes, personal responsibility should kick in, that's easy to say if you don't have a gambling problem. These machines are so good at getting you to risk a bit extra, to gamble your wins, to chase your losses. There's a reason there's always someone playing them. Bastards.

Anyway, onto lighter things. We spent the night in the Premier Inn Wakefield and only woke when poor Svetlanka brayed on the door like we were on the Titanic. We decided on one final naughty meal so nipped over the road to a Brewers Fayre. I'm not a fan of this type of pub – it screams 'Access Day' – but nevertheless, we ordered nachos, hunters chicken and something else so delicious that I've clean forgotten it. Well fuck me, we were back to English food alright – the nachos were a pack of Doritos with some guacamole shoved on it with all the care and panache that an arsonist applies petrol with, the chicken clearly died from thirst given how dry it was (I had to suck the beermat just to moisten me lips) and Paul didn't finish his meal. That's only happened three times in our relationship that I can recall and one of them was when I set the kitchen on fire making cherry samosas. We hurtled back up the A1, said hello to the brassy old tart known as the Angel of the North, and we were home. Cats welcomed us back warmly by showing us their pencil-sharpeners just in case we'd forgotten what they looked like and them immediately meowing to be fed. Don't know what their problem was, we'd left a tin-opener.

twochubbycubs on: saying goodbye

So, where have we been? Well, if you're following us on Facebook, you'll know that we posted a post to say we'd be away for a few days as we had received some bad news. My nana was taken into hospital on Friday morning, ostensibly with a bit of constipation (I had the first few numbers of Dynorod's number already dialled on my phone for once we got the news of a 'delivery'). I then got a text on Friday evening to say things were so much worse than we had imagined, and in the early hours of Saturday morning, she rolled a seven and shuffled off the mortal coil. My parents were by her side and she died peacefully, painlessly in her sleep, tripping the light fantastic on all the good strong drugs the NHS could muster. It's the way we all wished for her to go. She'd been diagnosed with bladder cancer a few weeks before and had decided not to undergo any treatment – she was knocking on ninety, had most definitely had a good few innings, and couldn't be chewed with the idea of being ill or a burden, which she never would have been. Anyway, there were Take a Break crosswords that needed filling in with all sorts of incorrect nonsense:

31 down. Auctioneer's hammer (5): G-A-B-L-E

A good friend of mine messaged me and summed it up nicely – when someone dies, you expect the world to stop, people to be wailing in the street in their widow's weeds, everyone to be so inconsolable that the only thing worth doing is eating Ben and Jerry's Peanut Butter cup by the tubful with watery eyes. It's what my nana would have wanted. But it's not how it works – the world keeps turning, everyone still keeps going and a mortal love becomes a cherished memory, alive only in our minds rather than a slightly inconvenient thirty mile drive away. I never minded really, it gave me an opportunity to do 90mph on the military road. I'm slingshotting between being upbeat and chipper to being despondent and melancholy, which is probably why I'm up this morning at 4am writing this. This post may be incredibly self-indulgent – I'm aware of my wiffly-waffly prose, and any other time I'd be leaning on that delete key until the arrow wore off – but I express myself best through writing and it's strangely cathartic.

See now, I grew up in the same village as my nana and saw her every day until I moved away – and even then, I was clearly a glutton for punishment and paper-thin pastry because we'd make the pilgrimage (first by three separate bus journeys and then finally, by car – she was the catalyst for me eventually learning to drive) to see her nearly every Sunday. My parents looked in on her every day, she had plenty of friends and she lived with my uncle, so she was well-liked, much-loved and well looked after. We were very close – I'd often spend an afternoon with her doing a jigsaw (her key tactic for completing a jigsaw seemed to be attaching random pieces to one another and then smashing them flat with her fist, so you'd end up with a charming vista of the

River Avon only with one of the tiny picnickers on the bank of the river having the exhaust pipe of a Nissan Sunny for a head). We would chat about nonsense, she'd tell me the story of when she had to jump off the bus into a six foot snowdrift for the 376th time, my sister and I would wrap her Christmas presents for her as her approach was to use more sellotape than wrapping paper. All sorts.

Oh, it was definitely Nana, mind. It was never grandma, she said that aged her horribly, though at 89 I don't think she was going to be fooling the Grim Reaper for especially long. She was an incredibly proud and wonderfully loyal person, with keen eyes and a sharp tongue. Her ears were fucked though – there could have been one of those gas explosions that rip a street asunder in the next room and she'd only think the phone was ringing. She never quite got on with her hearing aids, treating them as optional accessories the way one might keep a particularly ungainly set of beige earrings for best. We used to kid that she was receiving a fax when she had them in as they'd be whirring and whistling away. She couldn't hear that, but by god she'd hear if you so much as mouthed a swear word. I use to mouth the word 'VACUUM' (which looks like FUCK YOU if you're lipreading) at Paul across the room and she'd be up remonstrating at me for swearing at 'Poor Paul' and 'Eeee Paul how you put up with him'.

She never had much – she was widowed young with

three children and received very little in the way of support, so she had to balance working with raising children (long before it became socially acceptable to become a 'STAY AT HOME MUVVA' and let Jeremy Kyle and Quavers raise your son whilst you adorn yourself in rancid copperplate writing tattooes of your latest ballsack lover – sorry) and she did it with aplomb. And even then she'd turn that aplomb into aplomb jam. Haha, bit of wordplay for you there. What she did have she shared – you couldn't escape the house without running the gauntlet of:

- "have a slice of this cake, it'll not get eaten"
- "I've just baked this hundredweight of scones, but there's no-one here to eat them"
- "have a sandwich (a risk in itself, she remains the only person I've ever known to put her butter on with a plasterer's trowel and apply salt like one might apply gravy)"
- "I know you're on a diet but I've made you an apple and blackberry pie and it seems a shame to chuck it out"
- "Take this Breville sandwich toaster, last used for Queen Elizabeth's Accession, works just fine as long as you change the plug and the wiring and prise off the half slice of National Loaf stuck to the plates".

Ah it's no wonder I'm fat. Of course, one of the very best things about my nana was her tolerance – I can't remember how she found out I'm a mud-valve engineer but she welcomed Paul with open arms. How many people in their eighties can say they attended a civil partnership? To be fair she probably thought she was at a particularly low-budget version of Judge Rinder but she seems entertained enough. She'd talk of Paul as my husband or partner, none of this 'good friends' business. She did once ask me 'who was the woman' in our relationship but before I drew her a blisteringly hardcore and frank representation, Paul twigged on that she meant who did the cleaning and ironing (remember her age, now, before anyone goes all Millie Tant on me) and explained that heaven's no, we had a cleaner.

So yes, I love my nana, with every part of me, and I can't imagine her not being around, but everyone leaves the stage in the end. I'd swap anything to have her back for another few years of bellowing at me like she was hailing a taxi from across the Irish sea and trying to sneak an entire bag of Aldi Mint Imperials (Mint Industrials) into Paul's pocket because "he doesn't get his fair share". If only she knew! But there's no merit in wishing for the unobtainable, so, I'll suck it up and on we go.

twochubbycubs on: the funeral

Last Friday was the day we put dear old Nana into the oven on gas mark infinity and sent her back to her husband, like some hard-of-hearing Emmett Brown. It was a lovely service, and I didn't laugh once – which amazed me, as I have a nervous laugh. A teacher once told me her husband had hung himself over the summer and I had to excuse myself into the corridor to slap my knees and laugh into my blazer like she'd told me the filthiest knock knock joke ever. I have backwards emotions – it's not that I'm not sympathetic, I'm just emotionally incapable. Isn't that awful?

Of course, the service wasn't without humour – there I was at the front of the church, with the coffin in front of me like the world's most macabre coffee table – and I swear when everyone shut their eyes to pray I could STILL hear her hearing aid whistling away like a 56k modem. Plus doesn't All Things Bright and Beautiful have a lot of verses? Good heavens – even the charming lady playing the organ took a swig of Lucozade (think of the sugar, woman!). Thank Christ she didn't pull a Paula Radcliffe and piddle on the floor. Oh and I like to think my nana chose All Things Bright and Beautiful simply for the line 'The purple headed mountain', which I'm sure made everyone under seventy bite the inside of their cheek. It was a happy, cheerful affair and the vicar did her a great send-off, which is exactly what we (and she) wanted. The cremation was oddly impersonal though – I wouldn't have been surprised if we had been asked to collect a ticket and await our turn, ala Cashier Number 7, please. Ashes Number 7, more like.

The wake was in the village where she grew up and grew old, and the lovely ladies of the WI catered the event, which meant cakes, biscuits, scones you could prop a barn door open with, clotted cream, sandwiches, meringue, tea and fine china. It was delicious and a wonderful gesture which again, my nana would have loved.

twochubbycubs on: procrastination

I'm the world's worst procrastinator. If I can find a way of putting something off to do later, I will, even if it's something I enjoy doing like writing. Hell, a book about a wizard made JK Rowling insanely rich, even if she does walk around with a face like a franked stamp. Like she's seen her arse and doesn't like the colour of it, as my dad would say. Like she'd lost a fiver and found a pound, if you will. Like an abandoned sofa. I'm only jealous.

To give you a few examples, I painted our bedroom a charming slate grey last summer (Paul wouldn't let me put a slab of wipe-clean Perspex on the wall behind the bed, which I think was a mistake) and I had every intention of going around with a little scrubby cloth and getting all the paint of the windowsills, lest our gardener looks in and thinks I'm a cack-handed slattern. I am, but I don't want him judging me. But I've put it off and put it off to the point where I'd rather repaint the room than go at it with a cloth. For a year and a half in our old flat we had a bed that dipped in the middle almost to the floor because three of the slats snapped (sadly not through passionate love-making, but because I plucked one of Paul's bum-hairs as he walked past naked and he fell onto the bed in fright). Did we go to IKEA and get some new slats? No, we propped it up with a few DVDs and spent 18 months walking around with spines like question marks.

If I take a day off, it's always done with good intentions that I'll go shopping, get some nice food in, do tasks around the house, practice writing, have a walk. What invariably happens is that I'll spend three hours pressing the snooze button and the rest of the day watching Come Dine With Me on Channel 4 catch-up in my 'house boxers' – i.e. the ones I can't wear outside of the house because my knackers tumble out of a hole in the gusset. We've got several pairs of these, super comfy, but god knows what we do to our boxers to make them fall apart like that. Paul puts it down to friction, I put it down to his rancid farts burning through like when you toast the top of a crème brûlée. Nevertheless, they're handy for dossing around the house, though I do think my neighbours over the road have seen my balls swinging around more times than they would care to admit.

Speaking of neighbours, we seemingly have a new one, and I don't care for her at all. She can't reverse park. Now I know that's an awfully trite reason to judge someone, but she's got room enough on her drive to turn the space shuttle around on, and she's only got a shitty little Clio. We no longer bother turning the light on in the kitchen of an evening – the two hours of her reverse light bouncing off our tiles is more than enough to get us through cooking. I can't get my head around it – I throw my car onto my drive like the car seat is on fire, whereas she nudges it back and forth for time immemorial. She saw me silently judging her as I washed the pots the other night and I think I've managed to make her even more nervous. She'll probably take to leaving the car at work and getting a bus now.

twochubbycubs on: casual Saturday

We're mulling over whether or not to move house. I know, the people in the street would be bereft not seeing my knob hanging out of the front of my boxers as I absent-mindedly put the bins out on a Monday, but since we had some strange lads in our back passage a few days ago (not invited through Grindr, either, unusually) it's made us a bit unsettled. We don't think they were trying to break in, because there was an open window into our bedroom (though admittedly the flashing neon red light was turned off at the time) and they didn't do anything...but still. It makes you feel uneasy. Though saying that, had they climbed in through the bedroom window, they would have fallen onto our bed – and all I'm saying is I wouldn't have needed Tony Martin's shotgun to make them bleed from behind. The little smackrats. This is a nice part of the world!

So yes, we bundled into the car and decided to go have a look at some of the new estates that are being build, and to take the opportunity to view the showhomes. Well, they were awful. It didn't help that the chap on the front desk took one look at us – physically looked us up and down, mind you, taking in our dog-walking trainers, shaved heads and George jeans – and clearly decided we were there to steal the copper wiring and good silver. His opening gambit was that 'these houses are very difficult to get' and that we'd need excellent credit to get an appropriate mortgage. The cheeky, oily little oik – we own our house outright with no mortgage and I've got better credit than the Queen. Paul hasn't, because he bought a stereo from Kays catalogue on tick and then forgot all about it over ten years ago, but there you go. Always trust a Geordie with money. We spent ten minutes looking around and then left with a disdainful look at Captain Acne behind the desk and told him it was far too small and there were altogether too many Audis on the estate.

We didn't manage to leave quietly though as I managed to back the car over a child's football that had been discarded in the middle of the road, resulting in an surprisingly loud bang echoing around the estate which probably sounded like the car backfiring, which I suppose didn't help our image. We trundled over to The Parents and spent half an hour oohing and aahing at how well my nephew is coming along (I make him sound like a tomato plant) – without so much as a cup of tea mind, mother – and the highlight of that being when he pointed at Paul and called him Uncle Fatty. The kid has style!

After my parents came IKEA, and good lord IKEA is stressful at the best of times but even more so when you're breaking the rules and going anti-clockwise with seemingly all of Gateshead's unwashed masses bearing down on you, it's hell on Earth. Especially because when the weather is warm enough not to leave an icicle on your tit, everyone decides to throw on a scraggy t-shirt exposing their Neapolitan-ice-cream skin to the sun – blistered red from being out under a SKOL umbrella all afternoon, yellow from nicotine and jaundice, streaky brown wherever the Poundstretcher Fake-Bake took hold.

And the stopping! I know everyone needs a moment to sniff their eighty-dozen orange-scented KLIT tea-lights but for goodness sake, do it to the side. I genuinely think there should be two lanes in places like this – one of those who can glide with purpose and one for those dolts who walk like they have a ball-bearing stuck in their socks. I'm being glib, I appreciate that people have disabilities and of course, they're exempt, but if you can't move quickly simply because you're too much of a clot to remember to put one foot in front of the other in a reasonably rhythmic pattern, then just do everyone a favour and stay at home and have someone else pick up your ÖRGI bookshelf. Bastards. I didn't even get a bloody hot-dog at the end because I couldn't bear the thought of having my face stripped by someone's eye-watering B.O for ten minutes in the queue whilst I had nothing to do than count the skin tags on their neck.

Hark listen to me, you'd think I was Adonis. But Paul says I am, so there.

Costco next – and if you think IKEA is bad, then Costco is even worse. Here the aforementioned numpties are armed with a trolley big enough to fit a hot-tub and enough baked beans to keep a Toby Carvery going for a financial quarter. Oh and it gets worse – it was bloody tasting day, which meant crowds of people all pushing and pulling at one another with their 4×4 trolleys in a nugatory attempt to get their cracked hands on a postage stamp of lasagne or a bit of brioche you could start a fire with. We bought our usual forty tins of tomato puree, sack of pasta and catering jar of gherkins, which were crashed through the till by the cashier with all the care and panache you'd expect from someone who had tattooed her eyelashes on, and we were on our way to the final test – Tesco at 3.40pm on a Sunday afternoon.

Which, remarkably, was a fairly sedate experience, despite me shrieking at Paul 'STOP PLAYING WITH YOURSELF THERE ARE KIDS ABOUT' when he was adjusting his belt in the reductions aisle. I'm surprised he had room, the usual ballaches were waiting to tackle the poor Tesco lackey to the floor for their 35p breadbuns. I genuinely can't stand greed of this sort – but I've rambled on about these shitgibbons before who fill their trolley because they **can**, not because **they** need to. Nobody needs fifteen discount cauliflowers at 4pm on a Sunday. Take one, and fuck off.

So that was today. Goodness me.

twochubbycubs on: even more casual Sunday

We decided, after we got out of bed at an unseemly hour this **afternoon** that we would have a 'trip out in the car'. That's a sign we're both getting old, not least because the three places we considered were a) a garden centre b) an outlet shopping centre and c) a castle. I fear we're rapidly becoming one of those couples who drive to the seaside and then sit inside the car eating egg sandwiches before driving home again, the bitter resentment of each other thick in the air. I don't understand that – there was an old couple yesterday who had driven to the same beach we were geocaching at, only to park their Nissan Incontinent facing away from the beach and then proceeded to eat their sandwiches. Surely you'd want something interesting to look at – I can't imagine the 'Pick Up Dog Shit' posters were that enthralling. Perhaps they were enjoying the spectacle of two fat blokes bustling around in the undergrowth looking for a lunchbox with an ASDA smart-price notepad and an IKEA pencil in it. Who knows. Frankly, a trip out to the beach isn't a success for me unless I'm still picking sand out from under my helmet four days later.

There's an image, I hope no-one was eating mackerel.

Anyway, we decided to go to the Royal Quays Outlet Centre purely because there's a Le Creuset outlet there and I wanted a salt-pig. Listen, I know my rock-and-roll lifestyle is getting too much, but please try to keep up. This meant a trip through the Tyne Tunnel where I immediately managed to cock everything up by missing the tiny basket for the toll as I drove through, leading to 50p rolling under the car. Now, I'm an exceptionally tight person, but even I didn't think to get out of the car and retrieve it – I just made Paul find another one amongst the detritus in our ashtray and we were on our way. However, the driver of the car behind was almost out of his car and on the hunt for the pound coin no sooner had I pulled away. I was aghast – I mean, I'm stingy, but for goodness sake, he hurtled out of his car door like Usain Bolt looking for my 50p. I slowed down because I was trying to sync my phone with the radio and he hurtled past us at the entrance, pretty much cutting us up, so we spent the tunnel journey mouthing mean words at him – Paul mouthing TIGHT and me mouthing BASTARD in perfect unison. I hope he felt thoroughly ashamed – he was driving a BMW though so I very much doubt he had any sense of shame. Or pity. Or driving ability. Nobber.

However, catastrophe struck when we got to Royal Quays – the Le Creuset shop has gone! Where else will I buy my beautiful but overpriced kitchen ornaments now? The ladies on the checkout, who clearly saw our shaved heads and dirty shoes and assumed we were there to rob the place (though you'd be pretty hard-pushed to make a quick getaway with a bloody cast-iron casserole pot jammed down your boxers), always treated us with incredible disdain. But the deals were good so we kept going back. Alas, it is no more. We checked the information board and Paul suggested that we could get something nice from Collectibles. Well really. I'd sooner shit in my hands and start clapping than trawl through the tat in there. Not saying you can't get nice stuff, but when your window display is a pyramid of Nicer Dicer boxes then we're not going to get along. We left in a huff, didn't even bother going to Cotton Traders to pick up a marquee-sized flannel shirt. Our wardrobe is almost exclusively flannel shirts in varying pairs of colours – it looks like a test-card when you slide the door across.

twochubbycubs on: décor

Firstly let me apologise for any spelling errors that may arise during this post – we have finally unpacked our super shiny iMac and I'm not used to the tiny keyboard. I feel it is made for delicate, straw-like fingers to dance over, not having my hairy sausage digits pummel away at it like a sailor *applying lip gloss* to a £10 hooker. WOW there's a sentence you didn't expect.

We bought the Mac because it is a lot easier to edit the blog photos on, which means you better hurry along and buy a billion copies of my book to pay for the fucker. It wasn't hard to win Paul round – he has such a love of polished metal and smooth edges that I'm surprised he isn't dryhumping the Micra on the side. But everything about using a Mac is different from a Windows computer. Even navigating using this tiny mouse is proving a bloody chore, yes it's fair enough taking away the buttons and relying on me using gestures but so far the only gesture I've managed is calling it a dick and scratching my foot with it.

In fact, it almost looks like a sex toy, all slick and polished – but it would be a boring person's sex toy, something slipped into a pastel handbag and wheeled out between accountancy seminars at various Days Inn across the country. It would be called something yawnsome like 'Pleasure Max' or 'Orb'. Amateurs.

Everyone knows a good sex toy needs to be tapped into

the National Grid and come with an instruction manual on DVD, called something like 'The Ripper' or 'Uvula-nudga'. Anyway. One thing I do like is how sharp everything looks – it's in 5k, which is apparently like HD but even better. Even better than 4k. Great, now when I watch Jeremy Kyle on catch-up I'll actually be able to see the sheen of smugness that he has in every pore. I just hope the ultra high definition doesn't turn online pornography (a healthy part of any modern marriage) into a disturbingly accurate affair – god knows bumholes aren't pretty to look at in soft-focus, let alone splayed in billions of colours and filling the screen like a flattened sea anenome.

The Mac does look good in our new living room, and the good news is that we're almost finished with decorating. We've got someone coming around to hang our artwork on the wall, fix the TV to the wall and various other little odds and sods, someone coming around to fix the alarm and then finally, the house is our own and we don't have to make small-talk with anyone but the cats every again. Yesterday was a painful case in point – we had a chap around to install new blinds throughout and because I'd responded to his question of 'How do you like them hung' with 'Well', Paul retired me to the kitchen to research recipes.

What this actually meant was I got to eavesdrop on Paul making small-talk and the good news is that he's even worse than me at it. Clearly both Paul and the blinds man were hard of hearing because every sentence by one of them was met with a 'pardon' from the other, then an 'EH', then Paul clearly doing that thing where he hasn't heard a word of what was said but is too embarrassed to ask him to repeat it. At one point, he answered the question 'What do you do for a living' with 'absolute junkies' and that killed the conversation dead. Like the good husband that I am, I just spent the two hours laughing into my fist and trying not to fart too loudly.

One thing we've learned from all of this decorating is that buying furniture is a bloody chore. We can't buy stuff in shops because we're too common for the posh shops and too posh for B&M, so we're stuck buying things online, which is fine to a point until you order what you think is a cushion and you get a 7ft beanbag delivered. I mean it looks nice enough but work don't half raise their eyebrows when they have to hoick that into the lift. We've bought most of our new stuff from made.com which has been a revelation, but we've tried shopping local for all the accessories and bits and bobs. What a waste of time.

Since when did it become acceptable to half-arsedly rub a bit of sandpaper over a shitty chest of drawers from IKEA and call it vintage or even worse, distressed. Distressed? I certainly was, I could barely stop the tears. There's a shop near us absolutely rammed full of the sort of trinkets and sculptures you'd imagine someone who has the word 'healer' in their job-title to have littering their house and it is quite genuinely one of the worst places I've ever been to. And I've been to Southend, remember. (I'm joking, before I get any barely-understandable voicemails left). Who decides that what they really need for their house is a friggin' incense burner made from a rusty tin and a feeling of malaise?

My mother, god love her, looks a bit of chintz and tat, saying it makes a home – well, that's one gene that didn't make it down the line to me, I can tell you. For a woman of normal, reasonable taste, she refused for all of my teenage life to throw away what I consider to be the ugliest statue I've ever seen. It was a grinning monkey dressed as a waiter holding a tray. It looked to all the world like the final thing a demented mind might see before the hands of hell grabbed your ankle. I dreamed of kicking it down the stairs or accidentally setting fire to it (I'm not sure how well stone would burn in a Hotpoint oven but fuck me I longed for the chance to try) but my mother was fair attached to it. A quick look online suggests I can buy one for around £150, which might actually be money well spent if it meant I could fulfil a fantasy. I note you can buy a similar statue in the shape of a rooster – that would certainly be more suited to our house, given how much we're fans of large cocks in our bedroom, but still.

Mother, if you're reading this, it really is your only decorating faux-pas. We should send you off to Cuba.

The only thing I associate with Cuba, because I always revert lazily to stereotypes, is cigars. They're about the only thing I occasionally miss about smoking. Before I joined my current job, I almost took up a job managing a cigar and pipe shop in Newcastle. How different my life could have been, dispensing cherry tobacco to whiskery old buggers and burning my eyebrows with the cigar lighters.

Paul and I used to be members of a mail order cigar club that would send out a variety of different cigars every month – I always remember one month they sent a cigar that looked like a bloody roll of carpet – I could barely get it in my mouth, and let me tell you, that's a problem I almost never have. It took about ten minutes to light the bugger (I had to use the grill function on the oven) and it was enjoyable for approximately sixteen seconds before the emphysema kicked in. There's something inherently butch about cigars, well, decent cigars – mincing along with a Café Crème that you've lit with a novelty lighter shaped like a phallus doesn't quite have the same gravitas.

twochubbycubs on: technology

Note this is a joint effort – James' bits are in italics.

Technology really is marvellous, in't it? I'm happy to say that in a little over seven months we've managed to attract (at the time of writing) 2209 subscribers to the website and 2704 to the Facebook group! And thank you to each and every one of you.

I absolutely love technology – any kind. I'm a complete geek when it comes to anything like that. I once dragged James around an old nuclear bunker from the Cold War just so I could crane my neck to have a look at what their printer was like (very beige, if you were wondering). His latest thing is Twitter – I can't use the bloody thing, too complex for my liking (it just reminds me of someone mouthing off in the middle of a bus station hoping someone screams back – gah) and I recoil whenever I see a bloody hashtag so he's looking after that side of things. I'll stick with Facebook, thank you very much. It's where all the drama happens.

A thought entered my mind today as I sat at my desk at work trying not to think about Galaxy Ripples. I remember the feeling of amazement and wonder I had when I was just a little lad whenever I saw computers. Back then they were just these little boxes whirring away in the corner of the classroom (but only if you were good for that week) that didn't really do very much but were still fantastic and quite mystical. I also remember the excitement whenever I saw anything even vaguely computerish on the telly (I sat through an entire series of Bugs once. It was crap but it looked cool). I was always lucky enough to have a computer in the house. It started off with the Commodore 64 which unfortunately ended its life at the hands of an errant Lambert and Butler from mother. She used to be fixated with a game called 'Split Personalities' where you had to slide bits of a puzzle around to make a picture of a famous personality – mother, in the grips of a panic that only rearranging Elivs Costello's face in 16-bit can create, must've clamped her thin lips down a little too harshly on that tab of hers because the tip fell off and burnt its way through the keyboard. Turns out you can't load a tape without the use of the space bar.

Our first PC was smashing – a Packard Bell that we had to have the bedroom floor reinforced to stop it crashing through the ceiling. Well not quite, but you get the gist. I've never known a computer where you had to shovel coal in the back just to get Encarta 96 running at full speed. No internet at the time – just Solitaire, Rodent's Revenge and then completely knacking everything up by installing After Dark screensavers (flying toasters!) and setting a boot-up password, then promptly forgetting it. We had to call someone who 'knew computers' to come and fix it whilst we stood slack-jawed at the Windows 95 splash screen. He also installed Quake on it but that was far too manly for me so I just spent my time playing

Hover and Theme Hospital. No internet at that point see, so there were no long summer evenings spent flogging the dolphin. Anyway. Back to Paul.

From there we eventually moved up to a PC – we got some 'glorious' reconditioned box of crap from an iffy looking warehouse that disappeared the next week and where the workers had far too many gold earrings not to be up to something shifty. The only problem was that I used to love tinkering with it. As a curious twelve year old I loved nothing more than taking the case off and pulling wires out to see if I could remember where it went, or delete key files to see if I could fix it (I never could). I was able to get away with it by blaming the Millennium Bug until some smartarse actually pointed to the problems most likely being the massive amounts of smut I had hidden away on it. Eeh what am I like.

I soon got my comeuppance, though. Whilst fannying on too much I accidentally deleted the display driver meaning that it could only ever from that point on do things in sixteen colours. SIXTEEN. You've never seen complicated porn until you've watched it in only sixteen bloody colours. I didn't realise a bumhole wasn't an aurbergine colour until I saw one winking at me for real. Anyway, after a few weeks of aborted, frustrated attempts at having a wank I finally managed to sulk my way into getting another, nicer, newer one. It was still rubbish, mind, but at least I could finally crack one off in a few million different colours. It makes all the difference, believe me. The problem from then on though was that mother started to get her hands on it. No, not that (I know I'm from East Anglia, but come on) I mean the computer, and that's when it all went terribly wrong. You wouldn't trust a hamster with a bandsaw so whoever it was that decided a middle-aged woman that had only managed to figure out how to click a biro should be allowed access to a computer deserves a good kicking. There was no time for smut when I had to spend all my days uninstalling toolbars and iffy Bingo diallers and running up and down the stairs with a list of words to run through a thesaurus for her latest Puzzler. And when Bejewelled came along that really was the final straw and I decided to move out. I couldn't bear another question about a bloody Java installer.

I want to interject here and continue my bit and agree that, for my formative teenager years, technology was amazing – in that technology could get me any amount of debauched filth at the click of a mouse and an installation of Realplayer. Truly, it was a wondrous time to be a teenage boy. When I finally managed to get the computer put in my bedroom rather than downstairs I don't think I reappeared for a good two weeks, and even then I came out of my bedroom with a right arm like a Russian shot-putter and skin the colour of milk. You know when you were young and you used to slick your arm with PVA glue so that you could peel it off? That's what my bedroom looked like – like a giant spider had made a nest. My parents were responsible enough to put parental controls on, but nothing stops a teenage boy getting at pornography, and if you're sitting there reading this thinking little Oliver and Danrobért aren't bypassing every restriction you've put on there, you're so wrong. It's a wonder I got any GSCE coursework done.

Hush, you. Fancy lowering the tone like that.

twochubbycubs on: cold callers

I keep receiving phone calls from various 'Claims Management' companies who have somehow got my number and are adamant that I've had an accident and must claim now. I'm not one of these people who get hysterical about it, ultimately people are just doing their jobs, but they are parasitic vultures and I do enjoy wasting their time. The amount of different scenarios I've had for my fictional accident is beyond belief. I had some cheery chap on the phone the other day for fifteen minutes asking me about my accident – I told him I was driving a car ferry down the A1 and hit a bridge. His response? He asked me for the registration plate of the ferry. I told him I couldn't recall the registration plate and that I couldn't check because one of my eyes had fallen out on impact.

Today's call was a little shorter, I told him I'd hit a pollard. Admittedly, I'm not convinced English was his first accent, but I have a clear voice and clearly said pollard. He asked me to repeat. I said pollard. He asked again. Pollard. 'Bollard Sir? You hit a bollard?' – to which my reply was no, I'd hit eighties television star Su Pollard, who had strayed in front of my car whilst lighting a cigarette after turning on Durham's Christmas lights. I mentioned that I felt her trademark glasses crack under my tyre and I couldn't sleep for knowing there was so many Hi-De-Hi fans who'd never be happy again.

He hung up. No staying power at all, these cold callers.

twochubbycubs on: phobias

I'm writing in a bit of a huff.

See, I'm going to have to go to the dentist. A year or so ago I cracked my back tooth chewing on a hairbrush, which sounds fabulously fun but it hurt like hell. My dentist took one look, took it out and sent me on my way, with only a stiff jaw and a modest NHS bill to accompany me. All good. However, one of my wisdom teeth has clearly seen the gap left by my departed tooth and thought to himself that he would really rather like to move in. And it hurts. Not the tooth but rather a tiny bit of gum that I keep catching with my teeth as I shut my mouth. How can it heal if I keep biting into the bloody thing? It's bad enough that I have to sit with my mouth slightly open at all times like a pensioner stuck on her Sudoku, but now I have to go to the dentist to fix it? Bah.

It's not that I'm scared of dentists...well, no, that's a fib. I am, but who isn't, you can't get a kick out of a man pumping a tool in and out of your gob and finishing it off with a squirt of something acidic to set your teeth on edge. OR CAN YOU. No. Oddly, the drill I can deal with because it doesn't hurt, but when they use that little air-sprayer thingy I just want to bite his nipple off as he hangs over me in his dainty tunic. My skin is crawling up my back as we speak. I know where the unease about my dentist comes from – I had to have a tooth out when

I was little after I (again!) cracked one eating nuts. I swear my teeth are made of glass. Anyway, the dentist I had back then clearly hated life, children and smiles, so set about me with all the care and precision one might elect to us knocking down a brick wall. I remember even now his pock-marked face being within kissing distance from mine, his bloodshot eyes darting around and spittle-flecked lips pursed as he yanked the tooth out. It wouldn't come, so naturally he decided to put his entire bodyweight onto me, using his elbow in my chest as leverage. Fair enough, he got the tooth in the end, but he had to stop after forty minutes to have his brow mopped with a towel and Lucozade brought in and I had a collapsed lung and internal bleeding. No wonder I'm scared, though I'm not scared of much else. Rollercoasters? High as you like. Water? Chuck me in. Enclosed spaces? Pfft. As long as I don't get stuck and have to be 'popped out' of the tight space by a team of firemen, I'll be fine. That said...

Spiders bother us both, though Paul more than me. We once ran screaming from our Quayside flat when a spider the size of a small motorcar came trundling out from under the fridge. We were on the cusp of checking into a hotel when we realised our wallets were still in the flat, and without those, we'd be screwed. So we dutifully went back in only to see it, bold as brass, sitting in the middle of the laminate flooring. I swear if my vision had been good enough I would have been able to see his tiny little finger sticking up at me in defiance. Action was needed, so, screaming all the while, Paul ran to the balcony doors and flung them open as I dashed (I was skinny back then, I could dash) into the little office, got the giant (expensive) John Lewis waste-paper bin, emptied the contents on the floor, ran back into the living room (still screaming), trapped the little fucker and promptly ran to the balcony and threw him, the bin and almost myself over the bloody edge. I was surprised the little bastard didn't have a parachute and a distress flare he was that big. Good times. The bin disappeared down onto a road somewhere and when we picked it up the next morning, an electric bus had run over it. Serves me right eh.

Paul's also scared of all the boring things like being buried alive, and he doesn't like the idea of drowning or burning, which seems an altogether reasonable way to live, whereas all my fears are quite silly. For one, I'm scared of dams. Terrified. Even looking at the word makes my teeth jitter a bit (which doesn't help my sore gum). It's not the fear of them breaking – oh no – it's just how alien and unsettling they look. They have no business being there. Having a parent who works for the local water company means I have an unflinching and comprehensive knowledge of all the creepy things and secret pipes hidden just below the ground, ready to suck you away into oblivion. He once told me that a family crashed their car into a reservoir and the suction on an intake pipe held all the doors shut so they couldn't get out. Yikes. Sewers too. Pennywise I could handle, but the sluice gate at the end would have me sucking on Kalms like there was no tomorrow.

I'm also genuinely frightened of irregular holes. Har-de-har not bumholes, no, but irregular clusters of holes sets me on edge. If I have a crumpet, I have to have it upside down otherwise I can't eat it, and sponges make me feel uneasy if I look at them. I feel like I could have myself a story in Chat magazine surrounded by sponges, biting my nails, but alas I saw someone has beaten me to it. Things like sieves are alright because the holes are organised and clean, but I reckon I'm probably the only person ever to almost faint looking at Swiss cheese. Ah, aren't phobias daft.

twochubbycubs on: music and neglect

We've discovered a new app on our iPad — Wakie! Essentially it's an alarm clock but one that actually connects you to the person who wants waking up. For example, some bronzed god in Australia may want waking up because he has to go to work at 11am, and I'm sitting in the UK available to make the call, and the app will connect the two of us. It doesn't cost anything, it's just like making a phone call, and we LOVE it. At first we were shy — lots of 'So what's the weather like where you are' and 'what you getting up for', but now we wake people up by telling them jokes, or my most favourite, using the soundboard of Roy Walker's catchphrases that we found on the internet from the old Radio 1 days. Imagine that — you're fast asleep in New Zealand, your phone goes, you blearily answer it and you get 'GOOD MORNING CONTESTANT' blaring at you, followed by 'IT'S A GOOD GUESS, BUT IT'S NOT RIGHT'. Haha! It works the other way too, we had a wake-up call from someone in America this morning, who told us a joke and then farted down the phone. She sounds like just our type of girl to be honest. It's completely anonymous so there's never a way of finding out who you spoke to, but it's just great fun. Perhaps you should download it — you'll know if you get through to us because it'll be a litany of blue jokes, shrieks of laughter and ten seconds of Paul trying to press the hang up button and missing because he hasn't got his glasses on and there's four iPads in his field of vision.

Anyway, the good news is we've had no altercations with our neighbours today and it's been an altogether pleasant day, even though all we've done is our grocery shopping and beetled about in the car. Are we the only couple who go out in the car just for a drive? I mean, I know the price of fuel means arranging a small mortgage beforehand, but there's nothing better than just heading out on a sunny day, not knowing where you are going to end up. I think I get that from growing up with my parents, who would take us out on a drive to nowhere and always reply to the question of 'where are we going' with 'there and back to see how far it is'. Helpful. To be fair to them, my sister and I were proper nightmares in the back of the car. Not as bad as Paul, mind you. He kicked his sister so hard in the side of her head for turning off his 911 CD that she spent a car journey from Glencoe to Aberdeen with ringing ears. To be fair, I'd have ringing ears if I had to listen to Paul's music choices for more than ten minutes – I spend less time changing gears than I do pressing the 'Skip Track' button on my steering wheel to try and get past his Tracy Chapman nonsense. It's no wonder the clutch in the Micra is fucked.

I'M SORRY: TRACY CHAPMAN SOUNDS LIKE A BEE WITH A COLD TRAPPED IN A BOTTLE.

Actually, my parents once thought it would be a great

idea to transport my sister, me, a tent and two week's worth of camping impedimenta in a scalding hot Ford Escort to the bottom of France (from Newcastle). It wasn't, and I think my sister and I started fighting from the second my dad started backing the car down the lane from our house. Bearing in mind that we were quite fractious siblings at the best of times (though we're close now) this was a recipe for disaster. Anyway, clearly sick of remonstrating with us and smacking our arses, our parents threatened to leave us by the side of a road in the middle of rural France at some backwater petrol station. Of course, being kids, we were full of bravado, and we knew they wouldn't dare. But they did – they bundled us out of the car at the petrol station and proceeded to drive to the exit ramp.

Now, let me clarify, I believe their intention was to give us a little fright and stop a moment or two down the ramp and pick us back up. Only they hadn't factored in the massive lorry that pulled out behind them, clearly with Paris' entire shipment of Gauloises in the back and no time to wait for my parents to teach us a lesson in good behaviour. Being a one lane exit ramp they had no other alternative than to carry on down onto the motorway and leave us stranded, bawling. Oops. They came back around from the other side around fifteen minutes later after they'd driven like they had a bomb up their arse to the next junction and turned around and we were completely silent for the next couple of hours. So I suppose the threat worked. Anyway, don't judge, they are great parents, and certainly there were no more incidents of accidental neglect until they went out for tapas that night in Portugal a few years later.

twochubbycubs on: our cats

I really begrudge having to pay £200 to insure two cats who are healthy, worm-free and trackable. Especially when they're so spoilt they have their own water fountain and bloody ensuite shed.

Of course, insurance wouldn't be quite so necessary if our cats didn't dice with death on a daily basis, and entirely through their own choice. See, they recognise the sound of our car approaching, and the very second they see the bumper of my car appearing at the end of the cul-de-sac where we live, they sprint across the front lawn in front of the car and run ahead of us, like we're the star attraction in a tiny cat parade. They then proceed to run around the tyres, rubbing themselves up against the scalding chassis of the car, until one of us picks them up and they proceed to turn our face into mince with their razor-sharp welcome. I don't think they feel we're home until one of them has left an oily paw-print all over our shirts. They're also forever eating things they shouldn't and I've seen Sola, the tiny cat, fighting a dog and winning. To be honest, I wouldn't be surprised to learn she smokes.

Sola we retrieved from some chav on an estate who was selling kittens on the basis that if no-one wanted them, she was going to leave them by the side of the road. I'd like to have left her by the side of a road, preferably trapped by her legs in a burning labia-coloured Vauxhall Golf, but I digress. We couldn't drive at the time so we had to take two buses and by the time we got there, she was the last one, the runt of the litter. She meowed the way home and tried to commit instant suicide by falling off the balcony of our apartment. Thankfully, she only fell one floor onto the balcony below, but that made for a slightly awkward exchange because we weren't talking to the neighbours at the point since we inadvertently told his girlfriend that he was having an affair with someone else. Genuine mistake. We also thought he was belting his lass too, which was wrong. That made for a few difficult bus journeys on the Quaylink, let me tell you.

They missed out not keeping Sola, for although she's the most uppity bitch you'll ever meet, she has the nicest fur you'll ever feel. It's the type of fur you can imagine ultra-rich women making gloves from. That's partly because she never lets you stroke her – probably sick of trying to lick gravy and sweat from her fur to even entertain us. She's the epitome of aloofness although for all of her delusions of grandeur, she's certainly not averse to sticking her nose right up Bowser's arsehole like she's sniffing for truffles whenever he wanders back in from outside.

Bowser is the other cat, the tom, and we also got him from a very downmarket area. We heard on the grapevine that he was one of about ten trillion cats that had been found living in one of those houses you see on

Hoarders. We could only take one and so we took the first cat that came over. If we had our way, we'd have more cats than furniture, but we're realists – I already begrudge spending so much on Bite 'n' Chew, and not just because of that rebarbative little 'n'. He settled in straight away, walking around like he owned the place and battering the other cats until we had his bollocks cut off. Now he comes in each day missing massive chunks of fur from fighting but touchwood, they haven't got his eyes yet.

We also used to have Luma, and she was a lovely, fat cat who was painfully shy and used to hide, no matter how much coaxing, fresh tuna and fuss you tried to make of her. She had plenty of personality when she wanted to – she held us ransom for about two weeks by pissing on our Sky box because we had the bare-faced cheek to switch her to Tesco own brand cat food. Perhaps she was trying to electrocute herself, I don't know, but she managed to break my Doctor Who series link so I sulked for a week. Along similar lines, I was once lying in bed and she came bumbling over, wheezing away in that gentle fashion, for a stroke. Naturally, I made a proper fuss of her in this rare moment of tenderness and she turned around, showed me her tiny cigar-cutter bumhole and sprayed a tiny jet of foul smelling nastiness right in my face, before sauntering off as I screamed like it was ammonia. We gave her away to a family friend in the end because she was fighting with our other cat all of the time and she's far happier now, by herself, with an octogenerian who is too slow to catch her and rich enough to spoil her, though I did spot a packet of Viagra in his bathroom cabinet when I was dropping her off so god knows what she actually sees. No wonder she looks so haunted when I spot her.

twochubbycubs on: a night in a hotel

Quick post tonight as we're both knackered after our poor stay at the glamorous, salubrious Village Hotel just outside of Whitley Bay. We decided to spend a night there on the basis that "it can't be that bad", which is never a good reason to stay in a hotel. Now let me say this, I'm sure it's lovely for weddings or it has rooms that blow the mind, but we were given a room that resembled Barbara Cartland's bathroom, all bright colours and furnishings. The bed was that uncomfortable that we actually went for a drive at midnight as opposed to trying to sleep with the jizz-rusted springs digging into our back. We had a meal delivered by room service that was so forgettable I went for a bath halfway through my burger. It was very 'god bless, they've had a try at least.' I did feel bad for the room service people though – as soon as Paul ordered our meal I spent a good twenty minutes generously farting away under the duvet, with the effect that as soon as they knocked on the door and I barrelled to the bathroom, a veritable mushroom-cloud of trump went off in the bedroom. Paul tells me that the poor lass delivering our food physically blanched upon smelling, and I'm sure I heard her gagging away in the hallway.

You know what pisses me off though? The various ways they rip you off or let you down in places like this. For example, for £20, we could have been upgraded to

'Upper Deck' where such luxuries as Sky Movies and Starbucks coffee awaited. Choose not to upgrade, and your TV (I kid you not) picks up BBC1, BBC2, ITV, Channel 4, True Movies and Nickelodeon. Perfect if I want to watch the lass out of Cheers getting slapped about or Songs of Praise, but otherwise, fucking pointless. Not to mention the picture broadcast was so poor that I wasn't entirely sure there wasn't a tiny man behind the screen hastily drawing an approximation of what should have been on the screen at any given time. Why not just give us the normal TV channels rather than going out of your way to give a shit service? We had a drink in the bar – £13.50 for a gin (unbranded) and tonic (ditto) and a cider. I'm a tight Geordie, yes, but for that price I expect a hairy orchard-worker to come and squeeze my apples himself. Our room service cost £7 to be delivered (had they come in a taxi?) because we had two trays – fair enough, save for the fact that one of the trays held a tiny plate of cheesecake and could have easily been buried on the other tray. I'm surprised that they didn't have the lift shake the coins out of our pockets as we checked out.

It's foolish because all it does is create a shit impression – pay extra on top of your hotel stay and you'll get what you paid for originally. It's no surprise the hotel trade is dying on its arse with the likes of AirBnB chasing them – I'd sooner pay a flat rate and get everything than pay through the nose and then get asked for more.

Oh, and the coffee. I'd have got more taste and flavour if I'd pissed the bed and sucked it through the mattress.

Staff were lovely though.

twochubbycubs on: an online argument

I wanted to mention the most ridiculous argument I had last night with some absolute stream of arse-gravy who was trying to have a pop at me for explaining how to cook an omelette. Her 'proposal' was to find a zippable (?) sandwich bag, pour in four eggs, seal the bag, break the eggs up, open the bag, add all the toppings, seal it again, boil the bag in a pan full of water and then after a few minutes, out slides the "omelette' like a bright orange poo full of undigested tomato. Apparently, this saves time.

For goodness sake. An omelette is one of the quickest meals you can make as long as you're not so mentally deficient you don't know how to crack an egg, and if that's the case, you'd perhaps be better served colouring in and eating lead. Crack eggs into jug, beat the eggs, pour into pan, allow to stiffen, add toppings, fold over, finish under grill. If James Martin and some random bag of hormones from Hollyoaks can do it on Saturday Kitchen then so can anyone. I mentioned this and got "well we can't all be fucking mastercheffs', followed by lots of huffing and unbecoming puffing and argument style which felt like I was getting sassed by Dizzee Rascal, which doesn't quite suit a "full time mammy" from Surbiton. Ignoring the fact that she'd quite semi-literally over-egged the pudding with her 'recipe', I'd hardly call being able to make an omelette 'highly-skilled'. I chose a decent deal in Subway this morning and saved £1.35, that doesn't make me Lord bloody Sugar. Thank Christ, his earlobes terrify me. Why must we revel in ignorance? I exited the "conversation" when I realised she looked the double of H from Steps and I couldn't write anything without shoehorning in a Steps reference.

OK, I sneaked two in. I said it was a *Tragedy* that she was getting so upset, and that the conversation was *Better Best Forgotten*. What AM I like.

twochubbycubs on: a day to myself

Came home today to find a clear plastic bag on the front step with a bag of chopped up rabbit in it. This is the pleasure and joy of living next to an ex-butcher with a shotgun licence. I wish he'd be a bit more discreet about it though – my freezer is absolutely full of unidentifiable bags of chopped up flesh and blood. I feel like Fred West when I go to get the fish fingers out. We had someone valuing the house the other week and when I went to get the ground coffee out of the freezer, I saw her wince and suck her teeth like she was expecting a jar of severed cocks to come tumbling out.

The Other Half has disappeared down to Peterborough for a couple of days to attend to family matters, and as much I would have just loved to spend time with my in-laws, I've elected to stay behind and attend to all the various bobbins we need doing around the house. What this actually means is that I can lounge around unwashed for three days with Pringles crushed into my back hair, stop brushing my teeth and revert back to sloth form. I dread to think what would happen if Paul went into hospital for a week or something, I'd probably end up looking like Ludo from Labyrinth with half the house covered in newspapers and cats. I do think Paul and I balance each other's foibles and tics out very well but then see, we were always destined to be together – I'm the yin to his yang, the Myra to his Ian, the Arthur to his Martha (or vice versa if it's his birthday). He was a poor boy (from a poor family), as was I, but I came with the benefit of having a crazy rich friend who funded all my shenanigans. When I look back on that time in my life, it's astonishing what I got up to. Case in point: I flew down to Portsmouth to meet up with him on an absolute whim because he had a cold and I felt sorry for him. My friend bought the tickets and sent me on my way, and then bought me four new sets of tickets because I kept cancelling to stay another day. Clearly Paul was so impressed by the fact I flew down in a plane so small and old that I had to hand-crank the propeller before I got on that he decided I was a keeper and moved straight up to Newcastle with me.

At least, I hope that's what it was. There's a photo of us somewhere in history of us both lying in bed, taking a selfie (I know), with me looking into the camera with my usual boss-eyed squint, and Paul smiling dreamily at my wallet just at the edge of the shot. I had the last laugh there though, I'm in charge of the money. I'm like The Banker from Deal or no Deal, but that would make Paul Noel Edmonds, and as he's NOT a beard with a twat hanging off it, the analogy doesn't quite work. I'd be able to show you the photo if I'd been on board with Facebook and the like at the time but I wasn't.

See, it took me almost five years to move onto Facebook and embrace all the soporific self-aggrandisement that came with it, but once I took the plunge, uploaded 7.3 million pictures of my cat and some filtered photos of Paul, I can see how useful it is, even if I spend more time than is healthy tutting at people's poor choice of cutlery and inability to tidy away the fucking wires at the back of their telly.

Pardon me a moment.

...

...

...

I had to go and open the door for Sola, who was scrabbling at the glass on the front door like crazy. I half expected her to have her paw pressed up against the glass with NOT PENNY'S BOAT scribbled on it. She's been doing my nut in today because she's doing her passive aggressive trick of meowing to be out and then immediately scratching at the door like a man who has woken up in a body bag. I've mentioned before that she's loosened a bit of the door frame so that she can pull it back with her paw and rap it against the door, meaning for about twenty minutes you get LET ME IN THE HOUSE I'M HUNGRY AND COLD AND YOU'RE CLEARLY COMFORTABLE SO YOU MUST MOVE' in fucking morse code. It's so loud. Bitch. She'll waltz in with her tail in full 'FUCK YOU' mode, go to her water fountain and then immediately start meowing to be out again.

No recipe tonight as, with Paul away, I can't be arsed to cook for one, so I'm having a jacket potato with beans and a chat with the cat. Both cats are in a huff because they went for their injections yesterday, although Bowser is especially put out because I managed to drop his cat-box as I was putting him into the car and he went rolling down the drive inside the box like a Gladiator in an Atlasphere. Have no fear, he's alright because the box was stuffed with towels and a plate of cooked chicken, but we could barely drive for laughing. That'll be the RSPCA kicking down my door later then. I did go to Morrisons (the glamour – it never ends) to try and pick up some treats but I became so despondent with all the harsh yellow lighting and the dead-eyed 3.40pm reduced-item-clutching zombies that I picked up the first nauseating bit of pastry I could see and came home.

As it happens, I managed to pick up a Morrisons All Day Breakfast Pasty. Which is fine if your idea of an all-day breakfast is some indistinguishable orange gloop, potato with all the texture of a wet sneeze and a sausage with the meat content of a sofa cushion all wedged into a suitcase of fire-retardant pastry. For one thing, the pastry was so thick and dry that I had to be put on a drip just to finish the second half. And the smell! Listen, I wasn't expecting a Heston Blumenthal level of magic and wonder, but I prefer my food not to smell like someone has just cut a cat turd in half and basted it in a dying man's breath. I put most of it in the bin, and didn't even need to pour Fairy Liquid on it to stop me going back later in a fit of greed. YOU LISTENING MORRISONS?

Anyway, this potato isn't going to eat itself.

twochubbycubs on: tatalogues

OK, so only a quick one tonight – and I'm not entirely sure we haven't already posted this. But look, it doesn't matter. It was wonderful, and frankly you can forgive me any old shite when I've covered it in melted cheese. Half of our dishes come out of the oven looking like a burnt knee, but through the wonders of careful photography and judicious cropping, you just never know. Perhaps if I presented it on one of those fancy Slimming World plates you can buy, where someone has scribbled all over a nice white plate with some felt-tips to show 'what you should eat' – a concept immediately defeated when you then proceed to cover the plate with your dinner, I presume. I don't understand the concept of drawing out 'what I should eat' on my plate. It's the foodie equivalent to scratching the TV guide into the glass of your television screen.

Actually, I saw one of these plates advertised on a facebook group the other day and asked what she meant by 'for show only', given I was envisioning someone having it on their mantlepiece like a decorative clock or one of those god-awful 'jumping dolphins rendered in plaster of paris' statues that everyone had in the nineties. She advised me that it meant it couldn't be washed or indeed, eaten off. To me, that breaks the two fundamental rules of a plate. It's definitely not something you'd keep for best.

Before anyone starts, I'm not knocking the lass for being entrepreneurial and flogging a few plates — all the very best and good luck to her! Nothing but chipperness for those who make their own way in the world.

But honestly, Paul, if you're reading this, I'm telling you now: if I get a decorated plate, bloody chalk-heart board or a food diary with a cupcake and twattish inspirational message on the front for Christmas, I'm going to bite your cock off and set it on fire.

Speaking of nonsense items that I'd sooner throw into the sun than have in my house, we seem to be locked in a battle of wills with our local Kleeneze distributor. Every few weeks he pushes a tatalogue of nonsense through our door with the passive aggressive note that he'll be back within a few days to pick it up. We immediately put it somewhere out of sight so we don't succumb to temptation and end up buying all manner of plastic shite for the kitchen or a portable urinal. A portable urinal for men. Haway. The WORLD is a portable urinal when you're a guy. Fair enough a shewee allows a lady to have a dainty tinkle instead of grunting around a ditch squatting like a shitting rhino, but a male version? I once, in my more athletic and skinny days, pissed out of a moving car because we were late for a ferry. Don't worry, we weren't boarding the ferry at the time. And I wasn't driving. Dangerous when I think about it — an errant branch whipping into my knob at seventy miles an hour could have really changed how my life turned out.

Anyway, he always ends up knocking on the door and asking for his tatalogue back, and thus begins a hunt for the offending item and a request that he doesn't deliver to us anymore. But he never listens. Each time we spend a bit longer looking for it, but he still doesn't get the message. I'm not enough of a bastard to rip the catalogue up (plus our shredder is on the blink – I wonder if Kleeneze sell those awful scissors with four blades that 'replace a shredder...maybe I should look...just once) – after all, it's someone's business, but I'm telling you now, if it continues, I'll be putting a VERY passive aggressive terse note on their facebook page. It's the very British thing to do. He needs to be careful – remember we're always naked in this house (seriously, it's like the video for Sweet Harmony by The Beloved viewed through a heat shimmer), next time he does it I'm going to put the offending tatalogue in my bumcrack and poke it around the door.

twochubbycubs on: people in our house

Before we get started, can I just tell you something which made my piss rattle this morning – I was driving to work on a particularly bendy, twisty bit of road when some log-gobbler came hurtling towards me on the other side of the road, white BMW, naturally, easily doing 30mph more than she should have been – and she was PUTTING ON MASCARA. Mascara! At speed! I only noticed because she was doing that stupid jaw-on-her-tits mascara face that seems to be obligatory. I couldn't believe it. The urge to turn my car around and ram it into the back of her shitwagon was immense. How dare she put people at risk on the roads just so she can walk around with big cow eyes? With any luck she'd crash into the River Blyth and impale her walnut brain on her Max Factor wand. Bah! I can't begin to tell you how much it annoys me seeing people use their phones / do their make-up / complete a 1000 piece jigsaw whilst driving. It's fine if you want to crash and die, but don't take me with you just because you're so keen to post '*ROFL drivin on motoway mad tunes YOLO*' on fucking facebook, you insipid tart.

Honestly. I was so angry I couldn't finish my shave.

We have a tiny leak in our hallway. I've become fanatical about measuring the spread of this tiny leak – we've marked out the water stain on the chipboard in the hallway (we have carpet, but we pulled it up to view the leak, we're not that common) and I find myself compelled to check it every time I go for a jimmy riddle I'm down on my haunches staring wildly at the floor. So doubtless that'll need fixing, which is dreadful because it means having yet more workers in the house.

I can't cope with other people in my house – I get annoyed when I see myself in the mirror, let alone burly men with rough-hewn hands fingering my coving. We've got someone coming to plaster all the ceilings in the house soon, finally getting rid of the fucking Artex that haunts our dream. You know how sometimes Artex can be applied delicately in gentle waves? Not ours. No, clearly the old biddy who lived here before had the Artex applied via a fucking fireman's hose – I feel like a pea looking up at the top of an abandoned freezer. It's awful.

We've also just had a man come round to see about painting the entire house – all the interiors, the doors, the skirting boards, plus the greenhouse, shed and massive fence that runs along the property. He immediately started asking questions about what type of paint I was wanting to use – I fear my non-macho answer of 'a subtle white with a hint of colour' has already set us off on a bad footing, because he looked at me witheringly and said 'No, matt, gloss or satin'. Well I don't bloody know, I'm very much a man who pays others to do anything taxing.

We've got someone coming to flush our radiators (not a euphemism) and another bloke coming to fit a new boiler, taking away the current boiler which I reckon was salvaged from Titanic. There's a man coming to fit blinds and eventually there'll be a scrap-man coming to take away various shite we've accumulated. The last scrap man spent ten minutes chewing my ear about not being able to work (pronounced wuuurk) because of a "bad back" whilst hoisting a fucking tumble-drier onto his flat-bed lorry like he was shotputting in the Olympics.

Finally, we've got carpet fitters coming to recarpet the entire house, which means the cats have a blank canvas to smear birds across and do secret pisses every now and then just to keep us on our toes. Or indeed, in amongst our toes. They're generally very good cats who know to go outside, down the garden path and into next door's garden where they can shit with gay abandon, but every now and then they'll decide that really the only place worth anointing with half a litre of eye-watering cat piss is next to my shoes, or in a drawer, or, perhaps best of all, all over the top of the Sky-Box in a protest against hearing the Jeremy Kyle theme tune for the 655th time that week. We got rid of that cat in the end – she went to a better place. Under the wheels of my car. No no I jest, she's up the road turning into a footrest with paws, remember?

So this means, for me at least, weeks of making

awkward small talk and worrying that anything I say is going to look like I'm trying to seduce them in some kind of awkward Bangbus-esque scenario. Honestly, it's something I probably shouldn't worry about but I've seen too many jizzflicks to know this is how so many of them start. Plus I can't make small talk so I stay away but then I worry about looking standoffish so I spend my time in such a state of anxious flux that I almost want to pay them just to go away. Urgh. So pray for me.

twochubbycubs on: our Corsican holiday: part one

Paul's done his back in thanks to a bit of adventurous moving around of our giant new sofa last night, so I'm free to type away with gay abandon tonight. We're fretting that the new sofa is a smidge too big, given you could perfectly easily get a whole rugby team spread akimbo on there. Maybe that's our plan, thank fuck we bought the leather guard. I'm going to tell you – the recipe tonight looks so dreadful but it tastes amazing. I say it looks dreadful – it looked BLOODY AMAZING, but so bad for you...

So, what to talk about? How about our trip to Corsica? You know I love a good tale and well, with Paul off his tits on tramadol and a bit of Murray Gold playing, now is the time. Oh, about that – we've kitted the house out in SONOS speakers and it is absolutely fucking amazing. They're essentially very loud, very good, very connected speakers that allow you to play music in any room, all controlled by the iPad. The advertising shows a sophisticated couple listening to a spot of Debussy in their study before retiring to bed accompanied by Radio 4. The reality, in The Sticky Patch at least, is that Paul has to endure me caterwauling my way through Now That's What I Call Period Pain 85 whilst sitting on the shitter. Mind, the flipside of that is that we get woken up by Meat Loaf blasting away inches from my face first thing in the morning. A boy can dream, though I mean, no, Meat Loaf is amazing but he has a face like a chewed toffee, so perhaps not. Bloody sidetracked again!

Why Corsica? The answer I'd like to give is that I saw it once in a Guardian travel section and fell in love with the beautiful scenery and tasteful architecture, but actually, the real reason was that a good friend of mine at work, who always travels to impeccably smart places, raved about it – and I'm incredibly easily led. Wherever she goes I end up perusing and following. I hope she doesn't tell me when her next smear test is otherwise I'll find myself at Wansbeck Hospital with my legs in the air and a Magic Tree hanging on my willy before you can say 'I hardly think that's appropriate'. Listen I don't know how it all works. I honestly thought Corsica was a Greece island but no, it turns out that it's a wee island off the coast of France, full of mountains, white sandy beaches and men who drive their cars like they're in a video game. Take a moment to have a look. We booked it through Simpson Travel, another first for us because we normally like to plan and book the flights, villa and car hire ourselves. They were faultless – expensive, but you get what you pay for.

We decided to get the train down to London the day before our flight so we could "see the sights" and as a result, we found ourselves in a taxi at 5.30am trying awkwardly to make conversation with a man whose entire conversational skillset amounted to 'money now', 'where you go' and, presumably, 'don't scream and it'll be quick'. I've mentioned before that I worry that as soon as we've minced off into the sunset with our tasteful matching Calvin Klein suitcases the taxi will nip back to the house and the driver will steal all our silver. So, to that end, I spent a good ten minutes airily declaring that I hoped the neighbours 'didn't set off our alarm' and that 'our flatmate would be back early'. I can't act a jot, so god knows how we didn't return to an empty shell of a house. I'm such a ham.

The train journey was exactly what you'd expect from a three hour early morning jaunt into London – full of people coughing gently, snoring and farting. Certainly Paul kept his side of the bargain up within ten minutes of boarding. We were in first class but really, what does that mean in the UK? You get a seat that reclines an extra inch and the steward throws you a croissant ten minutes after boarding. Clearly they decided that any decent person wouldn't want more than one snack because the trolley never appeared again, despite me trying to catch the eye of the bustling steward who did nothing more than purse his lips at me. We did get several free cups of hot brown water from a kettle marked 'coffee' but as this tasted like enema run-off, I didn't bother. Time passed slowly – I couldn't very well fall asleep because I might have missed something free, plus I didn't want my unattractive sleep face to end up on Buzzfeed as part of a 'Sleep face or Cum face' quiz. Such is life.

We arrived into Kings Cross exactly on time and immediately headed over to Left Luggage to hand over our holiday belongings and give the woman behind the counter plenty of time to rifle through our medications and hold our boxer shorts up to the light. I asked how much it would be to leave them for a few hours and when she replied, I honestly thought she'd misheard me and thought I'd requested that she buys them outright. Fucking hell London, you so expensive. Now we all know London is expensive and busy so I'll try to avoid moaning about that too much, but rest assured dear readers that I spent a lot of time saying 'HOW MUCH' and 'COME AGAIN' and making jibes about needing to get out a mortgage just to pay the tube fare. Paul, to his credit, only rolled his eyes to the back of his head eighty seven times.

Our first stop was a quick ride on the cable car over the Thames. I wasn't sure what I was expecting, if I'm honest, but although it was fun being high up, I was too distracted by thoughts of tumbling into the murky brown Thames below to really enjoy it. I did enjoy the fact they market it as a round trip to 'savour all the sights' – presumably for those who can't crane their necks in both directions. We nipped off and into the A380 experience, which was a tiny museum dedicated to Airbus planes. There was a chance to pose inside a cockpit but we had to wait fifteen minutes whilst someone who'd clearly been cultivating his body odour for seven months took a photo of himself from every direction. I noted his unkempt hair and dirty trousers and genuinely thought – for the first time in my life – that poor bloke needs someone to love him and tidy him up. That, and his internet activity carefully monitored. As soon as I was able to sit down in the captain's chair (and remember I had to wait for his BO to disperse – I genuinely thought the oxygen masks might have dropped down, and this was a fake fucking plane) we started taking photos – Paul posing with the 'FLAPS' handle, me wearing a Captain's hat and straddling the chair like a slutty stewardess. Thankfully none of these photos will be making their way onto here, though I don't doubt we're on a 'Don't Let These People Into The Exhibition' poster in the staffroom, along with ole Vinegarpits.

We then furiously minced down to get a riverboat back into 'central' London, which was charming until the smell of the churned riverbanks hit me. Was London going to leave me with permanent wrinkles from all the time I spent trying not to gag? I've visited many, many times before and love the city, but I don't know whether it was the heat or something but it stank. We alighted at Tower Bridge and made our way to The Shard, which was something I almost did in my boxers when they told me the price for two blokes to get in a lift and wander around high in the sky – £60! They sneakily hide the price until you get to the register so you can't back out else you'd look like a tight-arse, but jesus, I can get the same feeling at work and I get bloody paid for the privilege. The lift was lovely but they let far too many people onto the viewing floor at once including a coach tour of elderly Welsh ladies – I feel like I spent £60 to glimpse tiny London through a mist of Steradent and blue-rinsed hair. We, sadly, left rather quickly. I always feel like this when I'm supposed to experience things – I know that I am supposed to be astonished by how wonderful the view is or high up we were, but I just end up angry by everyone else existing and how much the windows needed a bit of vinegar and newspaper. Bah.

We decided at this point to collect the luggage and head to our hotel instead for holiday bumfun and room service. I wish I could say that we chose a wonderful boutique hotel somewhere charming, but we actually spent the night at the Thistle Hotel at Heathrow Airport, which is very much a place where middle-aged stationery salesmen go to badly fuck their secretaries in a mist of regret and Joop. I've never been so underwhelmed by the exterior of a building, and you must remember that I spent a summer in Southend once. We chose this hotel for a reason, though, and it certainly wasn't the architecture. No, see, it's connected to Terminal 5 via the 'Pod' system, and that is AMAZING to us as two very geeky lads. It's essentially a little taxi service but you get your own 'Pod' and it drives itself! GASP. Press a button, and a tiny robotic chamber comes beetling down the track and you climb inside. They're sleek, purple and spacious, although it does feel a bit like you're wheeling your suitcase into a portable toilet. Then it silently trundles along a track by itself and drops you off wherever you need to be. It's the future! Of course, being the UK, we were immediately charged £5 each for having the temerity to take a driverless car to the hotel. What's that charge for? I certainly didn't see anyone behind the thing pushing it and humming. Bastards.

We were shown to our room, and of course, it was very conveniently placed only a short flight away from the reception desk, and it was...perfunctory. It had a bed, it was clean, the TV boasted colour and at least six channels, so we went to sleep, woke only to order room service (£17 for a burger that I could have planed my feet with) and watch Doctor Who, and suddenly it was time to depart for our flight. That's where we can leave it   for   now.

twochubbycubs on: our Corsican holiday: part two

...when I last signed off, we were asleep with a puck of beef resting in our stomach. I reckon it's still in there. We woke ridiculously early to give us enough time to walk the 27 miles to the Pod, only to have to walk back and get a code from reception before they'd open the gates. Nothing says 'home comforts' like a prison gate to get out of your hotel. The Pod remained amazing and we were in Terminal 5 in moments. I've never flown from Heathrow despite having done a fair bit of travelling, so it was all very new and exciting. Ah wait no, sorry, it was dull and tedious. I know airports are never the most exciting of places, but I get the impression that unless you were minted, the terminal wasn't really for you. It's still better than Newcastle Airport mind, but that's more due to the fact Newcastle Airport consists of a couple of bars, a duty free shop and some toilets that haven't been cleaned since the days of me being an early teenager and buying condoms from the machine on the wall because my then-f'buddy was too worried. Ha! Plus it's invariably full of at least 2,000 pissed up Geordies who think they're sophisticated because they've got a Stella Artois moustache at 4.30am in the morning. Oh honestly you know I'm right.

We decided on a light breakfast in The Pilot's Lounge, so-called because I went up-a-height when I saw the price. The waitress – a smile wearing a tabard and sensible shoes – forgot to give me my pot of tea, my toast and my hash-brown. It's alright though, I forgot to give her a tip, so that balances things. You know how I can't go anywhere without immediately discovering a new enemy? I'd barely buttered Paul's toast when I overheard an American chap behind me LOUDLY telling everyone south of Manchester how 'TERRABUL' the coffee was in England. Oh it was just 'AWFUL' (though he was strangling every vowel as he spoke). I couldn't eat my breakfast because my teeth were grinding so hard diamonds were falling out of my nose. I'm a proper moaner, don't get me wrong, but I'm awfully British about it – I'll twist my face to Paul about something that has upset me, but I'll wait six months and bring it up in the bath or something. He went on – it was all I could do not to hurl Paul's tea in his oily face. Listen, I've been to America and I've had what passes for coffee there – it looks, smells and tastes like what I've bled out of my radiators. When he wasn't moaning he was hacking away, coughing up phlegm like it was jet-fuel. No discreet coughs into a hanky for this chap, no, he preferred to let us listen to his chest echo and rattle. No wonder the coffee didn't taste good, chum, it has to sink through eight yards of lungbutter to get to your stomach. Fucker.

Having finished breakfast and realised to our absolute horror that there wasn't so much as an arcade for me to throw a month's wage into, we settled down for the two hours before our flight. Thankfully, I had my new phone, old phone and iPad to entertain me, so I just sat on one of the departure lounge chairs with them spread out in front of me like I was on the lowest budget version of 24 you could imagine. Paul ate a Toblerone. OF COURSE, though, the horsefucker from the restaurant was on our flight. Of course! So we had two hours of boredom punctuated by him mining for phlegm. Lovely. My sigh of relief when they opened the gate almost blew the Newcastle to London Cityjet service over. The good thing about flying British Airways is the allocated seating – I can't bear the undignified scramble for seats you get with the likes of easyJet and Ryanair. I don't understand it – it's not as if the flight attendants are going to auction off the spare seats if you're not jammed in the bloody doorway one minute after the gate opens.

We promptly boarded the plane and, as expected, immediately brought the average age of the passengers on board down by around thirty years – everyone, to an absolute fault, was ancient. I wouldn't have been surprised if British Airways had removed the back toilet and fitted an onboard crematorium. Normally I watch the safety demonstration like my life depends on it (boom boom) but I didn't bother – it was clear from the amount of creaking hips and whistling hearing aids that if the engine had caught fire and we needed to evacuate post-haste, both Paul and I would perish in the flames whilst Elsie in 22A blocked the aisle putting her good teeth in and trying to get the inflatable slide to come out of the toilet door. We did have a chuckle when the exceptionally posh older chap sitting behind us dropped something on the floor and burst out with the loudest 'FUCK' I've ever heard. My ears were still rippling as we flew over Nice. I love it when posh folk swear with gusto.

The pilot came on the radio (you'd think that would make it hard to grip) and announced that it would be a smooth flight all the way to Corsica and that it was gorgeous and sunny. Excellent! I like to hear the hairs on my leg crinkle when I get off the plane when I'm on holiday. Go hot or go home, or something like that. I don't know the hip sayings, I'm in my thirties now. Oh fuck I'm old.

As usual when I fly, I spent the entire time on the runway thinking about how it would feel if my face was burned off when the fuel tank exploded or what sound the bones in my leg would make as they were concertinaed by the crumpling metal of a crashing 737, but as soon as we were airborne I was fine and only concerned with making sure I didn't miss out on the onboard snack, which turned out to be a croissant I could have shaved with and a plastic cup of orange water. Delicious! I still ate every last crumb whilst moaning about it to Paul. Our flight attendant was charming but looked like Missy from Doctor Who, which was a little alarming, because I did expect her to wrest the controls from the pilot and ditch us into the sea.

The flight itself was uneventful, bar for a tiny bout of turbulence as we flew over the bottom of France which shook a few pair of dentures loose, and we disembarked in Figari after only two hours. Figari Airport is absolutely tiny and only seems to appear once the plane is low enough for me to look for a four-leaf clover amongst the grass. It was in no time at all that we were off the plane and through what was ostensibly called security but actually amounted to nothing more than a very handsome Frenchman saying bonjour to me and oppressing his smirk at my bong-eyed passport photo. Paul held us up with his pressing need to have a poo as soon as we arrive anywhere new (I touched on this when I wrote about our visit to Germany – it's like a nervous tic he has) and we were forced to wait behind M. Physema in the AVIS car hire queue.

The car hire process was unpleasant, not least because I had to listen to the guy in front churning his lungs for a good thirty minutes before we got anywhere. The unpleasant shrew behind the counter barked at me in what I'm not even sure was French, hurled a set of paperwork at me like I'd murdered her child and then spat in the general direction of a trillion parked cars and sent me on my way. I don't think I managed one word other than a cheery bonjour which might have caused her ire. We trundled our suitcases down to the little garage only for someone else to shout inexplicably at us. At this point, we were a little deflated, and when someone finally drove a car around to us my spirits didn't lift. It was a Peugeot 208. A new one, yes, but I've had farts with better acceleration. Plus, Paul and I are big guys and a tiny car doesn't quite suit our ample frames – I've never had to pour myself into a car like a glob of wax in a lava-lamp. Nevermind. They clearly hadn't cleaned the car either given there was someone's chewed off fingernail sitting on the dash. I made a mental note to leave a skidmark on the back seat and cracked on.

We didn't have the language skills to argue or beg a better car, plus I got the impression that had I gone back to the rental desk and complained, my face would have been taken off by the tongue of the angry pickled Nana Mouskouri lookalike behind the desk. So we set off, slowly. Oh so slowly. The road away from Figari airport takes you up a fairly steep hill and clearly I overstretched the car because it stalled on the first hill. Superb! Thankfully I was so distracted by trying to master driving this shitbox that I forgot all my worries about driving on the right, which was a relief given I'd built it up into being a terrifying experience in my mind.

Actually, a serious note. If you're nervous about driving on the other side of the road, don't be. It comes very naturally – the only thing of concern were the roundabouts, of which there are many, and the fact that absolutely no fucker indicates. Not one! Joining a roundabout becomes a terrifying guessing game of intentions and given the average Corsican drives like the interior of their car is on fire and they've got a mouthful of petrol, you really do just need to take your time.

Yes, the driving leaves a lot to be desired (or, another view, they all know the roads so well that they know where they can afford to take chances) – quite often on a mountain pass you'll be faced with someone hurtling towards you in a little Renault, fag in one hand, phone in the other, steering the car with their blanket of chest hair, leaving you with the choice of a solid wall on one side of the road and nothing but air on the other. Best of all is the look of absolute astonishment that they've found someone coming towards them on the opposite side of the road. I'm not a religious man but there were more than a few times I just shut my eyes and prayed for the best. It's not uncommon for someone to overtake you on a blind corner or on the crest of a hill and to blur alongside the car shouting something terrible. I finally discovered what it must feel like to have me driving up behind you effing and jeffing. What am I like. Our villa awaited, but my fingers are bleeding now, so I'll stop for the night.

twochubbycubs on: our Corsican holiday: part three

After landing at Figari, and wrestling the keys from a woman who probably could have brought the car in on her shoulders, we were on our way down the N198 (the main road 'around' Corsica) to the charming little town of Sainte Lucie de Porto Vecchio, which was a good half hour drive away. We didn't mind the drive, it gave us an opportunity to let the scenery sink in. Corsica is beautiful – a true island of contrasts, with white beaches, heady mountains, green fields and dusty trees – and not what I was expecting. Our car, protesting as it did every time I dared nudge it above 40mph, shuttled us towards the town, and, us being us, we drive right past the turn off for the villa. Good stuff! We realised our mistake a good twenty minutes down the road and pulled over in a dusty lay-by by a beach to take stock. I could have texted the rep for directions and assistance but Paul had packed away my mobile into the suitcase, locked the suitcase, and put it in the bottom of the boot. It was altogether too much effort to sort. Paul insists on locking the suitcases at every opportunity, partly because they're fancy-dan editions where the zips actually form part of the locking system. He locked them after we had wedged them into the boot of the car. He remained entirely non-plussed by my bewildered reasoning of 'who the fuck is going to nick anything from a moving car, a tiny Corsican gypsy hiding in the ashtray?'. Honestly, the things I have to put up with. Frankly, if someone is that desperate to be at my passport that they want to sort through my extra-extra-large t-shirts and his 'broken in' boxers shorts, they deserve a reward.

Paul nipped into the bushes for a piddle and came dashing out with an alarmed face – not because of snakes, or scary wild boars, but (in his words) 'there's SO MUCH SHITTY BOG PAPER IN HERE'. Oh lovely! That would be a bit of a theme mind. Corsica is astonishing, but by god don't venture into the bushes to change your clothes, empty your shoes of half a ton of sand or for a piss, because they sure do love shitting and leaving the paper for nature. Don't get me wrong, I wouldn't imagine anyone would take their skidmarked paper home like a flower pressing, but at least bury it, don't festoon the fucking branches with it. Honestly, it looked like Christmas in Worksop.

We stopped at a nearby Spar for groceries. Groceries isn't quite the right word for the food you buy on holiday, though, is it? The only thing we left the shop with that could provide any nutritional value was the receipt. I'm going to hazard a guess that it will be the only time in my life that a bottle of Limoncello, swimming googles, eight bags of Haribo, headache pills, Pringles and enough bread to build an ark would appear in my shopping basket together. We did buy a token bag of rocket which looked great in the fridge at the start of the holiday and even better in the bin at the end. As a 'car snack' we bought a pretzel the size of a steering wheel to eat in the car (I was reassured that I could have dislodged any errant blobs of dough from my teeth with the toenail clipping that the previous driver had generously left on the dash) and we were back on our way. Let me tell you – it's difficult to drive an unfamiliar car on unfamiliar roads whilst trying to make sure Paul didn't get more than half of the bread. We made our back, veering dangerously across the road and spraying crumbs everywhere until we spotted the turn-off.

I have to say, the approach to the villa wasn't very inviting – it looked like the start of every dodgy serial-killer film I've ever seen – and the architects had carefully and assuredly made sure to put as many possible pot-holes and boulders on the drive-way, so that the 100m drive up to the villa made me feel like a trainer in a tumble drier. It was worth it, though. It accommodates ten people, so naturally it was just the right size for Paul and I to mince around naked and use every single bed to get the full value out of the holiday. Anyone else do that? God forbid the maid would get a moment to herself, we were too busy crinkling the bedsheets and leaving chest hairs in every conceivable crevice to care. Paul went for a dump almost immediately, despite having 'freshened the air' at the airport a mere hour ago. He uses new toilets like one might stamp a passport – to say he's been.

Nevertheless, the suitcases hadn't been unlocked more than half a minute before I was fully undressed and scampering to the pool. That's a fib, I'm too fat to scamper. Let's go with trundle. Lumbered. Yeah – I lumbered excitedly to the pool. That doesn't work either, actually, because you can't lumber with enthusiasm. How the fuck do you describe that grotesque speedy 'shift' that us fatties do? Shall we say I galumphed to the pool? That means to move in a 'loud and clumsy way', which describes the way my thighs slap when I go at speed. I galumphed to the pool. Not quite 'Arnold raced out of the door', mind.

I spent five minutes teetering on the step of the pool because it was SO BLOODY COLD. Not because it wasn't heated, it was, but because I was so overheated in my 'English' clothes that anything less than a pan of boiling jam hurled in my face would have felt a bit 'nippy'. Paul shouted encouragement from the lavatory (thankfully that was a one-way process – I don't think the locals would have been especially pleased to hear my Geordie tones shouting 'PUSH' and 'IS IT CROWNING YET' across the fields) but that's rich coming from him. Paul has never, ever just 'got' into a pool. He has to inch himself in, letting the water hit each part of his body and letting out a tiny scream as it does so....OOOH ME ANKLES...OOH IT'S COLD...OOOH IT'S ON MY HELMET...CHRIST MY GUNT....and so on. He'll then spend ten minutes with it lapping just under his tits before finally he'll crack and tumble in like a falling mountain. A fatslide, if you will. I'm the opposite, I'll dither and fanny on for a little bit and then just jump in. I've got the luxury of all-over hair, see – the cold doesn't bother me so much because it has to penetrate my shag. It does rather look like someone has pushed an old persian rug into the pool, however. Even the air-filter gasped rather unnecessarily when I waded in, I thought.

Once I'd managed to acclimatise to the coldness of the pool and my scrotum had stopped resembling a Shredded Wheat, it was lovely. I swam around in that fat-person style – 2m of front-crawl, bob under the water, kick my legs about, lie on my back. I got a bloody fright when I felt something swim underneath me and envisioning some kind of aqua-wild-boar, I hurtled (again, however a fat man hurtles) to the other end of the pool only to realise it was the bloody pool cleaner. I hated it immediately. I have an inherent and deep phobia of machinery in water ever since I watched 999 and watched some poor horse-faced lady get stuck underwater when her pony-tail was sucked into a filter. Brrr. Although looking back, everyone was panicking and screaming but really, no-one thought to grab a pair of scissors? Anyway, this little device looked like a Roomba – a smooth circle of menace attached to a hose and with three turning wheels, and it's job was to beetle around the pool during the day (when normally, the guest would be out), sucking up leaves and hair and tagnuts. It was creepy. It moved silently through the water aside from a tiny electrical hum every now and then and all I could think was that it was going to either get entangled in my arse-hair (imagine THAT 999) or it'll somehow become live and fry me in the water like an especially fatty pork chop. I couldn't relax until Paul finished his dump, fished it out for me (the robot, not the poo) and placed it to the side, where it lay gasping and spluttering and wishing me dead. We did manage to turn it off before it drained the pool. Phew.

We then spent a hearty two hours getting in and out of the pool, lying on every sun-lounger and swinging in the hammock that rather put me in mind of a big metal bollock. By god they were comfy. I looked for them online when I got home only to discover they were over £1,000 each. I like comfort, but I don't think an afternoon lying in the mild air of Northumberland quite justifies the cost. Plus, I'd need to be dressed here, and it just wouldn't be the same. I was swinging away in my hammock telling Paul all my thoughts on the stewardesses and Corsicans when his lack of answering – and his rumbling snoring – told me he was off to sleep. Ah well. Regular readers will know that we can't go more than a few scattered minutes without impressing some kind of embarrassment on ourselves and it was my time to shine with a trip to buy yet more beer and bread. Beer and bread, it genuinely doesn't get better than that for a fatty. Don't worry needlessly however, we weren't forgetting our roots – the beer was an entirely unnecessary raspberry froth called pietra (recommended by a far classier and tasteful friend) and the bread a foccacia with pressed olives and bacon wedged inside. We're that fancy. Leaving Paul in the hammock to fart away to his heart, and indeed his arse's, content, I stole out of the villa with a view to restocking the fridge with all manner of local 'nice things' from the other grocery shop I'd spotted down the road.

You may recall that I can't speak a lick of French. I really can't. I only managed one year of 'French lessons' before I got so bored it was either transfer to Spanish or defenestrate myself. Actually, we used to take our lessons on the ground floor so the most I could have hoped for was a grazed knee and an audition for drama school. It didn't help that our French teacher had an eye full of blood for seven months. It's all any of us could look at. No wonder I never learned my pronouns for goodness sake, he looked like the Terminator 2 poster rendered in Microsoft Paint. After a year I transferred over to learn Spanish and well, no me arrepiento, right? That said, I'm always keen to at least try, so I spent the fifteen minutes walking down to the shop reading my language app and practising out loud anything I may need to say – '...huit tranches de jambon, s'il vous plaît', or 'une petite portion de fromage local, mon amour' or indeed, '...pouvez-vous me montrer aux préservatifs extra-forts?' I genuinely thought I'd be welcomed and praised for my attempts, that perhaps someone would admirably slap me on my back and strike up in French with me about the local political situation or Greece's turbulent economy. Thank fuck they didn't – me repeating 'QUOI' over and over wouldn't have quite the same effect.

Anyway, you can guess, that didn't quite happen. No. I minced around the shop, filling my basket with ham and eggs and cheeses and, somewhat inexplicably, a box of blonde hair dye because I had a fit of the vapours and thought about dyeing my hair blonde because I'm on holiday, which has to rank up there amongst the 'unlikeliest thing to do because I'm on holiday' together with having a colonoscopy or visiting the dentist. My basket was full of deliciousness and I was immensely proud of myself for engaging the various shop folk in stilted, bare-bones chatter. I spotted the beer I'd seen earlier and put two six packs in my basket. All good. No. In my haste to reach for a bottle of mixer, my basket tipped over and deposited everything I'd picked up all over the bloody floor, each beer bottle shattering at once in the most noisy fashion. It would have been quieter if I'd ramraided the shop in a fucking train.

Time stopped. Every single person in the shop – indeed, the island – span around to look at me in a most accusatory manner, as if I was some tiny-scale terrorist. I stood there, desperately fishing around in my head for any relevant French, but I could feel every last French word in my brain popping like champagne bubbles, rendering me entirely mute and confused in a sea of glass and blood-coloured beer. Finally, the silence was broken by the absolute harridan behind the till yelling and shouting at me in incomprehensible gibberish and waving her hands around like Tony Blair bringing in an aeroplane. After a good couple of minutes I FINALLY remembered and I blurted out 'je suis désolé' over and over until she FINALLY twigged I couldn't understand her. Do you know what is shameful? I only know 'je suis désolé' from a bloody Madonna song. Thank God for ole Vinegartits! Some genuinely tiny hairy man came bustling out from the back with a brush and set about clearing away the glass with such exaggerated sighs and harumphing that I almost emptied out my tomatoes and gave him the paper bag to breathe into. I wish I knew what the French was for FAT, ENGLISH, CLUMSY OAF. I felt paranoid that the cow behind the counter was going to put a tannoy announcement mocking my silliness so I hastily paid (her slapping the coins down into my hand with such venom that if I turn my wrist towards the sun, I can make out the imprint of a two euro coin under my thumb) and scuttled back to Paul, who hadn't so much as noticed I was out of the pool.

To make up for my folly, he prepared a delicious tea of French bread, cheese, ham, grapes and that great equaliser, Pringles. ROSEMARY FLAVOURED PRINGLES, mind you. Living the dream! We spent the rest of the evening lounging and watching Modern Family on the Chromecast.

Sweet Jesus. I've typed 3,000 words and all I've managed to do is get to the villa and drop some beer. I need an editor!

twochubbycubs on: our Corsican holiday: part four

I want to chunter on about our holiday. Can I remember the details? Of CORSICAN. It's exactly that level of shit-hot humour you bloody love.

The last time I wittered on about Corsica, I told you about how lovely the villa was, how appalling my French was and how I managed to make a complete tit of myself in the middle of a French supermarket only to be shouted at and admonished by a merrily-whiskered lady behind the till. I'm not going to write chronologically about what we did going forward because frankly, we spent an awful amount of time sitting around doing nothing other than eating bread and relaxing in the sun.

That was my first downfall. See, I managed to burn myself in the sun. I'm always so careful to protect myself against the sun (health anxiety, remember), and despite previous times when I've turned myself blue by applying too much sun-screen, I slicked it on with gay abandon. Listen, I'm a Geordie – we don't do bronzed and golden, we do either Philip Schofield's hair white or alarming-boil-red. There's no middle ground. I'm a big guy and I take a lot of sunscreen to cover me (I did think it would be quicker to use one of those hoses so dramatically employed in decontamination chambers) but I thought I had it licked. Nope. After three hours of merrily splashing around in the pool and sizzling gently on the sun-lounger, I noticed that my right buttock was a trifle sore.

This isn't uncommon – I use my bum-cheeks most of the day, so a little tenderness can be expected. Normally Paul just needs to tilt me to relieve the pressure. But no, this was a more serious pain – I had managed to half of my arse a charming post-box red. You genuinely don't realise how much your arse touches something until it feels like it's been pressed against the door of an industrial kiln for a few moments. Every sit was uncomfortable, every walk a mixture of chaffing and sadness. Plus, in my mind, my arse now resembled a block of Neapolitan ice-cream, only far less delicious. Paul had to spend five minutes gently kneading my buttocks with after-sun to bring comfort – it may have looked slightly erotic if it wasn't for me yelling that he was catching my arse-hair in the metal clasps of his watch.

Now now, don't get preachy, most men have a hairy button, it's just a fact of life. Paul was once climbing naked into the shower when I ran into the bathroom and clipped a clothes peg to his bum-hair for a laugh. I managed to just nip his sphincter in the peg mechanism. Well, honestly. I've never heard him scream so loud – there would have been a less dramatic response had I shot his foot off with a sawn-off shotgun. He didn't speak to me for the rest of the day and it was only after I bought him a 1kg bar of Dairy Milk from Amazon and allowed him to delete all my favourite programmes from the Sky Planner that his frostiness melted.

That was me injured. Paul's turn now. Dotted around the pool were three metal 'hammocks' which were shaped like open metal balls suspended from a frame.

I declined to get into them as I was worried the chain would snap under my weight and well, I hate to hear metal scream, but Paul is lighter and more daring so flung himself into one with gay abandon. As if we could manage any other kind of abandon, dearie me. He swung around for a bit until he realised he was going to struggle to get out, given he's only got little legs and the ball shape didn't lend itself to an easy exit. I watched as he valiantly declared he'd found a way off only to swing the entire frame over and land, quite literally, flat on his face, with the frame of the hammock smacking his on the back of the head a moment later. I couldn't tell if the loud 'ooof' came from me, his mouth or the air escaping from his fat, but it was hilarious. Me being a conscientious, kind-hearted husband couldn't do a jot for laughing – indeed, I laughed so much from the deep-end of the pool that I almost drowned myself (that'll teach me) and he lay for a good few seconds before laughing and moving. I'd be a shit paramedic – anything faintly slapstick and they'd be declaring death whilst I stood around slapping my knees with merriment. Perhaps it was karma from when something similar happened to me in Dobbies – we just don't do well with hammocks.

Once we'd wiped the tears from our eyes (mine tears of laughter, his tears of blood and ocular fluid) we took a moment to decide what to do and decided on a spot of lunch. I was clearly so upset and fraught with the worry that Paul's skull was filling with blood from his massive internal injury that it was really all I could do to take myself off for a long shower whilst Paul set about cutting up cheese and putting rocket in a bowl – well, it makes it easier to scrape into the bin later on. It was just as Paul was bending down (naked, remember) to get something from the crisper drawer when our rep appeared at the open living room door with a loud 'HELLO'. Paul, mortified, spun around on his heel and clutched a tea-towel to his genitals (the same tea-towel I later saw him cleaning my wine glass with – which explains why I wondered if we were having Brie with our sauvignon blanc later on). Paul doesn't do exhibitionism (even though he should, because he's lovely), unlike me. I'm not fussed when I'm on holiday, I'll cheerfully flop it out if it saves me carrying my swimming knickers to the beach.

I don't swear 'swimming knickers' I hasten to add, I just like how that sounds in my head'.

What followed (I had taken a moment to stop murdering Cher's greatest hits in the shower in order to gleefully listen) was a toe-curling exchange where Paul, frozen behind a breakfast bar with only a tea-towel and a packet of Pringles to hide his modesty, had to exchange polite conversation about how to turn off the pool alarm and where to leave the towels whilst the rep looked absolutely everywhere but his body. The rep was lovely mind, don't get me wrong, and he had the good grace not to shout 'YOU'RE NOT SUPPOSED TO LET CATTLE IN' to me as I came out of the shower towelled and pleasant. He then explained that as a gay nudist he had seen it all before, as though Paul was some spectacle designed to be peeped at through a hole in the door. In another world it may have been the beginning of a raunchy Xtube video but not ours – Paul was so shocked and frightened that he had to have half of my sandwich just to calm down.

I appreciate that this reads like some campy seventies farce but, as Mags is my witness, it's the truth. Worst part of it all? Paul was so distracted by not accidentally showing the rep his lid that he paid no attention as to how to turn off the pool alarm, and MAN was that alarm sensitive. Each morning we'd be woken by it screeching away if a leaf tumbled in or a water-molecule split. I swear I sighed once in bed at the other end of the villa and it was away, wailing and blaring like a rape alarm. Our poor neighbours. Whilst we couldn't see anyone nearby – it was forest that surrounded us – we knew there were people close-by by the laughter and sound of cars crunching over gravel. Knowing us, we were probably perched at the end of a housing estate or a nursing home and several dozen Corsican families were being treated daily to the sight of our naked buttocks (mine a fetching red) as we climbed in the pool. Ah well. Not like we'll ever see them again.

Final tale before I sign off for the night. We did a very British thing indeed. Perhaps not British, actually, but rather the domain of the bone-idle. We decided halfway through the holiday to have a trip along the island to the port town of Bastia, a good three hour drive away (taking into account Paul's need to stop every thirty minutes for a dump as we entered somewhere new). We planned the route the night before, made a couple of sandwiches for the car, set the alarm – all ready. We were in the car and making excellent time by around 8am. We'd researched local museums and excellent restaurants to try on our day out, oh what a lovely day. Hmm. The reality of it was that we drove for three hours and then couldn't find a parking space. Not one. The French seem to park their cars like they're dashing into maternity wards and haven't a moment to lose. Every side street is an obstacle course of Corsican Corsas, with cars parked parallel, flush and across the road. I couldn't understand it and the rage built up in me to such an extent that I yelled 'WELL FUCK THIS', did a 76 point turn in the middle of a one-way street and immediately revved the hell out of Bastia. Bastia? More like BASTARD.

It might have been a lovely town full of curios and

wonder, but all we saw of it was the back of a tour bus and the interior of a very large supermarket where we stopped for a calming round of bread and cheese. We'd managed the equivalent of driving to Durham from London, stopping at a Tesco Extra, buying a loaf of bread and driving home. The drive home was fairly silent – Paul slept, and I spent most of the time with my eye twitching and a renewed dislike of the world. I did switch the radio on but frankly it sounded like I'd tuned into a cockfight so that was snapped off in anger too.

I was at least reassured that when recounting this tale to a friend that she had done exactly the same, right down to the stopping at the supermarket on the way back. Phew.

We'll leave it there.

twochubbycubs on: our Corsican holiday: part five

If I'm honest, the rest of the Corsican holiday was a relaxed mix of beaches, eating out and sightseeing, and doesn't especially lend itself to long tales of hilarity and embarrassing ourselves and making the British look terrible. So, as I mentioned earlier, I'll rattle off a few vignettes from various points in the holiday instead.

First, the beaches. For weeks before I was in a state of flux, flipping between not giving a toss about what people thought of my body to agonising over the thought of harsh words and cold stares from the body beautiful as I clambered in and out of my beach towel. However, once we were there, it became a good honest case of "ah fuck it" and we didn't give so much as a thought to what anyone else thought. Life is too short to worry what the French is for "who's left an old settee lying on this beach". Always go into these situations with the knowledge that you're unlikely to ever see these folk again, and so what if they think you look like a solar eclipse of shifting fat.

The beaches – at Palombaggia and Pinarello respectively – are just marvellous. You know when you see those beaches in adverts where the sand is white, the sea is blue and everyone is tanned and terrific – well, it was just like that, only with two milk-bottle white Geordies standing glinting in the sun in their

George swimshorts like morbidly obese lighthouses. We divided our time between swimming in the sea, snorkelling and splashing about, and trying to lie on the beach like good tourists.

Neither of us can 'lie and sizzle' on a beach, though. I fidget too much for one thing, constantly picking up my book only to read two pages and get frustrated with the wind blowing the pages around, or worrying about whether I'm coated in enough Crisp 'n' Dry to make the visit worthwhile. Joking aside, after burning my arse the other day I was slicked up with enough sun-tan lotion that Greenpeace had to come and hose me down. Nah that joke didn't work, but I'm leaving it in.

One thing we both realised is how cavalier other nations are when it comes to nudity – the average Brit will huddle behind a beach towel changing cautiously lest anyone gets so much as a glimpse of tit, whereas other nations are content to flap their genitals around mere moments away from your face. This wouldn't normally bother either of us – we've seen more penises than we've had hot dinners, and more often than not the former has lead to the latter – but even so. It puts us in that awkward position where you don't want to look because well, that would be weird, but at the same time, you don't want to not look because you know, it's just nature, and well, all lads like to know where they stand on the length ladder. Cocks are inexplicably ugly things when they're on the flop, I think, and even worse when they're sweating in the sun like the last chipolata on the buffet.

We took a trip into the mountains for a drive, taking the D368 for a lovely afternoon. I say lovely, it was, but white-knuckle doesn't begin to describe it. I've touched upon the Corsican lack of driving sensibilities and no more so was that noticeable on the windy roads with a canyon on one side and a cliff wall on the other. It always amused / terrified me to notice these drivers hurtling towards me, in my lane, with scant regard for what was in front of them – normally fiddling with their phones, or completing a jigsaw, or flambéing cherries for a crepe. I almost had to crepe a few times swerving around them.

The road had a cruel trick up its sleeve – a surprise dam. The worst kind! I can't remember if I've ever mentioned it, but I have two major phobias – manmade water structures (dams, weirs, reservoirs etc.) and irregular holes. The holes thing is common, though I can't tell you the name of the phobia because it would mean googling it and I'm such a fanny that I'd probably have a panic attack. The fear of dams comes from my dad who works for the water company and filled our childhood with gruesome tales of creepy underwater machines and pipes to keep us from playing in the nearby reservoirs. Plus, dams have no business being there. They don't. They're ungainly and creepy and they're just itching to give away and release all that water in a fit of mischief.

In fact, it's not even the fear that they'll collapse that bother me about dams, it's rather that I'll fall into the water and be sucked into the turbines, or, even worse, encounter something truly terrifying called Delta P. Delta P is basically a change in pressure, but the reason it's dangerous is if you imagine a crack appearing in the dam wall and you're nearby, all the water will be trying to push you through, and well it would be like pushing jam through a letterbox. Yak. Paul thinks I'm being nonsensical and perhaps I am, but well, aren't all phobias irrational? We hastened over the dam as quick as the lawnmower-engine in our shitty Peugeot allowed and carried on our way. We did manage to get stuck behind a car full of old ladies who were going to slow they were being overtaken by their shadows, but that actually made a pleasant change of pace from the wall-of-death driving that pervaded the rest of the holiday.

The holiday rolled to its end and we were on our way back home in no time. Figari Airport had even less to look at leaving than it did arriving – once we'd carefully examined the rack of fridge magnets and been barked at by someone with a beard and a cracking set of tits for ordering the 'wrong coffee', we were on our way. Being so close to the runway and having nothing to do but gaze out afforded us the peculiar sight of our plane landing, everyone disembarking, our luggage being loaded and the plane being ready to board in less than ten minutes.

I'm not sure why that surprised me as much as it did – I guess in my mind I always imagine the plane has to rest for a bit, like a well-cooked steak or a marathon runner. Nevertheless, we were airborne and shaking our way through the clouds in no time at all. On making our way back to Kings Cross via the delighted of an overloaded Tube network (the rugby world cup being played out above us), we stumbled into the filming of a Channel 5 documentary about the Tube. So, if you're watching TV and you spot two fat blokes dithering in front of the camera whilst some hurly-burly tube worker throws a beggar on the floor, that's us, we're famous, and yes we'll sign your tits if you ask nicely.

One final recollection. We were in first class on the way home with Virgin, naturally, and a prim little man who looked like Charlie from Casualty brought the trolley around with our free drinks and sandwiches. We gobbled them up. He came flouncing past around ten minutes later and said 'Anyone want more food?' to which I put my hand up and requested another sandwich (we hadn't had anything to eat since the morning).

His reply was cutting and LOUD, to say the least:

"SIR YOU'LL NEED TO WAIT UNTIL I'VE FED THE REST OF THE TRAIN BEFORE I CAN GIVE YOU SECONDS"

The cheeky fucker. Why offer if you're just going to be a bitch about it? There was no need, I was genuinely mortified. Of course, being British, I didn't say anything in return — just went red and shrank back in my seat. I got a petty revenge later by tipping half of Palombaggia beach out of my trainers and into the aisle AND for good measure I flushed the toilet whilst in the station. I'm like James Dean me. Well, Dean Gaffney.

And really, that's all there is to say on Corsica.

We travelled with Simpson Travel, who specialise in luxury villa stays in Turkey, Greece, Corsica and Portugal. They arranged the entire trip — the villa, flights and car hire, and were impeccable to deal with. Our villa was the Casa Julia in Porto Vecchio and we flew with British Airways. I'd recommend Simpson Travel in a heartbeat, although a friend found them lacking after experiencing an emergency abroad. Something to consider.

twochubbycubs on: inappropriateness

Mild hysteria yesterday when, after both getting in from work and GASP, discovering the TV was covered in a dust blanket (which would have needed oooh...around 3 seconds to remove, but we were tired), we went straight to bed for a lie-down. As you do. I was winding Paul up by putting my finger in his belly button whilst he dozed only to pull out a finger covered in soft, brown, lumpy matter. I genuinely fell off the bed in horror thinking it was faeces. How and why didn't cross my mind. Paul woke up with a start (he tends to when I start shrieking, I'm like the campest alarm clock you could think of), saw the mess and looked equally confused.

Turns out it was a big old chunk of chocolate muffin that had spilled down his shirt whilst he wolfed it down in the car on the way home so I wouldn't know he'd cheated on his diet. See? Some people find out their husband is having an affair through errant text messages or boxer shorts that look like a painter's radio – I find out Paul has been cheating on his diet because his belly-button filled with chocolate. The poor bastard never gets a break, does he?

I managed to mortify him in Homebase yesterday when I told the woman behind the counter that the scented candle she proffered me 'smelled like my nana's house, and she's been dead for four months', then wandered off chuckling whilst Paul fished about for the Nectar card. I do that a lot, make comments and roll out of shot – we were once in ASDA behind someone describing (I think) a car crash by saying 'first he thrashed it over to the left, then the right, then it span out of control and four people got hurt', when I jokingly said 'Sounds like one hell of a smear test that' and disappeared into the magazine aisle. Paul's still got the burns from the glare he got off the poor lady. Ah well. It's all fun until someone gets punched on the tit.

Our house is still an absolute bombsite but at least, thanks to our excellent painter, all the painting is finally done. Excellent. Our cats decided to celebrate by dragging a bird through our cat-flap and splattering blood all over our hallway wall (Dulux Urban Obsession, since you ask). They're kind like that. How I chuckled and clutched at my sides as I pushed them back out the cat-flap with the toe of my Dr Martens and put the lock on. I think they knew they had upset me, they spent the next thirty minutes silently meowing at the living room window before giving up and resuming licking their arses with their back legs stuck up like a big fuck-you-finger to common decency.

The other bit of good news is that my absolute legend of a dad has finished building us our lovely patio outside in the back garden. Whilst that's smashing news for us as it means we can lounge about on our fabulous oak outdoor furniture, it's bad news for the neighbours as it means we can lounge about on our fabulous oak outdoor furniture, and they'll be sick with jealousy. Well, perhaps not jealousy, perhaps nausea. What kind of noise does a sweaty back peeling away from wood make? Like pulling the last rasher of bacon out of the packet I imagine. They've got that to look forward to.

Anyway, that's quite enough nonsense, I'm getting a pain from my back from typing this on the computer whilst sitting on a set of decorating ladders.

twochubbycubs on: a doctor's visit

So you may, or indeed may not, remember me prattling on about having a sore shoulder a while back which was resulting in a numb face and a painful neck. At first, I put it down to the extravagant swimming I pulled off in Corsica, or my particularly deft way of dragging a suitcase behind me with ne'ry a thought for my posture or the shins of passer-bys. I even had to go for an x-ray which was terribly exciting. Though not as exciting as the time I went for an MRI. Anyway, after the usual battling through a phone menu last revised back in the eighties and waiting the customary seven and a half years to get a doctor's appointment (on the basis I'm not 89, and thus unable to get up at 5am to queue up outside the surgery), I went in for my results. I didn't get my usual doctor. Instead, I got the doctor who I always try to avoid.

Now, let me say this. She's a brilliant doctor, exceptionally knowledgeable and concise, and I'd (luckily) trust her with my life. But I don't feel comfortable talking to her because she's very aloof. I like a doctor who I can crack a joke with to relieve the tension and who will patiently explain all of the difficult terminology to me, such as spondylosis or stenosis or irreversible anal trauma or leg. I once, at the very peak of my anxiety, asked whether or not my erratic heartbeat was to be the end of me, only to be told by a jolly doctor with a nose the colour of a postbox that 'I would still get the ladies to fit you up for a Christmas suit as opposed to a bodybag', before launching into a paroxysm of phlegm-filled chuckles. He was great, though I believe he's dead now, so who got the last laugh?

No, this doctor speaks to me in a very clipped, matter-of-fact tone. Very professional, which is probably why I don't get along. If I was a doctor I'd spend the entire time bringing out the giant arse thermometer with a wince on my face, only to poke it rudely in my patient's side with an 'only joking, no, seriously now, it's terminal'. I sat down in the chair and I was given a look that almost set my ears on fire – the results were discussed over…ooh, seven seconds, and I was told I had spondylosis and that was that. To me, spondylosis sounds like a Eurovision entry from one of the wildcard countries, like Azerbaijan. Or perhaps a packet of Belgian sweets. When I asked for a mite more information, she signed like I'd punctured her lung and explained it was a form of 'arthritis and a result of getting old'.

Getting old! I would understand if I was in my sixties but I'm only 30 – and whilst I've doubtless weathered my body disgustingly by years of smoking, drinking, casual sex and hilarious-obesity (well it's better than morbid obesity) – I don't think I'm 'getting old' just yet. Granted, I do make a noise like the air-brakes on a bus when I finally settle into my chair at the end of a working day, and I find myself picking up trinkets in garden centres and thinking 'well now isn't that just the ticket, a little foam pad for my knees when I'm weeding', but come on. There's a few years left in me yet, I hope. Actually, the fact that I put down in writing how often I'm in a garden centre is worrying – they were always the domain of ladies who smelled damp and men with cumulatively more hair sprouting out of their nose and ears than on their scalp – but then there I am on a Sunday, fingering the seed packets and worrying endlessly about my car being scratched. Hmm.

I courted her opinion on whether I should see a chiropractor and her reply was that she couldn't comment – I resisted to urge to ask whether she was being held against her will or if a rogue chiropractor was holding her children hostage. She referred me to have my bloods taken, which I'm beginning to think is just a ruse to build up supplies because I have a rare blood type and they're forever taking my blood. I swear, I go in for an ingrown toenail and they've got a needle in my arm before I'm so much as sat down in the reception flicking through a Home and Country. That's a fib. There's no Home and Country in our surgery. There's a few dog-eared OK magazines – 'It's true love for Anthea Turner!' and 'Happy future ahead for Princess Di' and a copy of Puzzler which I swear has been there since the centre was built – it's probably a load-bearing magazine – and will remain there evermore. Out of little more than spite, I've arranged an appointment with a chiropractor regardless. If anything, it'll give me something to twist my face about down the line. I do wish there was a way of discreetly asking whether or not their investigation table can stand up to twenty stone of fat slithered on top like cooling lava but no.

Anyway, enough about my day. It's hurting to type, so I'll need to hurry. I don't like having a neck pose that makes me look permanently inquisitive. I'm actually frightened that I'm going to end up like all of those silly people on facebook who cast their head to one side and pout into the camera in the misguided belief that it's hiding their chins, which are smartly avalanching into a fleshy heap under their right ear.

twochubbycubs on: getting through the night

That awkward moment when you're about to start writing, you open your blinds for inspiration and just over the road is the sight of a neighbour getting changed with his curtains open, his saggy back and 'Yes, I read the Daily Express' underwear on show for all to see. I hope he doesn't think I was peeking – I'd get more sexual gratification from reading the ingredients list on a Rustlers burger. It's only fair, they've seen Paul and I in the altogether enough time to draw a time-lapse of our bodies from memory, like a particularly gruesome version of the Take on Me video. They'd certainly need a big pencil. Fnar fnar.

I'm somewhat tetchy as sleep hasn't been especially forthcoming lately. No dramatic reason – Monday night I was awoken by Paul farting so loudly I thought someone had been shot. I couldn't decide whether my heart was beating so quickly due to the shock or because my body was trying desperately to dilate my nostrils as quick as possible in the hope of getting some fresh air. I appreciate that's crass but honestly, I couldn't drift off for another four hours. I had to get up and wash the dishes.

Last night was the worst, though. Went to bed full of good intentions and Chinese food at an entirely appropriate midnight. The blinds were drawn, our ceiling awash with stars from the little projector we have. All very serene. I was asleep before you could say 'Oh I wouldn't love, it's like a ploughed field back there'.

Woke up at 1am by the heating. Yes, the heating. Our house is now controlled by a tiny Nest thermostat which is apparently learning when we'd like the house to be warm and when we want it colder than a mother in law's kiss. For whatever reason, it decided that at 1am on a Wednesday morning I'd like to be cremated, because, not kidding, I woke up so hot I almost set off the smoke alarm. If Paul had hurled a pan of boiling sugar in my face I'd have been refreshed. I didn't even know our house could get to that temperature but somehow it managed it. I went to shake Paul awake because well, I wasn't going to get up, but touching him was like trying to catch a fish in a barrel full of lube, he was so slick with sweat. He's lucky, he could sleep through a plane crash. I wandered into the hallway to be bathed in light from our 'reassuring' smoke alarm (seriously, it lights up the hallway when you go for a piss so you don't stub your toe, how thoughtful), clocked the cat having a Solero to cool down, and adjusted the heating from 'Magma'. Perhaps it's trying to kill us.

I retired back to bed, after bailing all of Paul's sweat out of the bed and onto the floor, and drifted back off, comforted by the sound of my skin blistering as I slept.

At 1.45am, the cat, clearly refreshed, thought it was altogether too unfair that I had briefly teased him an hour ago, and proceeded to climb onto my pillow and start doing that 'knead-knead-purr' thing that cats do when they want your attention / want feeding. He was immediately (delicately) shot-putted out of the window (we live in a bungalow, it's fine, he bounces) and I tried to return to the Land of Nod.

Nope.

At around 2.30am, the cat came back through the cat-flap with such ferocity that he must have nudged the sensor on the back door just enough to set the house alarm caterwauling. Paul slept on, I stumbled out of bed calling the world a cunt, turned the alarm off and then furiously made myself a cup of tea. It's amazing how much rage you can funnel into boiling a kettle, honestly. At this point, after my tea, there was little chance of sleeping, not least because I wasn't entirely unconvinced I wasn't being pranked by the Big Man Upstairs (God, not some gimp we keep in the attic – though I don't believe in either). I had the impression that had I gone to sleep, the bed would have burst 'hilariously' into flames or someone would have driven a car through the window. I lay in bed, reached for my iPad, clicked it on and was immediately castigated by Paul who claimed the tiny 'tick' noise had woken him up 'AND IT'S NO BLOODY WONDER YOU DON'T SLEEP WITH THAT THING BLARING AWAY'. Blaring away! This from a man who would cheerfully sleep through someone cutting off his leg with a fucking butter knife.

So naturally I stabbed him to death and buried him in the garden.

I lay in bed some more, contemplating death and/or sleep. Neither came. I read somewhere that masturbation is nature's sedative but given Paul was on HIGH ALERT from the sound of one finger hitting a glass screen, ten minutes of my wrist fwapping away wouldn't have helped. It might have been worth it just to get revenge of Paul and give him a face mask for the morning, but no. I got my headphones, put on a podcast about funfairs in the vain hope that the polite chatter would lull me away, but no, ten minutes in and I was awaken by the sound of screaming kids on a rollercoaster channelled directly into my ear. At this point, I gave up entirely, had a bath for two hours, stared at Paul in the darkness and watched Jeremy Kyle with the subtitles on and someone gurning away in the corner. A signer, not Graham. I've never been so sick of my life as I was this morning, with dawn creeping in.

Still, other people have it worse, don't they?

twochubbycubs on: fire

Gosh, all terribly exciting this morning in Newcastle. Looked out of my office window to see a big column of black smoke billowing into the air and my first thought was sheer stricken terror at the thought it might have been Paul's mother arriving.

Just kidding, don't strike me off the Christmas list yet.

No, a great fire was busy raging at one of a shop in Newcastle and it looks like it has completely gutted the building. An awful thing to happen, and they have been unable to account for the whereabouts of one chap. Hopefully he'll be found. Watching the local press heralded such treats as 'there is a smell of smoke in the air' and 'the firemen are putting water on the fire'. Really? Not petrol? Perhaps hurl a chip pan through the window and see if that'll calm the flames? Christ.

It made me realise how cosseted and safe my job is, and how frightening it must be to be a fireman. Imagine having to enter a building where you can't see, the structure is unsafe and IT'S ON BLOODY FIRE. I get nervous turning the thermostat up, let alone having to battle an inferno to rescue someone from being roasted alive. I just can't imagine it. I used to be absolutely terrified of fire. No wonder, looking back, with three memories sticking in my mind like smouldering ashes.

Firstly, chip pans. To watch 999 and the like you'd think a chip pan – a proper one mind, full of fat and bubbling on the hob – was akin to a grenade sat there with the pin taken out. Because we were Northern and geet hard we'd have chips for nearly every meal, and my parents were forever putting the pan on and 'having a lie down' in front of Countdown, or taking the washing out, or driving over to the next village for a twenty deck of Lambert and Butler, leaving me sat in the living room just waiting for the invariable explosion and the feeling of my skin melting off my face. Clearly they knew what they were doing but good lord, I used to be terrified. Never quite put me off eating the chips afterwards, mind.

Next, anyone have a coal fire? For those who aren't a fan of bringing coal in from the outdoors and developing COPD over the course of a childhood, you often needed to make the fire 'blaze' at the start – essentially you'd cover the fire up with a solid object / covering, which in turn caused the air from the chimney to pull through the fire and 'get it going' (or, indeed, to go all Tim Healy-haway-Pet on you, 'take ahad'). One morning whilst we were playing at a friend's house (I remember the board game, it was a knock-off version of Frustration where you had to shake the dice yourself instead of popping the dome – probably called Inconvenient or For Fuck's Sake) and her mother decided to light the fire. Being a proper countrywoman that took no time at all and she decided that instead of using something sensible to make the fire blaze, she covered it up with A SHEET OF NEWSPAPER. She couldn't have chosen a more stupid material if she tried — I'm surprised she didn't swap out the logs for canisters of Elnett. To put the cherry on the massive third-degree burns, the child-hating witch then left the house to go up the street to make a phonecall, presumably to her lover, Ian Brady. Of course, simple physics took place, the newspaper set alight and promptly fell apart, scattering little burning embers into the air, onto chairs, in my hair, all over the living room, leaving us children to try and stamp them all out. We did, but that made my heart race faster than any game of bloody Frustration.

Finally, anyone who has grown up in the countryside will remember the colossal pyramids of round hay bales that used to be scattered around. Well, my sister and I were cheerfully ignoring my mother's stern-faced admonishments about playing on the bales and sitting atop a gigantic pile when we heard a terribly loud WHOOMPH and the whole pile went up in flames. Well, you've never seen two pairs of Naf-Naf trainers move so quickly. Turns out that tightly-packed hay holds a LOT of heat and only needs the slightest encouragement to burst into flames. Who knew? We certainly didn't — we were only ever worried about being crushed under the weight of the bales, and well, that never stopped us rolling them down the field and crashing them through the fences at the bottom and into the stream. Oops.

Turns out that it was a small broken bottle focussing the sun's rays onto the hay which started the fire. We were just the little dirty-faced urchins who just happened to be nearby.

I realise that my descriptive ways of talking about anything from my childhood makes it sound like we were the rough family from every single Catherine Cookson novel but of course, I always add that slight air of exaggeration into my description. My dad wasn't Robson Green and I don't think I ever had pleurisy from working down t'pit. Here's a little fact though – up until the age of…I dunno, whenever I discovered masturbation and thus had something else to occupy my thoughts alone in the night, I used to have a 'procedure' I had to do before I went to sleep to make sure the house didn't burn down – blink eight times in a row, whirl my eyes around in my head and then shut my eyes and go to sleep. Interesting how a child's mind works.

twochubbycubs on: Christmas shopping: part one

You have no idea how much it pains me to write sizzlin' in the recipe title tonight instead of sizzling, but Paul threatened to withhold sex if I didn't acquiesce, and so here we are. In a perfect world there would be no need for unnecessary shortenings of random words, but it's not a perfect world, and I'm not a perfect person. So sizzlin' it is. Sizzling puts me in mind of those awful pubs where they bring your food out and slide it out onto a scalding hot bit of stone so it 'sizzles' and you're supposed to sit there rapturous whilst your food bubbles. Perhaps it's because I'm a curmudgeonly-old-before-his-type fart but I don't get it – I've seen stuff heating up before, I've used a pan in my lifetime. If they brought it to the table and heated the food via some Rube Goldberg machine that involved flamethrowers and magnetite, I'd perhaps crack a smile. Those types of pub are always full of the same type of people:

- those who can't eat their Sunday dinner without the application of three separate condiments that have to be brought to the table by some harried waitress with a lot more consonants than vowels in her first name;

- access day visits from dads sharing wan smiles and thin conversation with the top of their iPhone-engrossed children; and

- the elderly, fussing and gumming their way through a special menu printed in Times New Roman Size 32 so everything looks like this:

"puree of turnip served with turkey paste and parsnip wisps"

OK, so I exaggerate, but still.

It's been an uneventful day. We had two things in mind – go to Costco to see if they had the giant bar of Dairy Milk that was 10kg, £160 and came with a tray of prepped insulin on the side, and to Dobbies – our local garden centre. It's a terribly posh garden centre, you can tell because the person blocking the exit tries to sell us an 'orangerie' on the way out, rather than double-glazing. An orangerie! Just the thing – I was beginning to grow concerned that my lemon tree was becoming a mite chilled in the North Sea air. Actually, confession: we've already got an orangerie, but because I'm not a pretentious tagnut, I call it a greenhouse. He's actually stopped asking us anyway, possibly because last time he did so I replied that 'I couldn't possibly, I'm Jewish' and rushed past aghast. I could almost hear his brain whirring trying to work it out, by which time we were away.

Costco, then. Costco on a Sunday. Four weeks before Christmas. On 'sample' day. On a list of fun activities, that sits just above peeling off my face with the edge of a corned beef tin and just below shitting out an armchair. Busy? We didn't walk around, we just blended with a group of around 200 into one giant shell-suited mass and went as one, gliding down the aisles grabbing things as we went. I was gutted – there's nothing I like more than taking my time, judging people who are buying 84 Andrex Quilted and wondering who the fuck decides on a Sunday that what they really need to buy is 24 jars of chilli peppers. Naturally, because it was sample day, every single aisle was capped by some poor dolt in a pinny handing out 'samples' and, as a consequence, 50 or so slack-jawed simpletons all jostling and pushing to try and get a paper cup with FOUR FUCKING HARIBO in them. I can't abide queues at the best of times and wouldn't have stopped if they were offering to tickle my balls and give me cold hard cash, but Jesus, the lack of dignity people display over a 'freebie'! I was tempted to spit my chewing gum on the floor and shout 'FREE PRE-CHEWED MINTS' to cause a stampede but the exit was far away and I didn't have my running shoes on.

You witness this ugliness on Black Friday and during the sales and I just can't get my head around it. I can't! You see them on the television, queueing up outside of Next so at 5am they can rush in and have the pick of all the shit that no person wanted during the only time of the year pretty much guaranteed to empty your stock room, so what's left is the absolute dregs. Wahey! I'm sure Aunt Marjorie will be delighted with her jumper stained with the greasy fingers of the desperate and the nonsensical. There was a guy on Look North the other day who had been queueing outside of Currys all night in anticipation of the bargains galore he expected from Black Friday. He was the only one who turned up. When they interviewed him on the television you could see in his eyes that he regretted his decision, but clearly didn't want to back down, and he was later shown staggering shamefaced out of the shop after two hours (TWO HOURS! The only way I'd spend two hours in Currys would be if I'd had a cardiac arrest in the TV section, and that's pretty bloody likely given how high their prices are). What had he picked up? I couldn't see everything, but there were at least four graphics cards, two blu-ray players and some speakers. Not good speakers, I add. It was as if he was the sole contestant in the world's most depressing version of Fun House – one where Melanie and Martina had long since died and Pat Sharp didn't have a haircut that looked like Stevie Wonder had done it as a favour. He claimed to have spent £4,500, and all I could say to Paul was 'Yes, but what price dignity?'. Takes all sorts.

It took us almost 45 minutes in Costco to pick up a wheelbarrow of tea-bags, a mountain of coffee and a box of Rice Krispies so big that I feel like I'm in a shit version of Honey I Shrunk the Kids every time I look at it. It then took us almost an hour to get out of the 'Metrocentre' area, which was awash with red-faced families in oversized cars all trying to cram into the same lane. Luckily, we had the audiobook version of Carrie to finish in the car, so we were fairly content, though god knows what passer-bys must have thought to hear some American woman screaming about dirtypillows and menstrual blood coming from our car. I'd love to be telekinetic but I'd definitely end up being sent to Hell afterwards – people who so much as blocked my way for a moment in Marks and Spencers would be sent flying up into the air-conditioning fans and turned to jam, or all those Audis that insist on cutting in at the last second and blocking the box junction outside of where I park – they'd end up crumbled into a cube no smaller than the dice from a Travel Monopoly set. The world would be on fire before the end of the week, I almost guarantee it. I already spend roughly forty hours a week looking crazily at the back of someone's head and willing their brain to start leaking out of their ears. Sigh.

Dobbies was an absolute no-no, too. Quite literally, we got there, and there was no parking and no hope of securing a spot, given the place was awash with those fucking awful white Range Rovers (oh look at me, I'm driving a car designed for mud, all-terrain and exciting driving, and I only ever use it to ferry little Quentissimo and Angelica-Foccacia to their organic flute lessons) (bitch) and other such 'luxury' cars. We drove around and around and around and around until I felt like Sandra Bullock in Gravity and we admitted defeat. Paul and I did get a colossal serving of schadenfreude though with the sight of a spotlessly white BMW being completely and utterly trapped on the muddy overflow parking field. The silly arse behind the wheel kept spinning his tyres, sinking him even further into the mud, whilst his granite-faced wife looked coldly at everyone who went past laughing. Hey, it's not my fault your husband is a useless tosser who doesn't know how to pull a car from mud. We did, along with everyone else, smirk in that very British way when he got out of the car and started shouting at it. KNOB POWER ACTIVATE. I like to think he went home and had a good hard look at his life.

twochubbycubs on: Christmas shopping: part two

We have a Christmas tree!

Every year the same argument, though. Paul wants new decorations, I insist we use the old ones until my spirit breaks and I'm buying decorations in a fevered haste. The tree – always a real tree. We did fuss about with buying an artificial tree a few years ago but, having had a real tree all of my life, it's just not the same. All that bending of branches and adjusting angles sucks the joy out quicker than a Christmas colonic. We have no eye for detail – our trees just end up looking like we've wrapped Victoria Beckham in tinsel and stuck a star on her head. Plus, if I'm not picking tiny pine needles from every conceivable crevice – both in the room and on my body – until at least July, Christmas hasn't been done properly. Way back when my dad would just sneak into a forest near our house and steal a tree, but Paul and I aren't very good at being subtle and I don't think his Micra can handle a soggy forest trail.

We went to IKEA for the tree, having heard that they were only £25 – and you got a £20 voucher to spend instore too. Wah-hey! We got out of bed early (well, Paul did, he had to come and physically roll me out of bed – harder when it looks when you've slept in the wet-patch and you're stuck to the sheet like PVA glue) and hustled down to IKEA on Sunday morning. As did, seemingly, every bugger else from Newcastle, Tyne and

Wear to Newcastle, New South Wales. I've never seen so many people get excited amongst woodland without someone flashing their interior lights off and on and some van driver wearing fishnets wanking away against my wingmirror. We looked for a moment from afar, realised that we weren't going to be able to a) get a decent tree and b) breathe in that sea of Lynx Africa and spent-tab-breath, and headed for Dobbies, where at least we could get a box of assorted Lindt chocolates to tide us over. We did nip into IKEA first for decorations.

Paul hates shopping with me because I lose interest in what I'm doing almost immediately and then just end up getting catty about everything – my responses to the various decorations he held up? 'Tacky'. 'Cheap'. 'AWFUL'. 'Looks like something Katie Price would have hanging off her clit'. 'Are we decorating the lobby of a forgotten Travelodge?' I know, I'm a monster. Thankfully we managed to settle on a nice collection within ten minutes and we were back on our way.

Dobbies was so much easier and civilised – we selected a tree from the pleasant looking selection, had it wrapped by someone who decided to show me so much arse-crack when he bent over that I almost popped a 7ft Norway Spruce in there and paid for it within a few minutes. The only delay was in bringing me around from my heart attack at the cost – it's a tree! Was I paying for its fucking ferry ticket too? Good lord. I bundled it into Paul's car (we took both, I didn't want to get sap in my car and nor did I want to be stuck under a tree all the way home – plus Paul will insist on playing Tracy Chapman in the car) and sauntered back to my car.

As I was walking back to my car, some beetroot-faced old fart started waving his hands impatiently at me because he wanted me to dash back to the car, vacate the space and allow his shitty Audi in, despite there being a great number of spaces a bit further away. He was keeping the traffic waiting rather than doing the decent thing and you know, dying in a ball of fire. Naturally, I ran over to my car (I say ran, remember, I'm fat, so really it was a 'every third step a bit quicker' shuffle), flung open the door and promptly sat and fiddled with the radio, read my phone, did my hair in the mirror...all the very important things. Listen, I know that doesn't paint me in such a good light either, but I don't care – he was so obnoxious with his hand-waving (mirrored by his wife, no less, who had one of those wrinkly pursed faces that looked like a Mini Cheddar Crinkly with a pair of lips rolled on) that he had to wait. It took him almost ten minutes before he screamed off, gesticulating wildly. I then, of course, smoothly reversed out, gave the guy behind me the space, and went cheerily on my way. I did spot him as I drove out the car park trying to manoeuvre his shitwagon into a tiny space next to the trollies. I barely had time to clasp my hand to my lips and shake my head in the internationally recognised gesture for 'oh how terrible' before I was out of the car park.

Paul beat me home and managed to get the tree across the lawn and into the house himself, although he told me all of the neighbours were at the window staring. Goes without saying. They'd watch a leaf falling off a tree if they thought they could gossip about it after. Actually, everyone seems to be getting along cheerfully this year – we might get decent Christmas cards this year, as opposed to 'GET THE FUCK OUT' written with shit on a photo with our eyes scratched out delivered in an envelope made of bile and sealed with blood. OK, I jest, you get me. Decorating took no effort at all, given I sat and watched Paul to do it, interrupting occasionally to tell him where there were bald patches (mainly on the back of his head, though the shiny circle did look fetching with the reflection of the lights bouncing off it). He did do a smashing job. I contributed at the final moments by heroically placing the star on top because Paul couldn't find the wee stepladder we keep for such occasions (well we certainly don't use it for DIY, do we?). Together, we did it. He didn't end up choking me with a line of tinsel, I didn't wind up smashing jagged baubles into his eye-sockets. And isn't that what Christmas is all about?

a reflection

What a year (and a bit).

No births, save for many struggled bum-departures from eating way too much pasta and carbs.

One death, with nana rolling a seven and getting her ticket on the Death Express. This led to the first funeral I have attended where I've sat in the front row rather than at the back stifling my giggles.

We did alright with the weight loss, but 2016 needs to be the year we take it all a bit more seriously, given we're both now in our thirties and we've started making fat-bloke-noises every time we rise from a chair.

We had three marvellous holidays – Ireland, Corsica and Iceland (the blog posts for which will appear in January 2016), and Paul desecrated each country with his foul arse within fifteen minutes of landing each time.

But, really, the most remarkable thing about 2015 has been the fact we've actually kept the blog going, and attracted so many wonderful followers and readers, who post cheery comments and acerbic remarks. We love it, we're attention whores, no denying. I'd write even if no-one was reading, trust me, but the fact that so many folks enjoy it makes all the difference. Please, if you've enjoyed this book or are a fan of our recipes, then share, share share. Leave a review! Tell everyone who either needs a laugh or frankly, their weight concerns you.

Who knows what we'll end up writing about next, but don't worry – I'm sure whatever happens, there will still be a ridiculous amount of nonsense to be enjoyed.

Thank you!
James and Paul

JAMES AND PAUL ANDERSON

Printed in Great Britain
by Amazon